T0301388

Entrepreneurship and the Creative Economy

Entrepreneurship and the Creative Economy

Process, Practice and Policy

Edited by

Colette Henry

Norbrook Professor of Business and Enterprise, The Royal Veterinary College, University of London, UK

Anne de Bruin

Professor of Economics, School of Economics and Finance and Director, New Zealand Social Innovation and Entrepreneurship Research Centre, Massey University, New Zealand

Edward Elgar

Cheltenham, UK • Northampton, MA, USA

Published by
Edward Elgar Publishing Limited
The Lypiatts
15 Lansdown Road
Cheltenham
Glos GL50 2JA
UK

Edward Elgar Publishing, Inc.
William Pratt House
9 Dewey Court
Northampton
Massachusetts 01060
USA

A catalogue record for this book
is available from the British Library

Library of Congress Control Number: 2011924190

ISBN 978 1 84844 769 1

Typeset by Servis Filmsetting Ltd, Stockport, Cheshire
Printed and bound by MPG Books Group, UK

Contents

Figures

Tables

Boxes

Contributors

Elaine Allen, Research Director of the Arthur M. Blank Center for Entrepreneurship, director of the Babson Survey Research Group (BSRG), and Professor of Statistics and Entrepreneurship at Babson College, MA, USA. She is statistical director of the US Global Entrepreneurship Monitor team. Elaine has published widely on statistical issues in meta-analysis, data mining, survey research methods and clinical research methodology. Her collaborative research on women and entrepreneurship has appeared in entrepreneurship journals and books. Her doctorate in statistics is from Cornell University. At Babson College she has received the Women Who Make a Difference Award and the Faculty Award for Outstanding Research.

Anne de Bruin, Professor of Economics in the School of Economics and Finance (Albany), Massey University, New Zealand and Founding Director of the New Zealand Social Innovation and Entrepreneurship Research Centre, established at Massey University in 2010. Anne's research interests are entrepreneurship, social innovation, sustainable employment and regional development. In entrepreneurship, she is particularly interested in entrepreneurship in the creative industries, new conceptualizations of entrepreneurship, social entrepreneurship and women entrepreneurs.

Ted Fuller, Professor of Entrepreneurship and Strategic Foresight and Head of the Business School at the University of Lincoln, UK. Ted has previously held academic posts at Durham Business School and at the University of Teesside. His academic mission is to understand how futures are created and to develop responsible people who can create futures. He is consulting editor for *Futures: The Journal of Policy, Planning and Futures Studies* and is on several editorial boards of entrepreneurship journals. Current research includes studies of emergence in entrepreneurial contexts, knowledge value co-production, internationalization and responsible futures.

Patricia G. Greene, F.W. Olin Distinguished Chair in Entrepreneurship at Babson College and former Provost (2006–08) and Dean of the Undergraduate School (2003–06). Patricia's research interests include entrepreneurship education with a special focus on the role of serious games. Her latest book is the forthcoming edited volume (with Fetters, Rice and Butler), *The Development of University-Based Entrepreneurship Ecosystems: Global Practices.* Greene serves on the national advisory boards for the USA Small Business Administration's Small Business Development Centers and for the Center for Women's Business Research. Prior to becoming a professor she worked primarily in the health care industry.

Colette Henry, Norbrook Professor of Business and Enterprise at the Royal Veterinary College (RVC), University of London. Colette holds visiting professorships at the Universities of Tromso, Norway and Birmingham City, UK. A Fellow of the Royal Society for the encouragement of Arts, Manufactures and Commerce (RSA), Colette is also the former President of the Institute for Small Business and Entrepreneurship (ISBE). Drawing on her sales and marketing industry experience, Colette has worked closely with aspiring entrepreneurs and designed enterprise training programmes for incubation tenants and local industry. She has published widely on entrepreneurship education and training, evaluation, and gender in veterinary medicine and the creative industries. Colette is editor of the *International Journal of Gender and Entrepreneurship.*

Colleen Mills, Associate Professor of Management in the Management Department, College of Business and Economics, at the University of Canterbury, New Zealand. An avid researcher, Colleen's research interests lie at the intersection between change and development and communication and sense-making. Although most of her research focuses on large organizations, she is particularly interested in the process of business start-up in the creative industries where micro businesses are the norm. Her most recent studies have examined the process of business start-up and development in the information technology (IT) and fashion industries from a sense-making perspective using business founders' enterprise development narratives. Her findings have been published in various management, communication and entrepreneurship journals.

Sally Jane Norman, Professor of Performance Technologies and Director of the Attenborough Centre for the Creative Arts, School of Media, Film and Music at the University of Sussex, UK. Her work on art and technology has involved collaboration with the Performing Arts Laboratory of the Centre National de la Recherche Scientifique, UNESCO and the French Ministry of Culture. She has led research initiatives at the International Institute of Puppetry (Charleville-Mézières), Zentrum für Kunst und Medientechnologie (Karlsruhe), and Studio for Electro-Instrumental

Music (Amsterdam), where she was Artistic Co-Director from 1998 to 2000. In 2004, Sally left France to create and direct Newcastle University's 'Culture Lab', a £4.5 million interdisciplinary research facility. Her research interests include performing arts and technology, history of scenography and theatre architectures, and she has published widely in these areas.

Erik Noyes, Assistant Professor of Entrepreneurship at Babson College, MA, USA and holder of the Martin Tropp Term Chair. Erik's research focuses on corporate new venture creation, entrepreneurial opportunity recognition and social networks as an entrepreneurial resource. Prior to joining Babson, Erik was a senior consultant for a growth strategy and innovation consulting firm working with global companies such as Nokia, Hewlett-Packard, Motorola, BMW, Guidant and New Balance. He publishes on entrepreneurship and the use of new media, including information visualization, to teach the dynamism of entrepreneurial phenomena. Erik earned a BA in international economic relations from Brown University, an MBA from the University of New Hampshire and a Doctorate in Business Administration with a focus on strategic management from Boston University.

Salvatore Parise, Associate Professor in the Technology, Operations, and Information Management Division at Babson College, MA, USA. Salvatore teaches multidisciplinary courses in information technology at both the graduate and undergraduate levels. His research focus is in the areas of social networks, social media applications, knowledge management and human resource development practices, strategic alliances and management pedagogical research. His research has been published in several academic and management journals including the *Journal of Organizational Behavior*, *MIT Sloan Management Review* and the *Journal of Management Education*. Prior to obtaining his Doctorate in business at Boston University, Salvatore was an engineer and researcher at IBM.

Andy Penaluna, Professor of Creative Entrepreneurship at Dynevor Centre for Art, Design and Media, Swansea Metropolitan University, UK. Andy is both a practitioner and a lecturer in design, having developed courses ranging from illustration to interactive multimedia and, latterly, design for advertising, a heady mix of creative art mentalities that are set within firm business contexts. He also contributes to business courses such as the MBA. Elected to the Chair of Enterprise Educators UK in 2010–11, Andy also chairs the Higher Education Academy's Entrepreneurial Learning Special Interest Group. His expertise is utilized by numerous higher educational establishments who employ him as an external advisor and examiner for a range of 'enterprising' undergraduate and postgraduate studies.

Kathryn Penaluna, Enterprise Manager at the Centre for Creative Entrepreneurship, Swansea Metropolitan University, UK. A former bank manager, Kathryn highlights the fact that she required significant mentoring when first teaching business skills to students from creativity-based study programmes. These experiences have had a significant impact on her approaches to teaching. One of the UK's first Entrepreneurship Education Fellows, Kathryn directs the Centre for Creative Entrepreneurship, working with a strong team of 'entrepreneurial enablers' who help graduates and students to commercialize their ideas.

David Rae, Professor of Business and Enterprise at the University of Lincoln, UK and Director of Enterprise and Innovation at Lincoln Business School. David's pre-academic career included management development and consulting, as well as government and multimedia publishing. David has a PhD in entrepreneurial learning from Nottingham Trent University, and his innovative research is recognized through numerous publications including his latest book, *Entrepreneurship: From Opportunity to Action*, published in 2007. He is also a keynote speaker on entrepreneurial development at many international professional conferences. David is currently Vice-President for Education for the UK's Institute for Small Business and Entrepreneurship (ISBE), chairing the Entrepreneurship and Enterprise Education track at the Institute's annual research conference. He has a track record in the leadership of business and enterprise in higher education.

Simon Roodhouse, Professor at Middlesex University Institute of Work Based Learning, UK; Adjunct Professor of Creative Industries, University of Technology, Sydney, Australia; and Director of Safe Hands (Management) Ltd, a strategic consultancy engaged in education and cultural industries (www.simonroodhouse.com). Previously, Simon was Professor in Creative Industries at the University of the Arts, London, UK; Adjunct Professor at CIRAC, Queensland University of Technology, Brisbane, Australia; Visiting Professor Creative Industries at the University of Bolton, and the University of Greenwich, UK. He has written extensively in national and international journals and has published four books including the *Principles and Practice of Cultural Quarters,* which is in its second edition. He is also the founding editor of the *Creative Industries Journal.*

Calvin Taylor, Chair in Cultural Industries at the University of Leeds, UK. Calvin has worked on creative industries, entrepreneurship, innovation and regional policy since the 1990s, working with a range of international, national and regional agencies. He is also a drafting co-author of the *UNESCO Framework for Cultural Statistics* (UNESCO, 2009). Calvin has written and published on the creative industries in regional and urban development, and the role of universities in promoting entrepreneurship and innovation in the creative industries (in *Entrepreneurship in the Creative Industries: An International Perspective*, edited by Henry, Edward Elgar, 2007). His latest publication is 'The Creative Industries, Governance and Economic Development: A UK Perspective' in *Creative Economies, Creative Cities: Asian-European Perspectives*, edited by Kong and O'Connor (Springer, 2009).

Brian V. Tjemkes, Assistant Professor of Management and Organization at the Faculty of Economics and Business Administration, VU University, Amsterdam. Brian's main research interests are decision-making in strategic alliances, value creation and appropriation in strategic alliances, open innovation in service firms and small and medium-sized enterprises (SMEs) in the creative industry. He is the coordinator of the Master's specialization, 'Strategy and Organization', a fellow of the Amsterdam Centre of Service Innovation and an academic partner of Kirkman Company, consultants in strategic sourcing.

Lorraine Warren, Senior Lecturer in Innovation in the School of Management at the University of Southampton, UK. Lorraine's research is underpinned by complexity theory and addresses disruptive innovation – how new business models and new value creation systems emerge in volatile new technology sectors. Projects in this area are focused on the mobile web, photovoltaics and new technology firms.

Acknowledgements

The editors are extremely grateful to all those who have contributed to this book. It has been our pleasure to work with such dedicated and experienced individuals who have shared their particular specialist research expertise within the field of creative industries entrepreneurship.

Thanks are also due to those who supported the editors by willingly acting as reviewers for the chapters in the book.

A special word of thanks is also due to the Institute for Small Business and Entrepreneurship (ISBE); the introduction of a dedicated Creative Industries Track at their 2009 Research Conference in Liverpool created the impetus for this book. Finally, we are grateful to the team at Edward Elgar for their ongoing support and guidance in helping us prepare the final manuscript.

1. Introduction

Colette Henry and Anne de Bruin

The creative economy, and the broad spectrum of creative industries that it encompasses, is an essential component of growth, employment and international trade in today's global age (Higgs and Cunningham, 2008; United Nations, 2008). Indeed, in a recessionary and post-recessionary era, this somewhat heterogeneous set of industries (Flew and Cunningham, 2010) becomes even more attractive as a source of potential employment and entrepreneurial endeavour. This has already been recognized in the UK, with policy-makers being urged to target investment towards the 'drivers of employment in the future', ensuring that knowledge-intensive sectors such as the creative industries are given the support they need to fulfil their critical role in the recovery process (Lee et al., 2010, p. 30; UK Trade and Investment, 2006).

The term 'creative industries' first emerged in the 1990s and was originally used to describe all industries based on creativity that generated intellectual property (Henry, 2009). However, as noted by Howkins (2002), this description was quickly narrowed to include industries with a particular artistic or cultural bent. Amongst the many sectors that feature within the category of creative industries, arts and crafts, designer fashion, film, theatre and performing arts, advertising, publishing, broadcast media and recorded music would appear to be the most prominent. Some critics have suggested that the inclusion of software development, computer services, digital media and communications in the creative industries' definition serves to inflate the sector artificially (Garnham, 2005), but others have highlighted the exclusion of particular industries such as tourism, heritage and sport (Hesmondhalgh, 2007). While this past decade may have witnessed a degree of consensus in relation to what constitutes a 'creative industry', many questions remain unanswered, prompting further debate on issues surrounding definitional and policy coherence (Flew and Cunningham, 2010).

Despite still being regarded by some as an emerging field of academic endeavour, it has been acknowledged that the creative industries constitute a valuable sphere of practice in their own right (Roodhouse, 2009).

With this in mind, and building on Henry's (2007) text, this edited collection of chapters addresses a range of pertinent issues within current creative economy debates from a process, policy and practice perspective. As editors, we have endeavoured to include diverse yet complementary research contributions that deal with pertinent issues within this agenda; that adopt both conceptually and empirically based methodological approaches; and that employ a range of social and geographical contexts to explore the very nature of the creative economy. In presenting this collection, and drawing on international scholars, we aim to enhance understanding of creative processes and practices, demonstrating their dynamic interaction and embedding the creative industries firmly in the global policy agenda.

Following this introduction, the book adopts a logical yet strategic structure, beginning with four chapters that help lay the theoretical foundation by discussing some of the fundamental, definitional and structural issues associated with the creative industries. Some of the more practical, experiential and process-driven concepts are covered in the next two chapters. The final group of three chapters focuses on sector-specific issues of the creative economy, such as those found within the designer fashion, serious games and music industries.

In Chapter 2, Simon Roodhouse discusses the fundamental issue of defining and, indeed, redefining the creative industries and their related activities. He suggests that the constantly changing boundary definitions, which have been developed for the creative sector by government and its agencies over the years, are devoid of clear rationale. Indeed, such boundaries are often constrained to match the particular resources available at any given time. The author refers to the chaotic organizational pattern of creative industries agencies that has led to an absence of overarching regional strategies and a lack of shared understanding of an appropriate definitional framework to operate and evaluate such strategies. Roodhouse suggests that if research in the creative industries is to be taken seriously, precision is required in the use of classicality systems. Essentially, the sector needs to cooperate in the building of shared definitional frameworks.

Chapter 3, by Calvin Taylor, considers the concept of creative industries, including its link to innovation, as socialized economic activities. This is discussed within the broader trend of applying social constructivist epistemological principles to accounts of organizational development and professional practice. The strengths and weaknesses of such an approach, as applied to the creative industries, are examined, with the author arguing that the intense social reflexivity present in these accounts leaves them open to the charge of paradoxically underplaying the role of creativity.

The chapter also explores contemporary developments in knowledge exchange research, and offers an alternative theoretical account of the role of sociality and reflexivity in the development of the creative industries.

In Chapter 4, Andy and Kathryn Penaluna set out the case for fuller collaboration between business educators and those experienced in developing creativity and innovation. Through an extended literature review that includes current government and policy reports as well as empirical evidence from national and international networks, the authors consider the type and nature of comments that have been offered on the subject of creativity in business. The chapter discusses the creative industries in both business and educational contexts, and investigates current trends and factors of influence. The authors illustrate that, despite gaining some momentum, the creative industries have been practically invisible to the academic enterprise community, which has located much of its thinking in business school environments. Essentially, the chapter calls for the creative industries to engage further with entrepreneurship education policy and development.

Chapter 5, by Ted Fuller, Lorraine Warren and Sally Jane Norman, presents a conceptual framework to capture the emergence of novelty in the creative industries, especially those operating in the so-called digital economy. The authors use empirical study, which includes observations of workshops over several days with creative groups and interviews with creative enterprises, together with literature reviews on creative industries, business models and value systems to inform their analysis and conceptualization. They move from the micro level to a wider analytical problem, which is how society changes itself. Their argument is that the increasing level of innovation and creativity produces greater levels of instability in social structures (habits, norms and so on). Completely new industries can arise (and 'creatively' destroy old ones) as new stabilized patterns form, particularly where entry costs are falling rapidly, such as in the digital milieu. Project-based, non-standard ways of work and organization epitomize creative industries in the digital economy. Dynamic, innovative and often unorthodox collaborations result in numerous large, small and micro-businesses coming together for the duration of a project and then disbanding and forming new partnerships for the next project. The authors contend that research designs must, therefore, address multiple contexts and levels, presenting an analytical challenge to researchers. Hence, methodologically, they suggest that their framework has potential to deal with this challenge. Conceptually, their work broadens the notions of the 'business model' to consider value-creating systems and particular states reached by those systems in their evolution.

In Chapter 6, David Rae reflects on the experiences of creating and running the SPEED (Student Placements for Entrepreneurs in Education) Programme, which ran in 12 higher education institutions in the United Kingdom between 2006 and 2008. The programme, which provided an action learning route for students to start their own businesses, supported over 700 participants. The chapter explores what is known about action and entrepreneurial learning in the context of new venture creation. The various types of businesses supported by SPEED, the majority of which were in the creative industries sector, are categorized, and the conceptual and practical learning gained from the programme is discussed. The author proposes a model of entrepreneurial action learning illustrating the connections between venture formation and 'pull' learning. Finally, recommendations for further developing the SPEED model in the post-recessionary economic era are proposed.

The focus of Chapter 7, by Brian Tjemkes, is organization development in the creative business services segment of the creative industries. He conducts a longitudinal case study of the establishment of an advertising agency in the Netherlands, to develop an integrative and multilevel process model of a creative business services start-up and assist with understanding of organization development. He explores how the firm's organization design evolves toward one that reconciles economic and creative performance. The case he examines sheds interesting light on how organization design progresses through positive and negative adaptation cycles, toward a design that would enable it to achieve the dual objective of economic and creative performance. Contrary to commonly held beliefs that organizational problems can be fixed with instant solutions, he concludes that economic and creative performance objectives can be reconciled over time through incremental steps as a new venture becomes established.

In Chapter 8, Patricia Greene focuses on a creative industries segment accelerating in importance: the serious games industry. Her chapter highlights the importance of studying emerging industries from a socio-economic platform. Given that the industry is still emerging and industry data are limited, Greene's study makes an important contribution to understanding this new industry. Pointing to the variety of terminologies that are used to describe the field such as 'edutainment' and 'digital game-based learning', she usefully sorts out what actually is a serious game and investigates what the industry looks like. She explores innovation in the industry to identify three sources: educational, technological and business models. She also identifies the types of businesses participating in the industry, discusses who is in the market for serious games and comments on the growth trajectory of the industry. Additionally, the chapter has valuable practitioner relevance since it suggests practical lessons to be learned and shared with entrepreneurs who are interested in working in this area.

Chapter 9, by Colleen Mills, delves into the New Zealand fashion industry to obtain insights into the start-up challenges of new designers. She employs enterprise development narratives to explore their experience of business start-up. Her chapter reveals how social capital and self-identity interact and structure the way these designers navigate the tension between creative expression and business practices that characterizes their participation in the designer fashion industry. She presents an enterprise development orientations framework to explain how nascent designers approach this tension. The word 'orientation' is used to capture how the designers positioned themselves in relation to creativity, business and the fashion industry. Three orientations are distinguished and designers' orientations mapped according to how strongly their self-identity, start-up motivation and aspirations match these three defining orientations. An important finding is that those who successfully navigate the creativity–business tension access quite different social capital from those who feel constrained by this tension.

In the final chapter, Erik Noyes, Salvatore Parise and Elaine Allen are interested in the pattern of creative influences that increases the likelihood that an artist will pioneer a new market. Their longitudinal research examines the unique creative influences of all major artists in the popular music industry between 1950 and 2008, to check if certain structural positions in the complete network of influences make an artist more or less likely to be a first mover in new markets. They apply network analysis to the social structure of the popular music industry to ask the question: do artists who pioneer new markets occupy and exploit distinct structural positions in the influences network? Applying resource dependency theory, they examine each artist's structural pattern of creative influences as an idiosyncratic resource base from which to fashion industry-shaping musical innovations.

This collection was put together after a widely circulated general call for contributions early in 2009 'for an exciting new book showcasing research on entrepreneurship in the creative industries, to be published by Edward Elgar in 2011'. While not a prerequisite, contributors were invited to present their papers at the 32nd Institute for Small Business and Entrepreneurship (ISBE; www.isbe.org.uk) Conference to be held in Liverpool, UK, 3–6 November 2009. For the first time, this conference included a dedicated 'Creative Industries' research track, chaired by the editors Colette Henry and Anne de Bruin. Following the conference time line enabled the editors to read and review submissions in advance, and facilitated the presenters in receiving feedback from other conference participants. It was especially significant that the ISBE Conference was held in Liverpool; as the European Capital of Culture in 2008, Liverpool continues to experience a renaissance of creative and civic enterprise, and ISBE conference delegates were able to see at first hand both the achievements of economic regeneration through enterprise as well as the challenges of moving from decades of decline into rejuvenation and growth. Potential contributors to the book who were part of the broader creative industries community of interest but who were unable to attend the ISBE Conference were offered an option to submit directly to the editors. This ensured a rich and robust basis from which to source appropriate research contributions, allowing for a more balanced collection of creative industry perspectives encompassing the process, policy and practice dimensions. We believe this text has moved understanding of the creative economy a step forward and trust it will encourage readers to explore further and contribute to the creative industries debate.

REFERENCES

Flew, T. and S. Cunningham (2010), 'Creative industries after the first decade of debate', *Information Society*, **26**, 1–11.

Garnham, N. (2005), 'From cultural to creative industries: an analysis of the implications of the creative industries approach to the arts and media policy making in the UK', *International Journal of Cultural Policy*, **11** (1), 15–29.

Henry, C. (ed.) (2007), *Entrepreneurship in the Creative Industries: An International Perspective*, Cheltenham, UK and Northampton, MA, USA: Edward Elgar.

Henry, C. (2009), 'Women and the creative industries: exploring the popular appeal', *Creative Industries Journal*, **2** (2), 143–60.

Hesmondhalgh, D. (2007), *The Cultural Industries*, 2nd edn, London: Sage.

Higgs, P. and S. Cunningham (2008) 'Creative industries mapping: where have we come from and where are we going?', *Creative Industries Journal*, **1** (1), 7–30.

Howkins, J. (2002), *The Creative Economy: How People Make Money from Ideas*, London: Penguin Books.

Lee, N., K. Morris, J. Wright, N. Clayton, I. Brinkley and A. Jones (2010), 'No city left behind? The geography of the recovery and the implications for the coalition. Cities 2010', July, The Work Foundation, accessed at www.work-foundation.com.

Roodhouse, S. (2009), 'The scope of the *Creative Industries Journal*', *Creative Industries Journal*, **2** (2), i.

UK Trade and Investment (2006), 'Prosperity in a changing world', UK Trade and Investment's strategy (2006–2011)', July, accessed at www.ukti.gov.uk.

United Nations (2008), 'Creative Economy Report 2008, The Challenge of Assessing the Creative Economy towards Informed Policy-Making', New York: United Nations.

2.   The creative industries definitional discourse

Simon Roodhouse

INTRODUCTION

Successive United Kingdom (UK) national governments and their agencies have defined and redrawn boundaries. This has resulted in continuous public cultural policy and practice turbulence since 1945, commencing with the establishment of the Arts Council of Great Britain (Pick and Anderton, 1999). The pragmatic determination of these boundaries – that is, definitions with no obvious rationale for inclusion or exclusion – lends itself to an interpretation of a public sector domain engaged in restrictive cultural practice, wherein boundaries are constrained enough to match the level of available resources at any given time. It is the government administrative machinery responding to national policy by providing manageable and controllable categories, classifications and frameworks for the allocation of public funds, rather than a rational, inclusive and empirically informed (and hence measurable) system that conforms to the requirements of evidence-based policy (Solesbury, 2001). Urban regeneration (Roodhouse and Roodhouse, 1997) and the creative industries policy (Roodhouse, 2003c) by the New Labour administration exemplify this practice.

This chapter explores the difficulties created as a result of defining and redefining the creative industries and their related activities. The various boundary definitions for the creative sector are discussed, and a historical perspective on their evolution is provided. The economical and statistical limitations of such boundaries are debated alongside the difficulties associated with weak and questionable data sources. An evolutionary model for classifying the creative industries based on core and related activities is then presented.

BOUNDARIES AND CHAOS

The impact of the obsession with continuous boundary redefinition through national government machinery and by political parties for the arts, creativity and culture (which commenced with the Department of Education, followed by the Office of Arts and Libraries, then the Department of Heritage and now the Department for Culture, Media and Sport) works against cohesion, interaction and connectivity; although much is said by politicians about joined-up policy and action. 'Joined-up government' is a key theme of modern government. The Labour government, first elected in 1997, decided that intractable problems such as social exclusion, drug addiction and crime could not be resolved by any single department of government. Instead, such problems had to be made the object of a concerted attack using all the arms of government – central and local government and public agencies – as well as the private and voluntary sectors (Bogdanor, 2005). In particular, the government encourages isolationism between national, regional and local government and agencies by relying on departmentalization and compartmentalization as the organizational means of delivery. As an illustration, culture resides within the Department for Culture, Media and Sport (DCMS) and is also found in the Foreign and Commonwealth Office, which funds the British Council (British Council, 1998, 2004); the Ministry of Defence, which resources a substantial number of museums, galleries and musical bands; the Department of Trade and Industry, which supports creative industries through the Small Business Service, including the export effort of these businesses; the Department for Education and Skills (Allen and Shaw, 2001); and the Higher Education Funding Council for England (HEFCE) which provides entry-to-work and workforce development in the cultural field (North West Universities Association, 2004). This, incidentally, excludes all the devolved cultural arrangements for Scotland, Northern Ireland and Wales, which are another area of chaos, as the studies referred to are focused on England. This chaotic organizational pattern is replicated at regional level with DCMS-sponsored Cultural Consortia, the Arts Council, the Museums, Libraries and Archives Council (MLA), the Sports Council, the Tourist Boards, Sector Skills Councils (SSCs) and local authorities, along with the Regional Development Agencies (RDAs) and the Small Business Service, including Business Link, not to mention the plethora of subregional intermediaries funded from the public purse, all pursuing differing cultural agendas and definitional frameworks (Hamilton and Scullion, 2002). Although attempts are made at over-arching regional strategies, there is not as yet a shared understanding of and agreement on a definitional framework to operate and evaluate the effectiveness of these strategies. This leads, for example, to data collection replication, which requires additional resource allocation for coordination. Selwood has recognized this, and suggests:

> If the lure of cross domain data remains attractive to DCMS and its agencies, there is a case to be made for a better relationship to be forged between the requirements of cultural policy and the collection of evidence. In short we should replace our reliance on the sometimes random data sets which already exist, and which are collated in a piecemeal fashion, with a coherent data framework. (Selwood, n.d.)

A BRIEF HISTORY

The above issues were foregrounded by the 1997 'New Labour' government engagement in the creative industries concept, which claimed to be a significant contributor to the UK knowledge economy (DCMS, 1998a, 2001). This concept, generated by Leadbetter and Oakley (1999), is a contemporary reinvention of the 'Old Labour' Greater London Council (GLC)-oriented cultural model. The Labour-controlled GLC provided a significant challenge to the definitional status quo in the early 1980s, at a time of high unemployment, significant industrial decline and diminishing public funds for the arts, by reintroducing the cultural industries model derived from popular culture theorists such as Bourdieu and reinvented by Walpole and Comedia in the 1980s. The introduction of the cultural and creative industries exemplars gave rise to a reappraisal of the role and function of the 'traditional' arts in economic terms (Myerscough, 1988), and in relation to new technologies such as instant printing, cassette recording and video making (O'Connor, 1999). So, the concept of culture as an industry in a public policy context was introduced. The arts, described by the GLC as the 'traditional arts', were subsumed into a broader definitional framework, which included 'the electronic forms of cultural production and distribution – radio, television, records and video – and the diverse range of popular cultures which exist in London' (Greater London Council, 1985). The eventual successor body, the London Assembly, and the executive Mayor of London have rekindled the theme (London Development Agency, 2003), this time with a focus on intervention in the creative industry networks and linkages. However, creative industries development is derived from a longer history associated with defining and redefining the arts as an industry sector (Roodhouse, 1997; Calhoun et al., 1993) and the relationship of the arts and media as cultural industries, for example, which others have addressed (O'Connor, 1999; Throsby, 2001; Pratt, 1997; Garnham, 1987).

The cultural industries' replacement creative industry concept, generated by Demos (Leadbetter and Oakley, 1999) and constructed as a component of the knowledge economy model, can be found in one of four key policy themes for the DCMS: that is, economic value (Cunningham, 2002). It is argued that the theme of economic value is a maturing of the Thatcherite ethos of efficiency, effectiveness, value for money and market forces. Smith, the first New Labour Secretary of State for Culture, Media and Sport in the UK, reinforced this interpretation, 'ensuring that the full economic and employment impact of the whole range of creative industries is acknowledged and assisted by government' (Smith, 1998), in his attempts to promote 'Cool Britannia'. As illustrated below, this was after all a continuation of the cultural economic rationale developed earlier by Ken Walpole (Greater London Council, Industry and Employment Branch, 1985):

> For the first time, the concept of culture as an industry in a public policy context was introduced. The arts, described by the GLC as the 'traditional arts', were subsumed into a broader definitional framework which included 'the electronic forms of cultural production and distribution – radio, television, records and video – and the diverse range of popular cultures which exist in London' [Greater London Council, 1985]. The London Industrial Strategy, The Cultural Industries, argued strongly that 'What is available for cultural consumption and what opportunities there are for employment in cultural production are, for better or for worse, clearly determined by economics'. Given the high levels of unemployment at the time, March 1985 (over 400 000 people were officially unemployed and there were a further 120 000 people wanting work in London), it is not surprising that the role of 'cultural industries' as an employment vehicle within London's economy was recognized. (Roodhouse, 2000)

Here, attention is drawn to a continuum of development, thus suggesting that the creative industries concept is evolutionary and certainly not radical. The connection with the knowledge economy provides a new dimension.

THE GOVERNMENT DEFINITION

The government, through the Creative Industries Taskforce, chaired by Smith, defined the creative industries boundaries. The definition employed is largely pragmatic, with little in the way of a rationale (Roodhouse, 2003a): 'those activities which have their origin in individual creativity, skill and talent, and which have a potential for wealth and job creation through the generation and exploitation of intellectual property' (DCMS, 1998a). The industrial activity subsectors within which this activity primarily takes place are: 'advertising, architecture, the art and antiques market, crafts, design, designer fashion, film, interactive leisure software, music, the performing arts, publishing, software, television and radio' (DCMS, 1998a). The representation of these activities as the UK creative industry sector generates structural and intellectual location tensions: for example, architecture relates to construction and marginally engages with the arts and antiques trade; similarly, the arts and antiques trade has little or nothing to do with interactive leisure software. It is an emerging policy construct that the DCMS has yet to embed both intellectually and practically in the consciousness of those working in the field, not least because there has been no consultation with those affected. As a consequence, the concept has more in common with the developing global economic interest in the knowledge economy (Leadbetter and Oakley, 1999; Howkins, 2001; Caves, 2000) than the DCMS-designated constituent activities (the subsectors). This is exacerbated by the DCMS's divisional structure, which does not attempt to reconcile the creative industries' subsectors.

PUBLIC AND PRIVATE

Of particular note in this definitional discourse is the equitable inclusion of both public and private sector activity in public cultural policy by redesignating cultural activity as creative industries and engaging with convergence arguments generated through advances in technology (Flew, 2002; Cunningham et al., 2003). Fundamentally, this growing reconceptualization facilitates a reassessment of the traditional forms of policy intervention in support of the arts and culture (Roodhouse, 2002). As elaborated by Cunningham (2002), the term 'creative industries' offers a workable solution that enables cultural industries and creative arts to become enshrined within a definition that breaks down the rigid sustainability of the long-standing definitions of culture and creative arts to create coherency through democratizing culture in the context of commerce, whereby creativity can become coupled alongside enterprise and technology to become sectors of economic growth through the commercialization of creative activity and intellectual property. Cunningham confirms this: '"Creative Industries" is a term that suits the political, cultural and technological landscape of these times. It focuses on the twin truths that (i) the core of "culture" is still creativity, but (ii) creativity is produced, deployed, consumed and enjoyed quite differently in post-industrialised societies' (Cunningham, 2002, p. 2).

THE ARTS

This, then, is a move from the traditional arts definition established by the Arts Council of Great Britain and successor bodies, recently reinvented as 'the value of the arts' argument (Jowell, 2004), to an economic reconceptualization of the creative industries that implies a democratization of the arts (Roodhouse, 2002) and opens the door to engaging seriously with the arts as business. Subsequently, these concepts were encompassed in an invited article for the Liberal Democrat policy journal, the *Reformer*, as a contribution to the arts policy debate:

> Such an alternative perspective allows us to consider a more sustainable future for the arts and heritage as creative businesses, with products, services and markets. Judgement of excellence is simple, and funding becomes based on a business model. The nature of public sector organisational roles can be re-evaluated in developing this industrial sector just like any other industrial activity. Large businesses and the education sector take over the role of research and development. Government should ensure that risk and innovation is nurtured. No special pleading should be required, though, and a wider range of funding agencies can become involved in supporting and developing the businesses. (Roodhouse, 2001)

ECONOMIC AND STATISTICAL LIMITATIONS

Since the early 1980s, attempts have been made by cultural economists, statisticians and cultural geographers to arrive at suitable categorizations for the sector (Myerscough, 1988; O'Brien and Feist, 1995; Pratt, 1997; Jeffcut, 2004; NESTA, 2006). A National Endowment for Science, Technology and the Arts (NESTA) research report (2006, p. 2) argued: 'the definition does not focus on how economic value is created. Most significantly, it does not recognize differences in market structures, distribution mechanisms and consumption patterns between the creative sectors'. Pratt endorses this by suggesting that value chain and domain categorization is a useful mechanism. This approach generalizes the problem and reduces the importance of subsectors and of specifying the activities within them. Meanwhile Jeffcut (2004), from a knowledge management perspective, suggests that the only way to understand the industry is as a cultural ecology. This relationship and interaction approach side-steps the key issue, which is a detailed explanation of the subsector activity categories. Cunningham, and particularly Hearn (Hearn et al., 2005), take this further by engaging with a value chain ecology, which relies on a thorough understanding of networks and shared detailed classifications

Table 2.1 CIRAC, ACLC, ANZSIC and UKSIC business activity concordance table

CMIC (1)	ACLC (2) AND UKSIC EQUIVALENTS	ANZSIC (3)
1. Music Composition (incl. Composers and Songwriters)	231 Music Composition 92.31 Artistic and Literary creation and Interpretation	9242 Creative Arts
5. Record Company or Label	233 Record Companies and Distributors 22.31 Reproduction of sound recording	2430 Recorded Media Manufacturing and Publishing 4799 Wholesaling n.e.c.

Source: Simon Roodhouse, CIRAC, 2007.

developed by the author. What seems to have emerged from this work is a recognition that the Office for National Statistics (ONS; a UK government agency) the Standard Occupational Classification (SOC) and the Standard Industrial Classification (SIC) provide a common, imperfect, but nonetheless verifiable structure to collect and analyse data, which corresponds with European, North American and Australasian systems. For example, Table 2.1 provides an integrated definitional model based on the Australian SIC and SOC system used to collect primary baseline data on the music subsector of the creative industries in Queensland, Australia (Cox et al., 2004). There are, in addition, arguments that suggest that a product classificatory approach may prove to be the solution to these issues, so Jacobs and O'Neil (2003) suggest that it is possible to avoid some of the problems associated with SIC by using databases (such as Kompass or Dash), which allow searches to be carried out on particular products or services. Others such as Kahle and Walking (1996) provide an alternative approach, namely the use of large-scale market research surveys such as those organized by the UK ONS, for example the Annual Business Inquiry Survey. However, economists and statisticians who are expected to quantify the creative and cultural industry and/or arts activity to provide informed data for policy evaluation and development continue to be dogged by this tortuous and contorted definitional history (Barrière and Santagata, 1997; Evans, 1997). In other words, it is difficult to provide the history with trend data.

WEAKNESSES AND INCONSISTENCIES

The weakness and inconsistencies of the definitional frameworks become apparent when used to quantify and determine the value of artistic and/ or aesthetic activity. The definitional chaos also illustrates a fundamental structural failure of the creative industries concept as defined generally by the UK's Department for Culture, Media and Sport (DCMS) and others, the problem being that the visual arts are not represented, but are instead located in the arts and antiques trade as products. In other words, this 'industrial activity' is referred to and classified as tangible output, such as sculpture, painting, prints and ceramics – that is, as product rather than as a creative activity or business or the creative process. This runs counter to the 'creative individual' argument enshrined in the DCMS definition, which the UK government, through the Creative Industries Taskforce, defined as it developed and implemented the creative industries policy. The 'creative individual' concept was derived from an interest in the knowledge economy, and the definition employed was largely pragmatic: 'Those activities which have their origin in individual creativity, skill and talent, and which have a potential for wealth and job creation through the generation and exploitation of intellectual property' (DCMS, 1998a). The sectors identified in this definitional framework are: 'advertising, architecture, the art and antiques market, crafts, design, designer fashion, film, interactive leisure software, music, the performing arts, publishing, software, television and radio' (DCMS, 1998b).

It is hard to conceive of the creative industries without identifying individual artists as creative businesses, but after detailed examination of the taskforce's subsectors and how they are defined, it becomes clear that artists are not defined this way. Visual arts activity can, however, be found in the 'arts and antiques trade' subsector (referred to earlier) and in the 'crafts' subsector. This chapter illustrates the confused conceptual analysis of the visual arts found in the DCMS creative industries mapping documents' definition (DCMS, 1998, 2001), which is at best a description of outcomes from a creative process that may or may not be recognized by the producers (Roodhouse, 2006, p. 1064).

FROM THE GENERAL TO THE SPECIFIC

There is a need for a shift from generalized descriptors and categorizations such as advertising to specific analysis of its component parts. Authors such as Baumol and Baumol (1994) and Heatherington (1992), who are interested in understanding the economics of the sector, with assertions that aesthetic pleasure has at least as much value as the difference in returns between works of art and financial assets, quickly find that there is no common understanding of art or aesthetics. This leads to the ultimate question: how to define a work of art? Another issue for economists studying the cultural industries is the differentiation between artistic and industrial goods. Part of the difficulty here is that the total assimilation of art into commodities creates serious problems because art goods escape the standard rules of utilitarian market exchange (Barrière and Santagata, 1997). The consequence of this failure to engage in establishing common workable definitions is summed up by Towse in considering the visual arts: 'The main point is that whichever definition is used, it is bound to produce different research findings.' This has led over time to: 'the paucity of alternative data sets with which to test the assertion(s) in practice' (Arts Council of England, 2003). Consequently, even if the definitional jungle referred to can be avoided, there are difficulties in successfully locating cultural product within the accepted norms of economic practice. The fault line for cultural economists in delivering convincing economic analysis is the lack of clarity and consistency in defining cultural practice and, therefore, generating any useful data. The rationale, for example, for including designer fashion as a discrete creative subsector and excluding graphic design is hard to find. Similarly, evidence to support the exclusion of the heritage sector, inferring that it is not creative, is difficult to ascertain from the published material such as the DCMS mapping documents.

QUANTIFICATION ISSUES

Twenty-eight years after the United Nations Educational, Scientific and Cultural Organization (UNESCO) report (Green et al., 1970), the DCMS published an audit based on these secondary data in 1998, with a follow-up in 2001, the Creative Industries Mapping Documents (DCMS, 1998a, 2001), which claimed that these industries generated £57 billion (1998) and £112 billion (2001) in revenues and employment of circa 1 million (1998) and 1.3 million (2001), as described in Table 2.2 by subsector.

There are the usual health warnings associated with these statistics, and recommendations for further work to be carried out in collecting and verifying the data underpinning the document. In particular, the DCMS recommends: 'Continuing to improve the collection of robust and timely data on the creative industries, based on a common understanding of coverage' (DCMS, 2001).

Table 2.2   UK creative industries headline data, 1998 and 2001, and 2005

Activity	Revenues 1998 and 2001 (£Bn)	Employment 1998 and 2001 (thousands)	Employment Estimates for 2005 (thousands)
Advertising	4.0 3.0	96 000 93 000	89 100
Architecture	1.5 1.7	30 000 21 000	83 100
Arts and antiques	2.2 3.5	39 700 37 000	22 900
Crafts	0.4 0.4	25 000 24 000	–
Design	12.0 26.7	23 000 76 000	–
Designer fashion	0.6 0.6	11 500 12 000	3 400
Film/video	0.9 3.6	33 000 45 000	51 000
Interactive leisure software	1.2 1.0	27 000 21 000	341 600 (incl. software and computer services)
Music	3.6 4.6	160 000 122 000	185 300 (incl. performing arts)
Performing arts	0.9 0.5	60 000 74 000	185 300 (incl. music)
Publishing	16.3 18.5	125 000 141 000	173 800
Software/computer services	7.5 36.4	272 000 555 000	341 600 (incl. leisure software)
Television and radio	6.4 12.1	63 500 102 000	95 200
Total	£57bn 112.5bn	Circa 1 000 000 1 322 000	1 045 400

Source: Simon Roodhouse, DCMS, 2007

THE REGIONS

The data on the interactive leisure software, designer fashion (Roodhouse, 2003b) and crafts subsectors were identified by the DCMS as particularly weak. When considering this matter at the regional level, the position is dismal, with little information available (Department of Arts Policy and Management, 2000). Consequently, one of the key issues identified was: 'The need for more mapping to provide a better picture of what is happening on the ground and help inform policy development. The mapping also needs to be based on a common understanding of the coverage of the creative industries' (DCMS, 2001).

However, the DCMS has attempted to develop a regional cultural data framework (Wood, 2004). This has not been accepted, because it does not universally conform to the national data collection classifications and relies on generalized notions of domains and a limited interpretation of value chains. Consequently, the DCMS has replaced it with a published guide (toolkit) to data collection:

> The main impetus behind the development of the toolkit was the urgent need, expressed by all the English Regional Cultural Consortia (RCCs), for a more robust and reliable evidence-base on which to develop future policies for culture, [however] there is currently no underlying taxonomic principle that guides whether certain activities fall within the realm of the DCMS or not. In turn, this is the result of the lack of a public definition of the area for which the Department has responsibility – that is, the 'Cultural Sector'. The only government definition that one could possibly identify is an operational, self-definition; that is, the Cultural Sector becomes defined solely as 'that for which the DCMS has responsibility'. (DCMS, 2004)

This can only be perceived as a fundamental structural weakness, when increasing emphasis is placed on evidence-based cultural policy and comparative international benchmarking.

Despite sporadic attempts (O'Brien and Feist, 1995; Arts Council of England, 2003), the paucity of empirical evidence available and the structural weakness of the definitional frameworks to inform cultural policy, management or practice, particularly in the fields of museums, galleries and the creative industries (Roodhouse, 2003c), to support the formulation and development of policy at local, regional (Devlin et al., 1998, 1999; Roodhouse and Taylor, 2000[1]) and national levels continues. A 2006 DCMS statement confirms this:

> As set out [above,] many of the calls for better evidence have focused on official statistics and the way DCMS uses these to estimate the economic importance of the creative industries. In particular, problems have been raised with the identification of creative industries within official classifications. Official statistics are drawn from ONS surveys which cover businesses that are registered for VAT and do not include those that are not registered or small businesses whose turnover is below the VAT threshold. This is problematic when trying to identify and measure the activity of the creative industries because many of the industries are very specific and small in terms of number of businesses, turnover and employment. There is concern therefore that official statistics are not totally representative of the whole creative industries sector. The only way to overcome this would be to carry out a separate survey of small creative firms and individuals but this would be a huge undertaking involving significant costs and potentially placing a considerable burden on the firms. (DCMS, 2006[2])

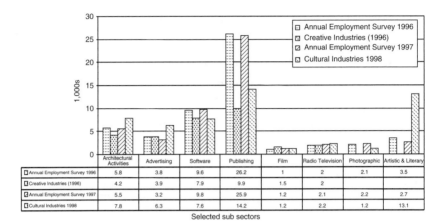

Source: Roodhouse (2003b).

Figure 2.1   Comparative Yorkshire and Humber regional employment by selected subsectors, 1996–98

Separate surveys to provide baseline analysis were pioneered in 2000 for the Yorkshire and Humber Government Office, involving a primary data survey of cultural industries businesses in the Yorkshire and the Humber region cited by the Arts Council of England (Hutton et al., 2004) and the University of Warwick, Institute of Employment Studies (Galloway, 2002). Figure 2.1 is an example of the primary data generated through baseline surveys of businesses.

QUESTIONABLE SOURCES OF DATA

Much of the statistical evidence used by the public sector agencies and government departments referred to earlier is traceable:

> National Statistics sources where possible – primarily the Annual Business Inquiry, the Inter-Departmental Business Register and the Labour Force Survey – meaning that the estimates are the best possible with the available data. Definitions are based on the UK Standard Industrial Classifications (SIC) and Standard Occupational Classifications (SOC); however, they do not accurately reflect the structure of the Creative Industries. As such, it is difficult to capture the full extent of the activity. (DCMS, 2006[3])

Eurostat has also been generating information in this field. However, in reality it is secondary data when used in the context of the creative industries, with all the inherent weaknesses of such an approach (Department of Arts Policy and Management 2000). This becomes worse, with questionable sources, when consideration is given to the data employed to support the DCMS creative industry mapping documents:

> Sources of data have included the Department of Trade and Industry, *Antique Trades Gazette*, Crafts Council, Design Council, Screen Finance, Arts Council of England, *Sunday Times*, *Screen Digest*, *BPI Statistical Handbook*, *The Value of Music*, Henley Centre, Association of British Sponsorship of the Arts, Society of London Theatres, Express Newspapers, Consumer Trends, Business Monitor and the *UK Media Yearbook*. Much of this information is unverifiable, collected over differing periods of time, using unrelated methodologies. (Roodhouse, 2000)

In addition, Companies House data are publicly available; however the SIC classifications are esoteric because the company chooses which classification it wants to describe the business best.

The Department has attempted to sift through these sources and select on the basis of compatibility. This process, however, reinforced the difficulties of using a variety of unverified sources that are not collecting data using a commonly defined framework. Smith confirmed, however, that collecting and analysing data to underpin creative industries policy is problematic, and past claims are difficult to substantiate (DCMS, 1998a):

> One of the problems in this whole area is that the precise figures (for the creative industries) are hard to come by. Many of these areas of activity are of course dominated by small and medium sized companies almost working on a cottage industry basis, with a handful of big players striding amongst them; it is a pattern that makes definition and accurate counting very difficult but even more essential if public policy is to be maintained. (Smith, 1998)

Rather worryingly, a similar view was expressed as long ago as 1970 in the UNESCO report, 'Cultural policy in Great Britain' (Green et al., 1970), referred to earlier.

What is apparent is the chaotic nature of the cultural sector at regional and national levels, reflected in the ad hoc collection of data and not least in the inconsistent use of definitional frameworks. This observation has subsequently been picked up by the DCMS in developing the Regional Cultural Data Framework and its successor, the DCMS Evidence Toolkit, by arriving at a working definition of culture as a starting point:

> Culture has both a 'material' and a non-material dimension. The definition of the Cultural Sector must focus upon material culture, and we understand this to be the sum of activities and necessary resources (tools, infrastructure and artefacts) involved in the whole 'cycle' of creation, making, dissemination,

exhibition/reception, archiving/preservation, and education/understanding relating to cultural products and services. We recognise that the range of activities defined as 'cultural' is mobile and changing. However, at their most inclusive, we propose that the domains (sub sectors) of the Cultural Sector cover the following: Visual Art, Performance, Audio-Visual, Books and Press, Sport, Heritage, and Tourism. (DCMS, 2006[4])

Although progress is being made in arriving at a commonly understood cultural definition, there remains a poor knowledge base: 'The evidence available is limited and patchy – more evidence needs to be collected to allow policy to be developed' (DCMS, 2006).

AN EVOLUTIONARY MODEL

This approach developed by the Creative Industries Observatory (CIO) builds on the pioneering work of Roodhouse and Taylor (2000) for the Yorkshire and Humber Government Office involving a survey of cultural industries businesses in the Yorkshire and the Humber region.

The first phase of developing the evolutionary CIO model consisted of identifying the core and related activities found in the DCMS Mapping Documents and matching these activities with the appropriate SIC codes. This was then related to NACE and ISIC classifications to provide a family tree of interrelated classificatory systems, which operate nationally and internationally.

In addition, the 2004 DCMS Evidence Toolkit (DET)[5] was evaluated because it included a wider definition of cultural domains and functions incorporating the creative and cultural industries. These categories were mapped against available UK SIC (2003) codes. However, the DET domains and functions have been reorganized based on institutional organizational theory to establish a closer 'fit' to the DCMS creative subsectoral industry definition. Consequently, if functionality is required, the definitional framework incorporates: origination (incorporates the DET creating and making functions); translation (incorporates the DET education, dissemination and exhibition functions); delivery (handing over the goods and services to the customer). This approach is informed by Scott's institutional theory (as presented at the European Group of Organizational Studies, EGOS 23rd Colloquium, Vienna 2007) based on an analysis of the professions so that: origination is a means of augmenting creativity and knowledge; translation concerns itself with transporting and carrying the results of origination to the point of delivery; and delivery focuses on the application of that knowledge and creativity to individuals.

A comparison of the definitional framework employed in data collection for the Creative Economy Programme[6] (CEP), launched by DCMS in November 2005, was also undertaken. There were differences but these can be explained. The emerging definitional framework had been constructed using the UK SIC 2007, so the comparative anomalies are largely the result of differences between the old and revised SIC codes. As a result of this analysis, explanatory tables were created to explain how core and related activities match with the relevant SIC codes and functions.

The approach adopted in the final definitional framework illustrated in Figure 2.2 is informed by the Office for National Statistics, where an activity is said to take place when resources such as equipment, labour, manufacturing techniques, information networks or products are combined, leading to the creation of specific goods or services. As a result, an activity is characterized by an input of products (goods or services), a production process and an output of products.

The DCMS and others have attempted to disaggregate the creative industries into core and related activities. The DCMS Mapping Documents (1998a, 2001) demonstrate this, with a subsector such as performing arts broken down as follows:

- Core activities:
  - Consumer research and insight.
  - Management of client marketing activity.
  - Identifying consumer tastes and responses.
  - Creation of advertising, promotions.
  - Public relations (PR) campaigns.
  - Media planning, buying and evaluation.
  - Production of advertising materials.
- Related activities:
  - Creative studios and freelancers.
  - Editing facilities.
  - Brochures, publications.
  - Photography, filming and digital recording.
  - Multimedia and Internet production.
  - Digital content generation.
  - Marketing consultancy.
  - Exhibitions.

However, the Mapping Documents did not provide an adequate explanation of core or related activity. Therefore, these have been revised as follows:

- Core activities represent the most important creative assets of the subsector that are a close match to the 1998 DCMS definition, that is:

CIO definitional framework for design

Core and related activities (DCMS mapping documents, 1998a, 2001)	SIC codes identified by the CIO (UK Standard Industrial Classification 2007)
Core activities	
Design consultancies (services include: e.g. brand information design, new product development). Design components of industry. Interior and environment design.	74.10 Specialized design activities.
Related activities	
Fine art. Craft (e.g. small-scale furniture makers).	90.03 Artistic creation.
Graphic design. Multimedia, website and digital media design. Research and development within industry.	74.10 Specialized design activities.
Television graphics.	No clear SIC code correspondence.
Interactive and digital TV design.	No clear SIC code correspondence.
Manufacturing industry design.	31. Manufacture of furniture. 32. Other manufacturing.
Modelling and prototype making.	No clear SIC code correspondence.
Retail (related industry).	47.19 Other retail sale in non-specialized stores. 47.59 Retail sale of furniture, lighting equipment and other household articles in specialized stores.

Source: Creative Industries Observatory (2008).

Figure 2.2   Summary of core and related activities versus UK SIC 2007

'those activities which have their origin in individual creativity, skill and talent, and which have a potential for wealth and job creation through the generation and exploitation of intellectual property'.
- Related activities constitute secondary sources of revenue, derived from the core activities.

Each of the revised subsectoral core and related activities were matched with a specific SIC code where possible. This has shown that there are no relevant codes in several cases. The revised subsectoral core and related frameworks and the SIC correlation were verified with the appropriate commercial associations, in order to establish a practitioner perspective. This resulted in further changes that have been incorporated in the final evolutionary model. The evolutionary framework example can be found in Figure 2.3.

So for example, the Design Council highlighted the complex structure of the industry, particularly significant overlapping activities with other creative subsectors including fashion, advertising and architecture. The results of the consultation with the Council provided a revised Definitional Framework for Design as shown in Figure 2.3.

The four-digit level UK SIC code that appears most frequently in the above framework is 74.10, 'Specialized design activities', which includes:

- Fashion design related to textiles, wearing apparel, shoes, jewellery, furniture and other interior decoration and fashion goods, as well as other personal or household goods.
- Industrial design, such as creation and development of designs and specifications that optimize the use, value and appearance of products, including the determination of the materials, mechanism, shape, colour and surface finishes of the product, taking into consideration human characteristics and needs, safety, market appeal in distribution, use and maintenance.[7]

It should also be noted that 'service design' has been identified as a new area of activity in development by the Design Council, which has not been mapped by either the UK SIC 2007 or the DCMS Creative Industries Mapping Documents (1998a, 2001). This approach was adopted for each of the subsectors and the revised definitional framework provided the basis for the selection of companies, data collection and the ability to relate findings to other SIC-related datasets. This emerging definitional framework is a fine grading of the basic DCMS definitions and enables the detailed organization and comparison of existing data as well as the collection of new data subsectorally and regionally; this is where the majority of the gaps in understanding exist.

CIO definitional framework for design

Activities	Corresponding UK SIC 2007 codes
Communication (graphic, brand, printing, information design, corporate identity).	18.12/9 Printing (other than printing of newspapers and printing on labels and tags) n.e.c. 73.11 Advertising agencies. 74.10 Specialized design activities (graphic).
Product and industrial design (Consumer and house products, furniture, industrial e.g. automotive).	71.12/9 Other engineering activities (engineering design). 74.10 Specialized design activities.
Interior and exhibition (retail design, work place design, display systems).	74.10 Specialized design activities. 82.30/1 Activities of exhibition and fair organisers.
Fashion and textile	74.10 Specialized design activities.
Digital and multimedia (website animation, film and TV, digital and interaction).	59.11 Motion picture, video and television programme production activities. 62.01 Computer programming activities. 90.03 Artistic creation.
Service design (developmental area).	*No clear corresponding SIC codes*

Core activities

[Bold] Additions by the Design Council [ ] UK SIC 2007 codes chosen by CIO and approved by the Design Council

Source: Creative Industries Observatory (2008).

Figure 2.3 Definitional framework for design

CONCLUSION

The introduction of a creative industries policy has inadvertently encouraged an emerging reconceptualization of the cultural industries, particularly arts practice: culture as business, not the 'Tate' effect; aesthetic, peer-group-determined public culture. As a result of this conceptual repositioning, arts institutions can be seen as creative businesses engaging with customers, developing markets, and providing services and products which contribute to the development of local, national and regional culture. This may, for example, require a re-examination of the role of local authorities or arts councils towards acting as contract and risk managers with a wider understanding of business development. Many local authorities see a long-term future for the cultural services and arts in contributing to regeneration, quality of life, social cohesion and economic development. What may be needed is the freedom to develop alternative strategies through the creative industries paradigm to recognize people's innate creativity, then capturing and building it into the creative businesses of the future.

If research in the creative industries nationally and internationally is to be taken seriously, we will need to be precise about the use of classicality systems and move towards an international standard. This calls for the sector and those involved in it to cooperate in the building of shared definitional frameworks. For example, care must be taken when applying value chain and ecology theoretical frameworks as a means of understanding the creative industries generally when, for example, we cannot yet quantify sculpture or sculpting or reach a common understanding of what graphic design represents. The implications, then, for cultural management policy and practice include the following.

First, unreliable data for management decision-making: if, for example, the visual arts officer for a regional arts council has no reliable definition of visual arts that is benchmarked nationally and internationally, how can he or she rely on the data (whatever their source) to support policy development? As a result it is very unlikely that the officer will know how many 'artists' exist in the region or be able to compare his or her data with the data for other regions and nations.

Second, unreliable comparative data for measuring performance: in the absence of a common definition at the national level, comparison of financial policy interventions at the regional level becomes at best generalized. This precludes interregional objective comparison of performance, which is an unsatisfactory position for a national government to be in. This does not happen in other areas of government, so why in the creative sector? No serious comparative research or evaluation can then take place across regions. If policy cannot be empirically evaluated and compared – which is common practice in the health and construction sectors – then creative industries and cultural policy are unlikely to be taken seriously. This is not a comfortable environment for cultural managers responsible for the allocation and administration of public funds.

Third, weak, unconvincing and unreliable advocacy: cultural managers are constantly concerned with attracting new resources to support their cultural activity. This forms a large component of most managerial roles in the sector and there is a constant cry for reliable data to construct the case, often manifested as economic impact studies. Another British example is the establishment, at a regional level, of cultural consortia, which include the majority of the DCMS cultural agencies operating at the regional level. The primary purpose of a cultural consortium is to produce at least a shared regional strategy and to act as an advocate. Reliable data on employment, income, participation and other factors are essential for this. However, there is little agreement on shared interregional definitional frameworks and, subsequently, a paucity of reliable and verifiable data. Consequently what is produced is ad hoc, unrelated and difficult to compare. This is dangerous territory for the advocate, as more of the data become discredited.

NOTES

1. These reports are available as supplementary evidence.
2. See http://headshift.com/dcms/mt/archives/blog_36/Evidence%20and%20Analysis%20-%20post%20cons%20final.doc, accessed 15 April 2007.
3. See http://headshift.com/dcms/mt/archives/blog_36/Evidence%20and%20Analysis%20-%20post%20cons%20final.doc, accessed 15 April 2007.
4. See http://headshift.com/dcms/mt/archives/blog_36/Evidence%20and%20Analysis%20-%20post%20cons%20final.doc, accessed 15 April 2007.
5. http://www.culture.gov.uk/Reference_library/Research/det/7_full_Technical_Report.htm.
6. http://www.cep.culture.gov.uk/index.cfm?fuseaction=main.viewBlogEntry&intMTEntryID=3104.
7. United Nations Statistic Division (2007), ISIC detailed structure and explanatory notes, available at http://unstats.un.org.

REFERENCES

Allen, K. and P. Shaw (2001), 'Continuing professional development for the creative industries: a review of provision in the higher education sector', Higher Education Funding Council for England.

Arts Council of England (2003), 'Artists in figures: a statistical portrait of cultural occupation', Arts Council of England research report 31, London.

Barrière, C. and W. Santagata (1997), 'Defining art, from the Brancusi trail to the economics of semiotic goods', AIMAC Proceedings, Golden Gate University, San Francisco, CA.

Baumol, W. and H. Baumol (1994), 'On the economics of musical composition in Mozart's Vienna', in James M. Morris (ed.), *On Mozart*, New York and Cambridge: Publisher?

Bogdanor, V. (2005), *Joined Up Government*, Oxford: Oxford University Press.

British Council (1998), *Britain's Design Industry: The Design Workshop of the World*, London: British Council.

British Council (2004), *Creative Industries*, London: British Council Creative Industries Unit.

Calhoun, C., E. Lupuma and M. Postone (1993), *Bourdieu: Critical Perspectives*, Cambridge: Polity Press.

Caves, R. (2000), *Creative Industries*, Cambridge, MA: Harvard University Press.

Cox, S., A. Ninan, G. Hearn, S. Roodhouse and S. Cunningham (2004), *Queensland Music Industry Basics*, Brisbane, QLD: Creative Industries Research and Applications Centre, Queensland University of Technology.

Creative Industries Observatory (2008), 'A report on the design sector in London'.

Cunningham, S. (2002), *From Cultural to Creative Industries: Theory, Industry and Policy Implications*, Brisbane, QLD: Creative Industries Research and Applications Centre, University of Technology.

Cunningham, S., G. Hearn, S. Cox, A. Ninan and M. Keane (2003), 'Brisbane's creative industries 2003', report delivered to Brisbane City Council, Community and Economic Development, Creative Industries Applied Research Centre, University of Technology, Brisbane, Australia.

Department for Culture, Media and Sport (DCMS) (1998a), 'DCMS mapping document', London.

DCMS (1998b), 'Creative Industries Task Force report', London.

DCMS (2001), 'Creative Industries Mapping Document', London.

DCMS (2004), 'DCMS Evidence Toolkit – DET', formerly the Regional Cultural Data Framework Technical Report.

DCMS (2006), 'Creative Economy Programme, Evidence and Analysis Group report', accessed 15 April 2007 at http://headshift.com/dcms/mt/archives/blog_36/Evidence%20and%20Analysis%20-%20post%20cons%20final.doc.

Department of Arts Policy and Management (2000), *Creative Industries Mapping Document Sources Review*, London: City University.

Devlin, N., S. Gibson, C. Taylor and S. Roodhouse (1998), 'The cultural industries in Rotherham', unpublished report, Bretton Hall College, Wakefield.

Devlin, N., S. Gibson, C. Taylor and S. Roodhouse (1999), 'The cultural industries in Rotherham', unpublished report, Bretton Hall College, Wakefield.

Evans, G. (1997), 'Measuring the arts and cultural industries: does size matter?' in Simon Roodhouse (ed.), *The New Cultural Map: A Research Agenda for the 21st Century*, Wakefield: University of Leeds, pp. 26–34.

Flew, T. (2002), 'Beyond ad hocery: defining creative industries', Second International Conference on Cultural Policy Research, New Zealand.

Galloway, S. (2002), 'A balancing act: artists' labour markets and the tax benefits systems', University of Warwick Institute of Employment Studies research report 29.

Garnham, N. (1987), 'Concepts of culture: public policy and the cultural industries', *Cultural Studies*, **1** (1), 23–37.

Greater London Council, Industry and Employment Branch (1985), 'London industrial strategy: the cultural industries', Greater London Council.

Green, M., M. Wilding and R. Hoggart (1970), 'Cultural policy in Great Britain', UNESCO report.

Hamilton, C. and A. Scullion (2002), 'The effectiveness of the Scottish Arts Council's links and partnerships with other agencies: a report to the Scottish Executive', University of Glasgow.

Hearn, G., C. Pace and S. Roodhouse (2005), 'The shift to value ecology thinking', unpublished paper, CIRAC, QUT, Brisbane, QLD.

Heatherington, P. (1992), 'Values in art: bases for making judgements of artistic value', Wimbledon School of Art and the Tate Gallery.

Howkins, J. (2001), *The Creative Economy: How People Make Money from Ideas*, London: Allen Lane.

Hutton, L., A. Bridgwood and K. Dust (2004), 'Research at the Arts Council of England', *Cultural Trends*, **13** (4), 41–64.

Jacobs, G. and C. O'Neil (2003), 'On the reliability (or otherwise) of SIC codes', *European Business Review*, **15** (3), 164–9.

Jeffcut, P. (2004), 'Knowledge relationships and transactions in a cultural economy: analysing the creative industries ecosystem', *Culture and Policy*, **112** (1), 67–82.

Jowell, T. (2004), 'Government and the value of culture', Department of Culture, Media and Sport, London.

Kahle, K.M. and R.A. Walking (1996), 'The impact of industry classifications on financial research', *Journal of Financial and Quantitative Analysis*, 31, 309–35.

Leadbetter, C. and K. Oakley (1999), *The Independents: Britain's New Cultural Entrepreneurs*, London: Demos.

London Development Agency (2003), 'The Mayor's Commission on the Creative Industries: improving links in creative production chains', accessed 2 June 2004 at www.creativelondon.org.uk.

Myerscough, J. (1988), 'The economic importance of the arts in Britain', Policy Studies Institute, London.

NESTA (2006), 'Creating growth: how the UK can develop world-class creative businesses', NESTA.

North West Universities Association Culture Committee (2004), 'The contribution of higher education to cultural life in the North West', North West Universities Association, Manchester.

O'Brien, J. and A. Feist (1995), *Employment in the Arts and Cultural Industries: An Analysis of the 1991 Census*, London: Arts Council of England.

O'Connor, J. (1999), 'The definition of the cultural industries', Manchester Institute for Popular Culture, accessed at www.mmu.ac.uk/h-ss/mip/iciss/home2.htm.

Pick, J. and M. Anderton (1999), *Building Jerusalem: Art, Industry and the British Millennium*, Amsterdam: Harwood Academic Publishers.

Pratt, A. (1997), 'The cultural industries sector: its definition and character from secondary sources in employment and trade, Britain 1984–1991', London School of Economics, Department of Geography and the Environment research papers in the environment and spatial analysis no. 41.

Roodhouse, S. (1997), 'Interculturalism, in particular the relationship between artists and industrial imagery', *Journal of Arts Policy and Management Law and Society*, **27** (3).

Roodhouse, S. (2000), 'What do we know about the creative industries in the UK?', conference proceedings, Australian Institute of Arts Management Conference, Brisbane, QLD.

Roodhouse, S. (2001), 'Creating sustainable cultures', Art Reach, New South Wales Museum and Galleries Foundation, Sydney, NSW.

Roodhouse, S. (2002), 'Creating a sustainable culture for everybody', *The Reformer, Journal of the Centre for Reform.*

Roodhouse, S. (2003a), 'Designer fashion: the essential facts', AIMAC 7th conference proceedings, Bocconi University, Milan.

Roodhouse, S. (2003b), 'Essential facts: the nature of designer fashion and its markets', Bolton Institute report.

Roodhouse, S. (2003c), 'Have cultural industries a role to play in regional regeneration and a nation's wealth?' *International Journal of Applied Management*, **4** (1)

Roodhouse, S. and M. Roodhouse (1997), 'Cultural intervention in British urban regeneration since 1945', *AIMAC Proceedings.*

Roodhouse, S. and C. Taylor (2000), 'Vital statistics: the cultural industries in Yorkshire and the Humber', Bretton Hall, Wakefield: University of Leeds.

Selwood, S. (n.d.), 'Creative industries', London School of Economics ESRC seminar paper, London.

Smith, C. (1998), *Creative Britain*, London: Faber & Faber.

Solesbury, W. (2001), 'Evidence-based policy – whence it came from, and where it's going', ESRC Centre for Evidence-Based Policy and Practice working paper 1.

Throsby, D. (2001), *Economics and Culture*, Cambridge: Cambridge University Press.

Wood, I. (2004), *Counting Culture: Practical Challenges for the Museum and Heritage Sector, Collecting Cultural Data – A DCMS Perspective*, London: Greenwich University Press.

3. Socializing creativity: entrepreneurship and innovation in the creative industries

Calvin Taylor

INTRODUCTION

Accounts of the growth and development of the creative industries have increasingly emphasized the social nature of their typical forms of entrepreneurship and innovation. This not only distinguishes them from other industrial sectors but also locates them theoretically and conceptually within wider notions of the 'associational economy' (Cooke and Morgan, 1999). This emphasis is made in a wide range of academic literatures, reflecting a growing interest in relationality and sociality: for example, in entrepreneurship studies (the role of social interaction in the formation of trust and the management of risk); in management and organizational studies (the role of social interaction in constructing knowledge and learning organizations); in regional studies (the role of proximity and clustering in the promotion of innovation); and in social geography (the role of social interaction in constructions of place and locale). The practical consequence of this insight can be readily detected in the wealth of creative industries business support initiatives that are based on it, for example networking activities, web-resources based on social networking principles, mentoring and leadership development initiatives and contract brokerage which in turn are a product of a tendency, especially apparent in UK policy discourse, to locate the creative industries within the national innovation system as a resource capable of delivering competitive advantage (Work Foundation and NESTA, 2007; DCMS, 2008a). Analysis has, however, moved beyond the systems approach to examine the specific social conditions necessary for the promotion of creativity and innovation.

This chapter is concerned with the ways in which creativity, and its complex relationship to innovation, has been incorporated into accounts of how the creative industries work as socialized economic activities. The chapter locates these developments within a broader trend to apply social constructivist epistemological principles to accounts of organizational development and professional practice. The chapter begins by examining the strengths and weaknesses of such an approach as it might apply to the creative industries, arguing that the intense social reflexivity present in these accounts leaves them open to the charge of paradoxically underplaying the role of creativity. The chapter then explores contemporary developments in knowledge exchange research with a view to offering an alternative theoretical account of the role of sociality and reflexivity in the development of the creative industries. The potential advantages of this approach are then explored, and the chapter concludes by outlining some of its practical consequences for further research and explanation.

THE CREATIVE INDUSTRIES AND THE ASSOCIATIONAL ECONOMY

Since the late 1980s there has been an explosion of interest in the socio-economic potential of symbolic production and consumption. Initially announced under the term 'cultural industries', then 'creative industries' and increasingly now under the terms 'cultural economy' and 'creative economy', this interest has been global in scope: in the United Kingdom (Pratt and Jeffcutt, 2009), North America (Florida, 2002; Markusen and King, 2003; Currid, 2007a; Currid and Connolly, 2008), Australasia (Hartley, 2005; Cunningham, 2004), China (Keane, 2006; Kong and O'Connor, 2009) and mainland Europe (KEA, 2006). For the purposes of this chapter the term 'creative industries' will be used throughout and is taken to refer to those activities of symbolic production, the reproduction of which is dependent on the public valorization of products, be that in a marketplace as exchange value, or as valorized aesthetic judgements within a civic milieu (Hesmondhalgh, 2007; Throsby, 2008). Research in this rapidly growing field is interdisciplinary in nature and covers topics as diverse as entrepreneurship (Henry, 2007), innovation (Cunningham, 2004), creativity and spatiality (Scott, 1999; Pratt, 2000), organizational and market structures (Potts et al., 2008), the means and mode of symbolic production (Pratt, 2004) and labour market and work patterns (Banks, 2006; Gill and Pratt, 2008). Although stemming from a wide range of disciplinary bases, this literature shares a common theoretical claim on the explanatory power of the idea of sociality (Lash and Urry, 1994; Scott, 1999; Kong, 2005).

In general terms, theoretical perspectives that place a central emphasis on sociality typically do so in opposition to varieties of methodological individualism which typically stress the explanatory role of rationally calculating individuals behind social phenomena. Perspectives that place sociality at the heart of their explanations tend to regard social phenomena as the products of the seemingly human predisposition towards interaction, suggesting that there is something importantly constitutive about those interactions. This emphasis on the associative dynamics of the creative industries can be seen in a wide range of contributions and forms of analysis. For example, claims that the creative industries are highly dependent upon lively ecologies of tacit knowledge (Grabher, 2001, 2002, 2004); or that they are especially sensitive to the particularities of place (Drake, 2003); or that they challenge the dominant models of linear innovation and knowledge exchange (Crossick, 2006) all draw on analyses that foreground the role of association.

The study of entrepreneurship has developed rapidly in the last few years, expanding beyond the boundaries of business and management studies (Casson, 2010). Clearly stimulated by the pressing needs of economies in transition (post-industrial economies seeking new sources of economic activity and heavily industrialized societies seeking sustainable economic activities), theoretical advances have moved ahead within a context of practical application. Innovation studies as an interdisciplinary field has also moved forward at an urgent rate, taking on board social interactivity (Rothwell, 1992, 1994; Dodgson, et al., 2005), openness (Chesborough et al., 2008) and disruption (Christenson 1997; Christenson and Raynor, 2003) in the formulation of new generations of innovation theorizing. Once a comparatively obscure corner of economics and management studies, it has become a major intellectual player, again closely linked to the real-world need for models, paradigms and ideas that can be operationalized either in pursuit of national or regional innovation-based competitive strategies; or, as is increasingly the case, internationally significant innovations capable of addressing such global challenges as climate change, security and development.

The study of entrepreneurship in the creative industries has also developed rapidly from a comparative standing start (Caves, 2000; Howkins, 2001; Rae, 2005; Bilton, 2007; Bilton and Cummings, 2010; Henry, 2007). However, when it comes to innovation, it was as recently as 2005 that one commentator on the creative industries was able to say: 'The creative industries don't as a rule figure in R and D [research and development] and innovation strategies. But they should' (Cunningham, 2004, p. 293). That situation is changing rapidly, but not without raising contentious issues. For example, Oakley et al. (2008) have opened an important debate about the innovatory capacity of graduates in one of the first studies to link human resource development (in this case, higher education) to innovation in the creative industries. In another contribution on the problematic relationship of artistic practice to innovation, Oakley (2009) has questioned the asocial assumptions that underpin the various attempts to harness the creative industries to the innovation agenda, including the 'Cox Review of creativity in business' (HM Treasury, 2005) and the McMaster Review of the future of the arts funding system (DCMS, 2008b). Removing society from innovation makes matters easier to deal with from a policy point of view, but as the sociality perspective would argue, it would also remove innovation from society.

This chapter examines the ways in which sociality has been incorporated into research on the creative industries. In particular, it points to the ways in which focusing on the associative character of the creative industries helps to develop non-reductive accounts of their specificity. However, the emphasis on the roles respectively of tacit knowledge, social milieu and cultural embeddedness tends to point analyses of entrepreneurship and innovation in the creative industries towards social constructivist explanations in which a deep methodological distrust of individual agency is predominant. This distrust is especially difficult to reconcile with ideas about creativity, unless creativity is regarded as a social property (as implied in some versions) and operative in the kinds of ways that might be encompassed by Becker's idea of the 'art world' (Becker, 1982) in which association and membership is bound by a particular 'epistemic culture' (Knorr-Cetina, 1999) or resides within a particular 'community of practice' (Wenger, 1998). The argument of the chapter is that the positive emphasis placed upon the associative dynamics of the creative industries as a way of avoiding either reductive individualism or reductive economism has led analysis to favour an oversocialized account at the expense of understanding the dynamics of creativity. It will argue that a socio-cognitive account of creativity complements the associative account of innovation in the creative industries without introducing either individual or economic reductionism.

The structure of the chapter and the detail of its argument proceed as follows. The next section presents a critical overview of the ways in which the specialist research on the creative industries has mobilized the concepts of social interaction and sociality in accounting for entrepreneurship and innovation. This is followed by an assessment of the limits of these analyses, showing the ways in which they leave important questions about creativity unanswered. The author then argues that possible solutions to these problems might be offered by an approach that combines a number of elements: an expanded account of the relevant forms and types of knowledge operative within the creative industries; a socially interactive model of the formation of innovation traditions, and a socio-cognitive account of knowledge exchange as a catalyst for innovation. Each of these ideas and their respective significance is explained, in turn and then in combination. While the purpose of this chapter is primarily one of theoretical development, it concludes by discussing some of the very practical challenges that may benefit from this theoretical work.

SOCIALIZING CREATIVITY

The forms of sociality through which the creative industries are reflexively constructed and articulated have been addressed explicitly in the literatures of cultural sociology, cultural geography and regional studies. Kong (2005, p. 62), building on the work of Scott (1999, 2000) offers a very clear typology of the ways in which sociality and creative production interact. Firstly, sociality provides the content and subject matter of symbolic production. Secondly, symbolic production is social production – we might say with Becker that symbolic production is part of an art world. Thirdly, symbolic production requires interpersonal norms and values to render it communicable; and fourthly, symbolic production relies on feedback mechanisms between producers and consumers. This emphasis on the role of social interaction in the creative industries has most recently been worked up into a fully fledged theoretical account of the creative industries under the rubric of 'social network market' analysis (Potts et al., 2008). The emphasis on how the behaviour of the individual subject is reciprocally both constitutive of and constituted by the behaviour of others (cultural choices, practices, communicated acts of judgement, and so on) in an informational economy, places this analysis clearly within a social constructivist model.

The strengths and weaknesses of this kind of approach are illustrated in the following short reviews of some of the key contributions on two typical topics: sociality and networks, and sociality and place.

SOCIALITY AND NETWORKS

Perhaps the most obvious way in which social interaction is seen as critical to the way the creative industries work is in the seeking, cementing, developing and exploitation of business relationships. Using ideas either directly inspired by or traceable to the work of Mark Granovetter (1973, 1985) in economic sociology in the 1970s and 1980s, the creative industries have been described as a 'transaction-rich' sector (Wilson and Stokes, 2005; Julier, 2006), one in which the reproduction of activity is dependent on the constant seeking out of opportunities, prospects and new clients.

The enlargement of one's own contacts by networking – the building and subsequent exploitation of the strength of weak ties (Granovetter, 1973, 1985) – expands the realm of possibilities and ensures a constant churn of market intelligence, potential collaborators and opportunities. The specific nature of business risk in the creative industries is reflective of both the high level of medium, small and micro-scale enterprise working, but also the existence of a small number of transnational corporations, particularly in media and media-related sectors that have a disproportionate ability to control the marketplace, not only for products and services, but also contract and work opportunities. It is also a sector in which there is a high degree of gatekeeping – by large industry players, industry bodies, funding bodies, and so on – and in which opinion-making and breaking by critics and audiences is absolutely central. The constant leveraging of significant opinion, keeping 'irons in the fire' and being alert to new possibilities is a central part of how risk in an intrinsically high-risk industrial sector is managed. Transaction-intensive trading through social interaction is one of the ways in which trust between economic agents is engendered (Banks et al., 2000; Bilton, 1999) and through which creative activities can be sustained and replicated.

However, this emphasis on the networked nature of the creative industries can become circular. These models, developed to address the formation of common practices and epistemic repertoires in a range of professional settings, whilst having several advantages, are limited in two important and critical ways when applied to the creative industries. Whilst they are effective at explaining the normalization of changes within a professional community – expressed as received wisdom, good practice and so on – they are much weaker at explaining the originating innovation and the causes of innovation. This limitation originates from the way that these particular models, in oversocializing creativity and the sources of creativity, distance knowledge development and appropriation from the processes of human cognition. In a piece that resonates with this argument, Thompson et al. (2007) argue that dominant accounts of the creative industries evacuate the space between conception – the development of new symbolic products – and their consumption, leaving a number of important considerations unexamined: that is the organization of work, management processes and employment relationships. This chapter argues that in emphasizing the epistemic efficacy of community, the model also evacuates the space in which human cognition and creativity play a critical role.

The second limitation stems from the tendency in epistemic culture and community of practice models to divine professional cultural significance in any form of social interaction, however prosaic or incidental. Whilst this can expose these models to charges of triviality, more importantly, in collapsing the socio-ontological distinction between the interactivity and relationality necessary for social reproduction, they seriously compromise the ability of analysis to account for persistence and change in a given social phenomenon. Paradoxically, as we shall see from the next discussion, given the emphasis that these accounts place on the role of tacit knowledge, the absence of relationality – the precondition for tacit efficacy – coupled with an aversion to the cognitive, undermine any effective account of tacit knowledge.

SOCIALITY AND PLACE

The second area in which analysts have identified a particularly important role for social interaction is in the association of creative production with place. Central to this is the notion that the relationship of individuals to each other is mediated by place – a definite sense of spatiality and its extension; and vice versa, that individuals relate to place via their social relationships, most readily felt in the tacit knowledge that is shared between inhabitants of the same networks. How one feels about a place – a city or town, district, neighbourhood or quarter for example – is an essential component of the creative identity one needs in the currency of the creative marketplace. How that is manifested is described in the literature in a number of different ways, but they all point to the same central idea: that is, that place and creativity are mutually energizing. This has been expressed in a number of ways including the idea of creative cities (Landry and Bianchini, 1996); occupied by a creative class of socially interactive professionals (Florida, 2002); the idea of the creative milieu (Tornqvist, 2004); and, most commonly now, the sense of a 'scene' or 'buzz'. Whilst these ideas can seem ephemeral to a point beyond analytical coherence (Markusen, 2003), what underpins them is the sense that a transaction-intense industry thrives on the constant turnover and circulation of information, opinion, rumour and gossip, in key social arenas of interaction: events, parties, launches, first nights, premiers, exhibitions, gossip columns, Internet sites and blogs.

However, this insight has developed beyond what could be described as a way of doing business to becoming the business in its own right (a further instantiation of Thompson et al.'s critical observations). In a series of papers and a book-length contribution, Elizabeth Currid (2007a, 2007b, 2007c) describes how the creative production of New York has become an extension of the intense networking activities that characterize the creative industries there, the art and fashion markets in particular. In this context, business efficacy is seen less as the realization of a business idea, but rather as the product of immersion in a particular 'scene', with its own characteristic 'buzz'. The attractions of this type of argument are clear. From a policy-maker's point of view such arguments offer positive affirmations of local creativity, possibly attracting more people to the locale by creating an attractive sense of identity and its related visibility. In a paper that is sympathetic to the forms of analysis offered by arguments about 'buzz', Asheim et al. (2007) argue that this emphasis on such evanescent activities should not, however, overshadow important consideration about the knowledge base that underpins the development of an industry in a given place. 'Buzz' may be an important way in which short-term market knowledge (contract opportunities, professional reputations, 'inside knowledge') is circulated and acted upon, but it does not necessarily explain how or why a particular industry develops in a given location, or provide any sense of how it may develop over time. The importance of the particular nature of the knowledge base underpinning particular kinds of industry becomes important later on in the chapter.

The emphasis placed on sociality, especially that concerned with intense social interaction, can provide a rich insight into the habitus of the creative entrepreneur and creative practitioner (Banks et al., 2000), but stepping back from the immediacy of those activities it is difficult to see how it can account for the development of creativity in a given context. The next section will argue, drawing on Asheim et al.'s argument, that this requires an understanding of the knowledge base from which creative industries activities draw, and further, the forms of knowledge exchange which realize that creativity.

SOCIALITY, CREATIVITY AND INNOVATION: A CRITIQUE

Whilst the critical literature on the creative industries has readily advocated the role of social interaction in the production and reproduction of the creative industries, it has two conspicuous problems relating to the locus and nature of creative agency. First, it is difficult not to conclude that the concept of social interaction has undergone extensive dilution, in which even the most fleeting or temporary interaction becomes invested with significance. It is not too difficult to see how a mass of interactions could induce a sense of the importance of interaction per se. It is then not too difficult to make the jump to the idea that it is interactivity itself that motivates creativity, thereby diminishing the role of agency within the creative process. Furthermore, this emphasis on social interactivity points towards the kinds of social constructivist epistemologies that have become dominant in organizational and professional studies, and which arguably can now be seen routinely at work in studies of the creative industries. Within these models – the notions of epistemic culture (Knorr-Cetina, 1999) and community of practice (Wenger, 1998) come specially to mind – but also within the recently developed social network market approach (Potts et al., 2008), innovative agency can be vested in the norms and practices of an interacting community, with such norms and practices becoming the heritable habitus of its members. Again, creative agency is assumed by the 'social'. The emphasis that these models have on the social construction of professionally relevant knowledge places constraints on accounting for innovation in the creative industries, arguably at best marginalizing it to the periphery of analysis where it can be dealt with as either a psychological or an aesthetic given; or at worst, evacuating the concept altogether. These models also tend to privilege the idea of the professional community as a consensus-seeking community, possibly even one subject to some degree of closure, thus creating little space for innovation based on openness or even the considerably less predictable effects of disruption.

Does this mean, therefore, that if creativity is to be acknowledged we have to fall back on older ideas about creative individuality? This has certainly been argued as a consequence of at least one particular definition of the creative industries that has been in widespread use. Garnham (2005) observed that the particular definition adopted by the UK Department of Culture, Media and Sport, with its emphasis on individual skill and talent, could not help but reinforce old-fashioned ideas about the relationship between artistic agency and subjectivity; in effect, in terms of this chapter, placing creativity itself beyond the realms of investigable innovation. It appears, therefore, that to the extent that we wish to maintain the idea of creativity as a socialized acquisition, we appear to be forced into surrendering creativity to the reflexes of symbolic economy of meaning-making (Lash and Urry, 1994; Hesmondhalgh, 2007). On the other hand, should we wish to maintain some meaningful sense of individual creative agency, we appear to be condemned to the narrow and one-dimensional view of creative subjectivity (Garnham, 2005).

There is a challenge, therefore, to account for creative agency within the creative industries without falling into old-fashioned dualistic analysis: that is, creativity being seen as either a uniquely social or a uniquely individual acquisition. There is, however, a contemporary literature – allied closely to both innovation and organizational studies – that may offer a useful way through this challenge. Contemporary innovation and organizational studies have increasingly focused their attention on knowledge transfer as a social process. The process of knowledge transfer, it is argued, is a key process enabling innovation, organizational adaptability, efficiency, the circulation of market knowledge, and so forth. Central purposes in this literature are the exploration of the interactive dynamics of knowledge production; the mediating role of social interaction; the integrative role of knowledge exchange; and the social processes by which new knowledge is embedded and subsequently challenged and transcended. To that extent it can easily be assimilated to the social constructivist accounts as an explanation of the mechanisms of knowledge circulation processes in the reproduction of organizational and professional cultures. Indeed, this is how it is often seen, with practical initiatives being designed to assure the most efficient circulation of knowledge within an organization or professional community. This has been seen most recently, for example, in efforts to promote knowledge circulation between universities and potential users of knowledge in industry, government and the third sector.

However, recent critiques within the knowledge transfer literature show a growing dissatisfaction with social constructivist accounts and a refocusing on knowledge, the conditions of its production and its circulation. The next section explores a range of this literature and considers the potential for developing an account of creativity and innovation in the creative industries that can maintain the insight developed in the sociality literature, but without relinquishing the efficacy of creativity to sociality per se.

SOCIALITY, CREATIVITY, INNOVATION AND KNOWLEDGE

At a meta-level this debate centres on one of the seminal problems of social science; how to provide an integrated account of the relationship between micro-interactivity and macro-structural efficacy without falling into dualism and/or determinism. Epistemic culture and community-of-practice models presume a consensus-seeking community and, therefore, deal with this problem by arguing that the operative agency is, in effect, the community itself. The creative industries superficially exhibit such tendencies, but the core activity is driven by a non-trivial sense of novelty. The very nature of the activity constantly threatens the integrity and stability of the community, even – as the pervasive sharing of digital music files illustrates – to the point of threatening the community as a whole. The challenge then is how to account effectively for creativity and innovation in the creative industries in a way that can allow for the integrative role of social interaction without reproducing the limitations of the social constructivist model.

The argument of this section is constructed from three insights, each of which will be explained in turn before assembling them into a putative account of innovation in the creative industries. The first is Asheim et al.'s (2007) insight that sociality matters because of the particular type of knowledge base that underpins innovation in the creative industries. This, in turn, calls for an approach that is capable of combining the cognitive (knowledge) and the social (the context of its creation and application). Recent trends in the knowledge transfer literature have returned to the importance of making this connection. Here the section draws on the work of Nightingale in the 1990s (Nightingale, 1998) and the idea of the 'innovation tradition' as a way of mediating the macro and micro perspectives. Nightingale's approach reinforces the role of cognition which is a point taken up by Ringberg and Reihlen's work from 2008; these can be combined in a putative socio-cognitive account of the knowledge exchange process as a knowledge-constituting process.

Asheim et al. (2007) point to the essential but differential role of sociality in a range of industries. However, they develop this insight by offering the view that sociality plays different sorts of roles, to differing degrees according to the specific epistemological character of the knowledge that underpins different industrial sectors. Their account differentiates the 'symbolic' knowledge base of, for example, the creative industries from the 'scientific' knowledge base of, say the life science industries, or the 'analytical' knowledge-base of the engineering industries. As Asheim et al. (2007) explain, following Brink et al. (2004): 'A "knowledge base" refers to the area of knowledge itself as well as its embodiment in techniques and organisation' (Asheim et al., 2007, p. 660). This idea neatly captures the sense of how knowledge can be thought of as a body in itself and also be subject to the necessary processes of embodiment – which are evidenced both in technique and in organization – both of which in turn are socially mediated. Asheim et al.'s argument concerning the specific character of the knowledge bases thought to operate in different industrial sectors is not important here (although some readers might question the extent to which their characterization of the symbolic knowledge base is accurate). However, what is important is the implication of their analysis.

Innovation studies, as an interdisciplinary field of inquiry has sought to reconsider the relationship of tacit knowledge to innovation processes by developing an integrated account of their cognitively embodied and socially embedded nature. Such an account of creativity and innovation has a number of distinct advantages over its social constructivist rival. Where the latter posits creativity as an immanent quality of social interaction, the former can account for it as both individually developed acquisition through practice, learning or skills development – in other words through processes of disciplined embodiment – and the formation of organizational knowledge as a heritable and transmissible social acquisition. There are important and well-recognized consequences – epistemological, explanatory, ethical and political – at stake in the development of such an account. At one level these consequences provide an important counterweight to current time–space compressing, weightless (that is, immaterial) accounts of creativity; at another level, they restore creativity to its proper place at the conjunction of human agency and social structure and their spatial extension. The growing interest in craft and skill, in path-dependent technological choices, and in the apparent 'stickiness' of creative talent to place, can all be cited here as examples of the ways in which accounts of creativity and innovation in the creative industries can benefit from such analysis. However, we need to be able to see how the cognitive and social dimensions can be brought together. A possible route into this is through a critique of the linear positivist model, a critique that has been mounted robustly in recent years.

In a paper published in 1998, Nightingale noted how the positivist, linear model of innovation was wholly inadequate to the task of dealing with the complexities of actual innovation. He demonstrates how, confined to a highly simplified information system approach, the linear model based on the radical separation of knowledge production activities from application or development can only deal with the sociological fact of path-dependency or 'stickiness' as either market failure or informational inadequacy. Current attempts to promote the development of the creative industries tend to make the same assumption in their reliance on information and network dissemination initiatives. To deal with the complex, iterative nature of innovation, Nightingale proposed a model based on three insights. The first and critical one for our exploration is the restoration of the humanly cognitive to the account of creativity. Cognition in this context rests on the existence of a pre-learned human capacity to recognize patterns. Pattern recognition and transference can be subsequently developed and refined through cognitive development, socialization and education. Such pattern recognition can also be borne by social networks as that knowledge which is tacitly understood and accepted (cf. Asheim et al., 2007 for a similar account). The second element regards knowledge as the social practice of mapping and codifying patterns. A wide range of accounts of cultural knowledge – structuralist and ethnographic accounts come to mind most readily – point to the basic model of pattern recognition and its ability to be communicated. The third element rests on a specific account of technology as a function-driven endeavour, that is, the functions of technology are not intrinsic to the particular apparatus of technology but are implicit in the tacit knowledge base – pattern recognition processes – by which solutions to one sort of problem are transferred and translated to another. This is the basis for innovatory potential.

The distinction between knowledge and technology is important for understanding why it is incredibly difficult to trace the direct relationship between, for example, specific scientific endeavours and technological development. There may be indirect and multiple relationships but these are difficult to describe, impossible to predict and largely beyond meaningful quantification. If we are to account for innovation we need to develop our understanding of the ways in which tacit knowledge from both practice and reflection are embodied in the cognitive processes of individuals, but also crucially form the basis of what Nightingale refers to as innovation traditions. Such traditions provide the localized repertoire of tacit knowledge accumulated within a given social and spatial context and within which individuals develop their own creative repertoires.

Such interactivity presents a question about the precise mechanisms by which this is effected. The concept of knowledge exchange has been developed since the 1980s to account for the means by which tacit knowledge is both accumulated socially and rendered accessible individually. Nightingale's distinction between cognitively embodied knowledge and socially embedded knowledge can be elaborated further by drawing upon the work of Ringberg and Rheilen (2008) who concentrate on the forms of knowledge exchange and their outcomes. They argue that current understandings of knowledge transfer are too closely wedded to a perspective of knowledge as categorical information. This perspective is evident for example in accounts of knowledge transfer such as that offered by the Organisation for Economic Co-operation and Development in its *Frascati Manual* (OECD, 2002). In this model knowledge is seen as the product of verified basic research (verified through, for example, peer review processes). Such knowledge is turned into information (through publication) and is then subsequently circulated. Knowledge transfer is then seen as the specific means by which such codified and categorical knowledge is transferred between different domains, for example between a university research laboratory and an industrial application. The matter of how knowledge is transferred between domains can then be attributed to the routine norms and rules that exist within the epistemic culture of a given community of practice.

Ringberg and Reihlen (2008) argue that this model leads to two specific limitations in traditional understandings of knowledge transfer. Firstly, it unnecessarily restricts what counts as knowledge within the innovation process. In its place, Ringberg and Reihlen (2008) offer a spectrum of possible forms of knowledge that vary according to their respective degree of categoricalness and reflexivity. This greatly expands the range of forms of knowledge that might be considered here, including tacit knowledge. Secondly, it overestimates the role of environmental feedback in the protocols that govern the interpretation and application of knowledge. This observation is based on their specific account of the combination of cultural (that is, public) and private models that regulate the conversion of information into meaningful knowledge – that is, knowledge with a specific efficacy in a given situation. Ringberg and Reihlen (2008) posit three arguments in the development of what they call a socio-cognitive account of knowledge transfer. The first, and highly redolent of Nightingale's account, is the view that social constructivist accounts of knowledge fail to take adequate account of both the private and cultural models by which individuals decode the data of their sense-experiences. Such decoding is always provisional, with varying degrees of tentativeness ranging from the categorical (knowledge which is largely taken for granted or assumed) to the reflective (knowledge that is open). Therefore, knowledge exchange is primarily not to be thought of as the transmission of ready-made codified knowledge, but is primarily a site of provisionality in which the cognitive feedback of environment plays a key but not overdetermining role.

When social interaction is brought into their account of the knowledge transfer process, four possible outcomes are suggested. They illustrate this by mapping possible outcomes onto axes oriented from north to south, high social interactivity to low social interactivity; and from west to east, reflective thinking to categorical thinking. Four types of knowledge outcome can be identified. The upper-left quadrant combines high social interactivity with a high degree of cognitive reflection, resulting in a high degree of what they describe as knowledge negotiation. This type of model assumes a high degree of interactivity between different private and cultural models where social agents are engaged in a high degree of negotiation. It is typical of the types of knowledge exchange required between different social and professional groups, for example where collaboration is being conducted on an interdisciplinary or multidisciplinary basis. The upper-right quadrant combines a high degree of social interactivity with what for the time being constitutes seemingly settled categorical knowledge. This is typical of the knowledge processes most closely associated with, for example, the community of practice model. Outcomes are more or less scripted by the shared and assumed categories that operate within a particular community. Such forms of knowledge transfer may bind one community together, but they are equally likely to inhibit exchange between different social and professional groups (one might want to consider the academic community here). The lower-left quadrant combines both low social interactivity with categorical knowledge, resulting in a category of knowledge exchange that Ringberg and Rheilen (2008) describe as stereotypical knowledge: that is, knowledge which has become routinized and requires little negotiation – knowledge which is not untypical of large bureaucracies in which low social interactivity coupled with an unreflective approach to knowledge results in little knowledge development. The fourth quadrant, at the lower-right, combines a high degree of reflection, that is, intense reflection on private and cultural models with low social interactivity. This produces forms of knowledge that step outside of those that are currently socially sanctioned and which may challenge accepted wisdom.

How might this apply to processes of innovation in the creative industries? By focusing on private and cultural models of interpretation, the model restores the processes of individual cognition to the process of innovation itself. It allows analysis to break out of the idea of innovation in the creative industries as simply the recycling of an existing cultural repertoire. However, by cross-referencing degrees of cognition – from the reflective to the categorical – with degrees of social interaction it not only provides a framework for a much more nuanced account of creativity but also points out the limitations of a unidimensional account of sociality. This lends theoretical support to Nightingale's idea of the 'innovation tradition' (Nightingale, 1998) as the enduring context within which knowledge is created, embodied and absorbed into the repertoire of tacit knowledge.

One implication of the kind of conclusion offered by Ringberg and Reihlen's (2008) argument is that innovation processes cannot be attributed to the working out of a wholly social logic of innovation (innovation as a structural feature of social processes); nor can they be seen as the product of an individual innovating subject. The social dynamics of innovation are mediated by processes of cognition; conversely, the processes of cognition are mediated by the operative cultural models of a given context. Innovation processes can, therefore, be said to be situated acts, combining both cognition and context – the basis for the formation of 'innovation traditions'. Once this is admitted, the 'ideal typical' innovation process offered in, for example, the Frascati model becomes at best an unusual exception. As Nightingale (1998) compellingly argues, the ideal type is defeated by the many common empirically observed discontinuities between knowledge and innovation (Nightingale, 1998, p. 691):

> Reading the broad sweep of history backwards, from the present to the past, it is common to find a link from technology to previous science. The historical extent of these links is an empirical matter. What is not clear is why when we turn and look from the present into the future the linear model falls apart, as it fails to explain how today's science can be turned into tomorrow's technology. The notion that the output of science is information that can be directly applied to produce technology cannot explain many of the key features of innovation

such as, the importance of tacit knowledge, why so much science is done in industry, why so much technology seems to be produced without much input from science, why in many instances the technology comes first and the science that can explain it comes later, why technical production is so localised, and why different industries have very different 'scientific' requirements.

Much of what Nightingale says also applies to the creative industries. Why is it that some forms of cultural knowledge are taken up within the creative industries and others are not? Why is it that the creative industries appear to relate to centres of knowledge production such as universities only indirectly? Why do creative industries businesses tend to cluster in some places and not others?

CONCLUSIONS AND APPLICATIONS

It is a commonly made observation that the creative industries are emblematic of the growth of the economic significance of symbolic production and its extension into other spheres of economy and society. Research has rightly abjured the asocial approach to the creative industries often presented in public policy and which becomes replicated in the kinds of initiatives that are designed to support it; that is, an emphasis on mechanistic approaches to interaction and information rather than an understanding of the role of knowledge, its formation through innovation traditions and its embodiment in the work of individuals and organizations. However, as this chapter has argued, this can be corrected by taking a critical view of the knowledge exchange process, restoring cognition to our interpretation of creativity and then beginning the process of understanding how the different forms of knowledge are worked out in the real day-to-day worlds of the creative industries.

So what can we use this for? There are two real purposes here – one relating to research and one relating to the business of devising intelligent business support mechanisms – but, as the analysis of this chapter implies, these two things need to work together. In research terms, the model offered here potentially allows an opportunity to break out of the circular account of the creative industries in which creativity is seen as very little more than the mobilization, representation and recycling of existing symbolic products. The reintroduction of cognition into the picture helps to tie creativity back to socially situated individuals as creative agents. The innovation tradition concept allows research to investigate the specific conditions that account for why the creative industries develop in the particular ways that they do, and in the particular places that they do. The application of Ringberg and Rheilen's (2008) account of knowledge transfer processes similarly offers the opportunity for research to examine the specific character of the knowledge base drawn upon by the creative industries and to compare that with the knowledge used in other industries. This might then open up interesting research questions about, for example, the relationship of the creative industries to higher education.

The development of this research area could potentially have important consequences for how the creative industries are fostered and developed. At the present time, business support initiatives have focused disproportionately on association without considering how new ideas are generated or how the resources for ideas-generation should be managed or directed. If sociality was an effective antidote to reductivism in theories of the creative industries, a clearer understanding of the sources of innovation will provide an effective antidote to simplistic and circular understandings of how the creative industries actually develop.

REFERENCES

Asheim, B., L. Coenen and J. Vang (2007), 'Face-to-face, buzz, and knowledge bases: sociospatial implications for learning, innovation and innovation policy', *Environment and Planning C: Government and Policy*, **25**, 655–70.

Banks, M. (2006), 'Moral economy and cultural work', *Sociology*, **40** (3), 455–72.

Banks, M., A. Lovatt, J. O'Connor and C. Raffo (2000), 'Risk and trust in the cultural industries', *Geoforum*, **3** (4), 453–64.

Becker, H. (1982), *Art Worlds*, Berkeley and Los Angeles, CA: University of California Press.

Bilton, C. (1999), 'The new adhocracy: strategy, risk and the small creative firm', University of Warwick Centre for Cultural Policy Studies research papers no. 4.

Bilton, C. (2007), *Management and Creativity: From Creative Industries to Creative Management*, Oxford: Blackwell.

Bilton, C. and S. Cummings (2010), *Creative Strategy: Re-connecting Business and Innovation*, Chichester: John Wiley & Sons.

Brink, J., M. McKelvey and K. Smith (2004), 'Conceptualizing and measuring modern biotechnology', in *The Economic Dynamics of Modern Biotechnology*, M. McKelvey, A. Rickne and J. Laage-Hellman (eds), Cheltenham, UK and Northampton, MA, USA: Edward Elgar, pp. 20–42.

Casson, M. (2010), *Entrepreneurship: Theory, Networks, History*, Cheltenham, UK and Northampton, MA, USA: Edward Elgar.

Caves, R. (2000), *Creative Industries: Contracts between Art and Commerce*, Cambridge, MA: Harvard University Press.

Chesborough, H., W. Vanhaverbeke and J. West (eds) (2008), *Open Innovation: Researching a New Paradigm*, Oxford: Oxford University Press.

Christenson, C.M. (1997), *The Innovator's Dilemma: When New Technologies Cause Great Firms to Fail*, Boston, MA: Harvard Business School Press.

Christenson, C.M. and M.E. Raynor (2003), *The Innovator's Solution: Creating and Sustaining Successful Growth*, Boston, MA: Harvard Business School Press.

Cooke, P. and K. Morgan (1999), *The Associational Economy: Firms, Regions and Innovations*, Oxford: Oxford University Press.

Crossick, G. (2006), *Knowledge Transfer Without Widgets: The Challenge of the Creative Economy*, London: Royal Society of Arts.

Cunningham, S. (2004), 'The creative industries after cultural policy: a genealogy and some possible preferred futures', *International Journal of Cultural Studies*, **7** (1), 105–15.

Currid, E. (2007a), *The Warhol Economy: How Fashion, Art and Music Drive New York City*, Princeton, NJ: Princeton University Press.

Currid, E. (2007b), 'The economics of a good party: social mechanics and the legitimization of art/culture', *Journal of Economics and Finance*, **31** (3), 386–94.

Currid, E. (2007c), 'How art and culture happen in New York: implications for urban economic development', *Journal of the American Planning Association*, **73** (4), 454–67.

Currid, E. and J. Connolly. (2008), 'Patterns of knowledge: the geography of advanced services and the case of art and culture', *Annals of the Association of American Geographers*, **98** (2), 414–34.

Department of Culture, Media and Sport (DCMS) (2008a), *Creative Britain: New Talents for the New Economy*, London: DCMS.

Department of Culture, Media and Sport (DCMS) (2008b), *McMaster Review: Supporting Excellence in the Arts: From Measurement to Judgement*, London: DCMS.

Dodgson, M., D. Gann and A. Salter (2005), *Think, Play, Do: Technology, Innovation, Organisation*, Oxford: Oxford University Press.

Drake, G. (2003), '"This place gives me space": place and creativity in the creative industries', *Geoforum*, **34** (4), 511–24.

Florida, R. (2002), *The Rise of the Creative Class: And How It's Transforming Work, Leisure, Community and Everyday Life*, New York: Basic Books.

Garnham, N. (2005), 'From cultural to creative industries: an analysis of the implications of the creative industries approach to arts and media policy making in the United Kingdom', *International Journal of Cultural Policy*, **11** (1), 15–29.

Gill, R. and A.C. Pratt (2008), 'In the social factory: immaterial labour, precariousness and cultural work', *Theory, Culture and Society*, **25** (7–8), 1–30.

Grabher, G. (2001), 'Ecologies of creativity: the village, the group and the heterarchic organisation of the British advertising industry', *Environment and Planning A*, **33**, 351–74.

Grabher, G. (2002), 'Cool projects, boring institutions: temporary collaboration in social context', *Regional Studies*, **36** (3), 205–14.

Grabher, G. (2004), 'Learning in projects, remembering in networks? Communality, sociality and connectivity in project ecologies', *European Urban and Regional Studies*, **11** (2), 99–119.

Granovetter, M. (1973), 'The strength of weak ties', *American Journal of Sociology*, **78**, 1360–89.

Grannovetter, M. (1985), 'Economic action and social structure: the problem of embeddedness', *American Journal of Sociology*, **81**, 481–510.

Hartley, J. (2005), *Creative Industries*, Oxford: Basil Blackwell.

Henry, C. (ed.) (2007), *Entrepreneurship in the Creative Industries: International Perspectives*, Cheltenham, UK and Northampton, MA, USA: Edward Elgar.

Hesmondhalgh, D. (2007), *The Cultural Industries*, 2nd edn, London: Sage.

HM Treasury (2005), 'The Cox Review of creativity in business', HM Treasury.

Howkins, J. (2001), *Creative Industries: How People Make Money from Ideas*, London: Penguin.

Julier, G. (2006), 'From visual culture to design culture', *Design Issues*, **22** (1), 64–76.

KEA (2006), 'The economy of culture in Europe', Brussels: European Commission Directorate-General for Education and Culture.

Keane, M. (2006), 'From Made in China to Created in China', *International Journal of Cultural Studies*, **9** (3), 285–96.

Knorr-Cetina, K. (1999), *Epistemic Cultures: How the Sciences Make Knowledge*, Cambridge, MA and London: Harvard University Press.

Kong, L. (2005), 'The sociality of cultural industries', *International Journal of Cultural Policy*, **11** (1), 61–76.

Kong, L. and J. O'Connor (2009), *Creative Economies, Creative Cities: Asian–European Perspectives*, London: Springer.

Landry, C. and F. Bianchini (1996), *The Creative City*, London: Demos and Comedia.

Lash, S. and J. Urry (1994), *Economies of Signs and Space*, London: Sage.

Markusen, A. (2003), 'Fuzzy concepts, scanty evidence, policy distance: the case for rigour and policy relevance in critical regional studies', *Regional Studies*, **37** (6–7), 701–17.

Markusen, A. and D. King (2003), 'The artistic dividend: the arts' hidden contributions to regional development', University of Minnesota Humphrey School of Public Affairs Project on Regional and Industrial Economics.

Nightingale, P. (1998), 'A cognitive model of innovation', *Research Policy*, **27** (7): 689–709.

Oakley, K. (2009), 'The disappearing arts: creativity and innovation after the creative industries', *International Journal of Cultural Policy*, **15** (4), 403–13.

Oakley, K., B. Sperry, A.C. Pratt and H. Bakhshi (eds.) (2008), *The Art of Innovation: How Fine Art Graduates Contribute to Innovation*, London: National Endowment for the Sciences, Technology and the Arts.

Organisation for Economic Co-operation and Development (OECD) (2002), *Frascati Manual 2002: Proposed Standard Practice for Surveys on Research and Experimental Development*, Paris: OECD.

Potts, J., S. Cunningham, J. Hartley and P. Ormerod (2008), 'Social network markets: a new definition of the creative industries', *Journal of Cultural Economics*, **32** (3), 167–85.

Pratt, A.C. (2000), 'New media, the new economy and new spaces', *Geoforum*, **31** (4), 425–36.

Pratt, A.C. (2004), 'The cultural economy: a call for spatialized "production of culture" perspectives', *International Journal of Cultural Studies*, **7**, 117–28.

Pratt, A.C. and P. Jeffcutt (eds) (2009), *Creativity, Innovation and the Cultural Economy*, London: Routledge.

Rae, D. (2005), 'Cultural diffusion: a formative process in creative entrepreneurship', *International Journal of Entrepreneurship and Innovation*, **6** (3), 185–92.

Ringberg, T. and M. Reihlen (2008), 'Towards a socio-cognitive approach to knowledge transfer', *Journal of Management Studies*, **45** (5), 1–24.

Rothwell, R. (1992), 'Successful industrial innovation: critical factors for the 1990s', *R & D Management*, **22** (3), 221–39.

Rothwell, R. (1994), 'Towards the fifth generation innovation process', *International Marketing Review*, **31** (1), 7–31.

Scott, A. (1999), 'The cultural economy: geography and the creative field', *Media, Culture and Society*, **21** (6), 807–17.

Scott, A. (2000), *The Cultural Economy of Cities*, London: Sage Publications.

Thompson, P., M. Jones and C. Warhurst (2007), 'From conception to consumption: creativity and the missing managerial link', *Journal of Organisational Behaviour*, **28** (5), 625–40.

Throsby, D. (2008), 'The concentric circles model of the cultural industries', *Cultural Trends*, **17** (3), 147–64.

Tornqvist, G. (2004), 'Creativity in time and space', *Geografiska Annaler, Series B, Human Geography*, **86** (4), 227–43.

Wenger, E. (1998), *Communities of Practice: Learning, Meaning and Identity*, Cambridge: Cambridge University Press.

Wilson, D.C. and D. Stokes (2005), 'Managing creativity and: the challenge for cultural entrepreneurs', *Journal of Enterprise and Small Business Development*, **12** (3), 366–78.

Work Foundation and the National Endowment for Science, Technology and the Arts (NESTA) (2007), 'Staying ahead: the economic performance of the UKs creative industries', London: Work Foundation and NESTA.

4. The evidence so far: calling for creative industries engagement with entrepreneurship education policy and development

Andy Penaluna and Kathryn Penaluna

INTRODUCTION

Both the UK's Treasury Department (Cox, 2005) and Department of Trade and Industry (DTI, 2005) have indicated that design, as a discipline, has much to offer business. Indeed, the former Chancellor of the Exchequer, Gordon Brown MP, highlighted the government's intentions not just to encourage creative industries but also to ensure that all industries are creative (Brown, 2005). However, in 2010, business school educators and researchers still dominate this emerging entrepreneurship research agenda. Though some advances have undoubtedly been made, it would appear that creatives who could respond to the calls for a paradigm shift to develop right-brain entrepreneurial capabilities as well as left-brain analytical skills (Chia, 1996; Kirby, 2003; Nieuwenhuizen and Groenewald, 2004) have yet to be fully engaged. As creativity increasingly becomes a buzzword in our knowledge-based economy, and entrepreneurship is increasingly considered to be about applied creativity (Rae, 2007), it would seem that design educators are a valuable and potentially underutilized source of expertise.

The UK's Higher Education Academy (Ramsden, 2008) recommends that new models of curriculum and assessment should encourage interdisciplinary study. However, we argue that business paradigms remain in '*einstellung*', and have yet to break out of their own boxes of comprehension and experience (Penaluna and Penaluna, 2008a, 2009). We also argue that design curricula already offer parallels to strategies advocated by acknowledged entrepreneurship educators. Echoing emergent literature in 'design thinking', our chapter seeks to establish a case for fuller collaboration between business educators and those experienced in developing creativity and innovation.

An extended literature review, encompassing government and policy reports as well as entrepreneurship and creativity literature, supported by empirical evidence from national and international networks, are the primary vehicles of our investigation. We consider the type and nature of comments that have been offered on the subject of creativity in business. Following this, we look at the creative industries from two perspectives: the business context and the educational context. This leads us to discussions about the pedagogical approaches that have evolved in creativity-led entrepreneurship education, and enables us to move on to the parallels that we perceive between design education, and entrepreneurship education. Finally, we investigate current trends and factors of influence before closing our arguments and concluding the chapter.

CREATIVITY IN A BUSINESS EDUCATION CONTEXT

In discussing creativity, we acknowledge that businesses and organizations described as 'entrepreneurial' and 'innovative' are defined as creative if they have developed a 'creative' workplace or climate (Goodman, 1995; Handy, 1985; Henry, 2001; Lumsdaine and Binks, 2006), and that integrating creative approaches and skills into entrepreneurship education provides students with the competencies to interact with the dynamic marketplace of today (Hamidi et al., 2008; Lumsdaine and Binks, 2006). Indeed, it is our view that the terms 'creative' and 'innovative' have become aspirational and positive descriptors for a successful organization. Thus, managers at all levels and across disciplines appear to have much to gain through a better understanding of how to foster a creative climate (Vidal, 2004), one that encourages rather than kills individual creativity (Amabile, 1998). We also recognize that the nature of business learning is changing dramatically; for example, manufacturing and production are no longer the gateway to international success, and prowess is increasingly measured in terms of innovation and entrepreneurship, hence 'creativity' has become a buzzword in the UK's knowledge-based economy. However, we must point out that this frequently employed descriptor's reliance on knowledge brings its own dilemmas to creative thinkers.

The World Economic Forum's (2009) report, 'Educating the next wave of entrepreneurs', suggests that in the current financial crisis, and with the global challenges of the twenty-first century, building sustainable development, creating jobs, generating renewed economic growth and advancing human welfare means that entrepreneurship has never been more important. The report views entrepreneurship in the widest of terms: entrepreneurial people in large companies, in the public sector and in academia, as well as those who launch and grow new businesses. The report proposes that:

> Now more than ever, we need innovation, new solutions, creative approaches and new ways of operating. We are in uncharted territory and need people in all sectors and all ages who can 'think out of the box' to identify and pursue opportunities in new and paradigm changing ways. (Wilson, 2009, p. 12)

The UK's Chartered Management Institute (CMI), through collaborative research with the National Endowment for Science Technology and the Arts (NESTA), broadly concur. The CMI discusses an 850-response survey of the CMI membership, noting that 'innovation is recognised by managers as an important factor in many organisations' strategic agendas' and that 'it has remained paramount over the last 12 months' (Patterson and Kerrin, 2009, p. 28). Their research further indicated that 'the leadership role is critical to successful innovation', highlighting personal development and motivational activities that integrate innovative behaviours and skills as important (Patterson and Kerrin, 2009, p. 29). However, we must highlight that leadership and management training 'was not found to be a good indicator of levels of idea generation, even though it is the most available resource and thought to be most effective . . . [it] has a greater impact on the implementation of ideas than on their generation' (Patterson and Kerrin, 2009, p. 27). This indicates a cultural deficiency in terms of initiating creative thinking. McWilliam's (2008, p. 263) observation that current mainstream pedagogic approaches in universities are un-creative could also indicate potentially critical oversights, but as Smith et al.'s (2006) conclusion was that the least useful type of creativity in entrepreneurship was the 'arty type', we must ask ourselves: what specific opportunities could we be overlooking?

A study prepared for the European Commission's Directorate-General for Education and Culture entitled 'The impact of culture on creativity' (European Commission, 2009) addresses this issue. The study highlights that 'the cultural and creative sectors are an important motor of creativity and innovation in Europe' and, in evidence, offers a 32-indicator 'Creativity Index' that links 'the economic contribution of the cultural and creative industries to a Member State's GDP [gross domestic product]' (European Commission, 2009, p. 193). The report suggests that: 'structured exchanges between art and other disciplines are particularly fruitful ways of promoting creativity' (European Commission, 2009, p. 114). Most pertinent to our discussion, the Commission makes recommendations that concur with the general theme of our debate. Describing progressive institutions that blend certain features of art and design schools with those of business schools, and 'focus on experiential learning that enables students to challenge ideas and concepts' (Penaluna, in European Commission, 2009, p. 115), they emphasize the importance of being able to develop 'visioning and scenario-planning skills, which are essential in problem-solving situations and, therefore, relevant for business managers' (European Commission, 2009, p. 115). Of specific note is the comment that:

> Designers and design thinking is [*sic*] more and more involved at the decision-making level. It is important for future business managers to understand designers' visions and for designers to understand the business implications. (180° Academy in European Commission, 2009, p. 115)

Considering the benefits of what have been described as knowledge-based approaches, there are indications that this perspective might be limiting our thinking. For example, Leadbeater (2000) does not feel that we are becoming a more knowledgeable society. In the context of a knowledge-based economy, where a robust knowledge base is important, this may have serious implications. In Leadbetter's opinion, and given technological advancements, we have far less understanding of everyday technologies than our forbears had, and therefore, have never been more ignorant. Taking this view, and given the breadth and availability of information, it is the accessibility of information that becomes a key issue for enterprising businesses, and the ability to creatively harvest information, as and when required, becomes potentially more important than a knowledge base of 'what is right'.

Pink (2008) takes an interesting look at the same problem and offers an alternative view. He suggests that people who can recognize patterns within confusion, and who have the ability to draw upon the right side of the brain to harness diverse connections, have a significant role to play in future business models. He sees society as being in the third stage of the industrial revolution, and his perspectives are useful in this context. According to Pink (2008), the first stage of the industrial revolution needed strong bodies and resolute minds to achieve success, whereas leadership skills that were based on knowledge acquisition later took precedence. However, with knowledge now so easily accessible via the worldwide web and enhanced networks of communication, successful individuals will be those who can source and resource flexibly according to perceived demands. Martin (2007, 2009) applauds those who can hold and maintain diametrically opposed ideas for as long as possible before reaching their conclusion, often synthesizing the two (or more) ideas to evolve a new solution (Abrams, 2008). This is very much the territory of the right-brain thinker.

Developing this argument further, there are times when ignorance of established approaches brings new light to a problem and its potential solution, such as when Tim Mott and Larry Tesler suggested the metaphor of a desktop for a computer interface, or when Barnes Wallis conceptualized the bouncing bomb that destroyed the Ruhr dams. These examples of innovation link emotional engagement with practical engagement and surpass traditional analytical strategies of 'the known'; they are very much solutions found through experiment and naive personal engagement. If we agree with the premise that creativity is based on new associations and combinations of existing knowledge (Schumpeter, 1934), then the implication for teaching and learning specialists in business-related studies becomes clear. Any 'ignorance' should be integrated into an evolving knowledge base, and pedagogical approaches should take account of this 'we didn't know that we needed to know' way of observing and learning.

The positivistic and predictable nature of assessment in business education contexts could, therefore, become a barrier to development. Consider that creativity, amongst other things, is the 'ability to challenge assumptions, recognise patterns, see in new ways, make connections, take risks and seize upon chance' (Herrman, in Vidal, 2004). While it is formed in the past, it constantly seeks the future; it embraces uncertainty and asks questions such as 'What if? Why not? How can?' Hence, a dichotomous position between traditional business education and creativity-enhanced education is revealed. Conversely, design-led, 'Tailor-made entrepreneurship education seems to better prepare arts students for establishing themselves as creative entrepreneurs' (Raffo et al. in European Commission, 2009, p. 113). Therefore, is it not conceivable that a broader understanding of design values could also benefit those engaged in business-based education?

Reinforcing the World Economic Forum's (2009) observations discussed earlier, cultural theorists have long argued that creative industries professions not only drive economic growth, 'but that they necessarily encompass social and cultural development as well' (Matheson, 2006, p. 55). This establishes the creative industries' position at the centre of civic and commercial life (Gans, 1999; Kunzmann, 1995; Volkering, 2000). Anderson and Ray (2001) and Florida (2002) think that the creative industries are leading to a new economy that incorporates social, cultural and environmental priorities: 'The deep and enduring changes of our age are not technological but social and cultural. These changes have been building for decades and only now are coming to the fore' (Florida, 2002, p. 17).

To conclude this introduction to relationships between business and creativity, one perspective adds potential clarity as to ways forward: 'It is hard to imagine a time when the challenges we face so vastly exceeded the creative resources we have brought to bear on them' (Brown, 2009, p. 3). Brown, who heads up one of the world's most innovative companies, IDEO, believes that while 'aspiring innovators may have attended a "brainstorming" session or learned a few gimmicks and tricks . . . rarely do these temporary place holders make it to the outside world' (Brown, 2009, p. 3). This is significant, as without creative capacity, many businesses will struggle to compete. Moreover, if it is mindset change that is required, not merely observation or short-term attempts to 'fix things', we need to look toward those whose business is creativity, because, as indicated previously by the CMI/NESTA survey (Patterson and Kerrin, 2009), the business school approach to leadership does not appear to work when it comes to being creative.

UNDERSTANDING THE CREATIVE INDUSTRIES SECTOR

The Business Context

The UK's creative industries sector has an enviable reputation: 'International comparisons of the Creative Industries sector are very difficult but most studies put the UK at or near the top' (DCMS, 2008a). The sector includes advertising, architecture, the art and antiques market, crafts, design, designer fashion, film, interactive leisure software, music, the performing arts, publishing, software and computer services, television and radio. As this is such a diverse and complex environment, we must firstly consider the 'knowns' that we can confidently include in any contextual discussion. The following snapshots help us to gauge the levels of activity that have been recorded in recent years.

> Britain is a creative country and our creative industries are increasingly vital to the UK. Two million people are employed in creative jobs and the sector contributes £60 billion a year; 7.3 per cent to the British economy. Over the past decade, the creative sector has grown at twice the rate of the economy as a whole and is well placed for continued growth as the demand for creative content – particularly in English – grows. (DCMS, 2008b, p. 6)

Software, computer games and electronic publishing have had the highest average growth (8 per cent per annum) contributing 31 per cent of the £16 billion of creative industries' goods and services exported in 2006 (DCMS, 2009, p. 1). The software, computer games and electronic publishing sector, and the design and designer fashion sector, both showed growth in employment of 5 per cent per annum between 1997 and 2007, the highest across the creative industries (DCMS, 2009, p. 2).

In 2008, there were 157400 businesses in the creative industries on the Inter-Department Business Register (IDBR), representing 7.3 per cent of all companies on the IDBR. Two-thirds of the businesses in the creative industries are contained within two sectors: software, computer games and electronic publishing (75000 companies), and music and the visual and performing arts (31200 companies). It should be noted that the IDBR covers all parts of the economy, other than some very small businesses (the self-employed and those without employees, and those with low turnover), and some non-profit organizations; thus, the true proportion is likely to be higher as certain sectors such as crafts contain predominantly small businesses (DCMS, 2009, p. 2).

In 2004 The Arts Council of England observed that: 'about 39 per cent of individuals working in the creative industries are classed as self-employed' (in Carey and Naudin, 2006, p. 519). However, it is acknowledged that being self-employed is not synonymous with being entrepreneurial (Carey and Naudin, 2006), as many enter the creative industries because of the flexibility that self-employment offers those with family responsibilities, thus making them particularly attractive to women (Carey et al., 2007; Henry, 2009). However, we must also be mindful that Carey et al. (2007) found that the number of women running businesses within the sector is comparatively low.

Creative entrepreneurs are diverse, from self-employed artists to owners of global businesses (Björkegren, 1996). Rae's 2005 case-study research, undertaken with four creative businesses over a two-year period, notes the 'cultural diffusion' in a creative enterprise: 'what works is a combination of the enacted values of innovation, emotional engagement and responsibility to people together with the "feel" and "approach" that have been learned through experiences' (Rae, 2005, p. 191). The UK-based Forum on Creative Industries (2009) recognizes the strong economic contribution made by the creative industries in terms of wealth creation and employment:

> They are multi-skilled and fluid; they move between niches and create hybrids, they are multi-national and they thrive on margins of economic activity; they mix up making money and making meaning. The challenge of the creative industries is the challenge of a new form of economic understanding – they are not 'catching up' with serious, mainstream industries, they are setting the templates, which these will follow. (FOCI, 2009, p. 1)

When we look at overarching categories within the creative industries, the discipline of design is acknowledged as one of the most dynamic and diverse. In 1999 it was judged at a global level to be worth US$140 billion, with an average annual growth in design jobs over 1995–2000 being recorded at 21 per cent (Cunningham, 2005, p. 7). Recent research undertaken by the UK's Design Council for the period between 2005 and 2010 suggests a continued growth rate of 29 per cent in terms of design jobs, and an estimated 15 per cent rise in terms of fees and revenue generation (Design Council, 2010). Considering the economic landscape of the period under review, this must be considered an impressive achievement. In broader terms, Cunningham (2005) observes that: 'there is a distinct correlation between design-intensity in enterprise activity and product development and broad economic competitiveness' (p. 7). Moreover, Cunningham also cites PricewaterhouseCooper's research, which demonstrated that: 'design is seen as a strategic asset by the highest performing enterprises, while less successful businesses give design a lower level of importance' (Cunningham, 2005, p. 8).

In the UK, the design industry is recognized not only in terms of the creative sector, but also through its relationships with other sectors (Cox, 2005), and central government has already highlighted that design has been significantly undervalued as a means of improving business performance. Of particular note is that even the UK's Department of Trade and Industry (DTI, 2005, p. iv) offered the view that the lack of engagement with design is a 'possibly under utilised resource of competitive advantage' (see also Penaluna and Penaluna, 2006).

The Educational Context

Before we start to consider any specific details about pedagogies and approaches, we must first acknowledge that the creative industries sector is one of the most educated, with around 43 per cent of employees educated to degree level or higher, compared with only 16 per cent of the workforce as a whole (NESTA, 2003). This is a factor that immediately adds resonance to any discussion, as the impact of education is clearly relevant.

The UK Higher Education Academy's work is a useful place to start any investigation into the nature and type of work involved, as its Art and Design Subject Centre has undertaken one of the few robust investigations into entrepreneurship education in the creative industries. Of primary interest is the proposition that entrepreneurship has already been embedded in most courses in the UK: 'Entrepreneurship is inherent to effective creative practice . . . over 80% of respondents include this type of delivery as a credit-bearing course and many of these situate this learning in the core practice of the subject' (HEA-ADM/NESTA, 2007, p. 14).

The UK Higher Education Academy's Art, Design and Media Subject

Centre (HEA-ADM) research, which was undertaken collaboratively with NESTA, was a unique first attempt to consolidate understanding through fresh investigation. The report is underpinned by a case study (Kellet, 2006a) of the UK's provision. It identified examples of teaching that fully engaged creative industry learners in the entrepreneurship agenda. Five 'in-depth' studies explored in Kellet's research provide: 'a distinct model for delivering entrepreneurship education to art, design and media students in higher education' (HEA-ADM/NESTA, 2007). Kellet openly states her intention to: 'champion the innate power of the creativity of entrepreneurial talent within art and design schools and Creative Industry businesses' (Kellet, 2006b, p. 3). Importantly, her findings indicated: 'a new and emerging currency of creative enterprise education within the UK, with a distinct subversion of the more traditional academic frameworks of teaching entrepreneurship' (Kellet, 2006b, p. 4), thus reinforcing the dichotomous observations made earlier.

The report highlights that there is a high propensity towards self-employment and entrepreneurship among graduates from creative disciplines. Graduate Prospects (www.prospects.ac.uk, April 2006) showed that only 2.1 per cent of graduates entered self-employment within six months of graduation, but that 9.3 per cent of design graduates are self-employed within the same period and of the top six subjects for self-employment five are 'creative subjects' (HEA-ADM/NESTA, 2007, p. 58). Moreover, many graduates regard employment as an essential part of their long-term plans to start a creative business.

We must acknowledge that within the creative industries sector there is a continued discourse between those supporting an ideology of an economic framework for the arts, that is, one that embraces industry and business constructs, with those that completely resist the categorizing of the arts into industry constructs (Caust, 2004). Moreover, Blackwell and Harvey's (1999, p. 82) in-depth study of the careers of 2000 art and design graduates from 14 institutions found 'the biggest area that was regarded as absent from courses was the link to the "business" or "real world"'. As this is the connective tissue between creativity and business that we wish to investigate, we move the focus of our discourse toward specialist educators within the creative industries who understand and value entrepreneurial traits in their approaches to educational constructs within art and design.

To add some clarity to this observation, one potentially important omission in the HEA-ADM/NESTA data is the lack of distinction between comments from the two differing disciplines of art education and design education. These two are often banded together for convenience, yet clear distinctions can be drawn between them. Kellet's (2006b) research on existing provision and comments from 'the student voice' (HEA-ADM/

NESTA, 2007, p. 123), suggests that in the continuum between the two sides, it is the design aspect that is most connected to the entrepreneurship agenda. However, once again we observe an educational disconnect, for while 93 per cent of designers believe business skills are essential or useful, only 54 per cent of heads of UK design schools agree (Design Council, 2005). This disparity could indicate a serious area of concern. Is it the case that traditional pedagogical methodologies for entrepreneurship education are ineffective for the creative sector (Kellet, 2006b; Leadbeater and Oakley, 2001; NESTA, 2003; Penaluna and Penaluna, 2005; Rae, 2004; Raffo et al., 2000), or that business professors, who are often dropped in to fill gaps in arts-based curriculum, do not concern themselves with alternative pedagogical approaches (Fregetto, 2006) and may not be best placed to stimulate interest? While no research into these important questions has been found during this investigation, the authors' perceptions are that this has been very much the case.

What we do know with some degree of certainty is that the term 'entrepreneurship' elicits many negative responses from students consulted in the HEA-ADM/NESTA review, with students associating the term with negative forms of behaviour such as confrontation, poor performance and commercial gain over social benefit (HEA-ADM/NESTA, 2007, p. 57). When pressed, however, these students ascribed inherently entrepreneurial characteristics that they recognized and valued in themselves (HEA-ADM/NESTA, 2007, p. 67). The issue of the language of business and the language of the creative being dissimilar, therefore, appears to exist at a surface level only. In terms of sense-making and sense-giving, issues of figurative language and their layers of associated meanings might well be clouding our interpretations and understandings of the terms we employ (Nicholson and Anderson, 2005). The dominance of business school approaches, especially in terms of communication strategies, may therefore be counterproductive in this context. Creative students typically wish to study their creative specialism, to learn the ins and outs of creative music-making or art forms, not 'dry' business studies (HEA-ADM/ NESTA, 2007; Penaluna and Penaluna, 2005). Issues of relevance and appropriateness are key to such students, and the people they trust most are from their own disciplines, those who have real and appropriate experiences to share (Penaluna and Penaluna, 2005). They see business as a means to enhance and develop their creativity, not as a means for businesses to exploit their creative minds.

These findings are supported by earlier research. For example, Hesmondhalgh (2002, p. 70) observes that 'most creative workers make very little money. Great sacrifices have to be made to achieve even limited autonomy'; many art disciplines attract those with a non-conformist

personality that potentially precipitates a desire to start their own business, so as to avoid employment and the subsequent regulations imposed
within a large organization (Kets de Vries, 1977). Motivational constructs
are clearly not business related; they are more an extension of personal
development and career plans. Business, per se, is often perceived as 'a
necessary evil', and comments such as 'I am not here to prostitute my art'
are regular responses during introductory lectures that the authors have
led, especially within the fine arts. This is one aspect that Kellet's (2006b,
p. 2) research clearly identifies. She describes it as a 'hidden curriculum',
one that requires the business or enterprise educator to elicit support and
interest and curiosity early in the process, otherwise the students remain
disengaged.

To help contextualize these comments and observations, we must take
into cautionary account that the inherent characteristics of these types of
students can be aligned to personality characteristics that are possessed
by successful entrepreneurs: specifically, their conceptual ability, creativity and innovative ability (Timmons, 1998), and their strong desire to
be independent (Meredith et al., 1982). Extended observation of these
students suggests that from the eight Myers–Brigg Type Indicator preferences for 'the way in which they like to focus their attention, the way they
like to take information, the way they like to decide, and the way they
like to adopt' (Myers, 1992 in Routamaa and Miettinen, 2007) 'perceiving (P)' – interested in acting by watching, trying out, adapting – is the
most prominent. This is borne out in quality control measures and benchmark statements for art and design. As perceiving is the most visible personal preference of entrepreneurs, according to Routamaa and Miettinen
(2007), we can conclude that what dictates creative individuals' behaviour
'is not a rigid inner structure, but the demands of the interaction between
them and the domain in which they are working' (Csikszentmihalyi,
2001, p. 23). Issues of relevance to ambition and motivation are thus
highlighted again; accordingly, design education students are challenged
through briefs that engage them in problem-solving within highly realistic
scenarios. It is this interaction that leads the learning process, and almost
everything is assessed in context, not through examinations.

Art and design students traditionally engage with pedagogical styles
that are experiential; they are seen to develop right-brain creative skills,
in addition to the left-brain analytical ones. Educators from the creative
disciplines already respond to the calls from entrepreneurship researchers
such as Chia (1996), Kirby (2003), Niewenhuizen and Groenewald (2004)
for right-brain development, and from others for whole-brain development (Bragg, 2005; Brodie and Laing, 2007; Pink, 2008). This extensive
experience suggests that pedagogical styles from the creative industries

could be relevant to a more wide-ranging, cross-disciplinary enabling strategy (Carey and Matlay, 2008; Penaluna and Penaluna, 2009). If we are looking for graduates who 'are well placed to be effective in all sectors of a knowledge-based society through their capacity for creativity through learning' (Higher Education Academy/Council for Industry and Higher Education, 2006, p. 45), as opposed to graduates who can simply 'demonstrate knowledge and understanding' (Higher Education Academy/ Council for Industry and Higher Education, 2006, p. 51), then such a discourse has added impetus and extended resonance.

If we accept the premise that creative industries disciplines attract students who already exhibit entrepreneurial characteristics, who value autonomy and want to make their own personal mark, then the recruitment strategies that attract appropriate teaching specialists might also offer valuable insights. Of significant importance is that the 'teacher practitioner' (Walker, 2008) role is encouraged in creative disciplines, and that connectivity with real-world scenarios is encouraged. For example, Carey and Matlay's (2007) investigation into recruitment strategies evidences that practitioners are highly valued contributors to creative disciplines. Conversely, in business schools, academic achievement and research contributions are more significantly valued. In a snapshot of over 30–35 job advertisements for each discipline, industrial experience was only called for in 17.5 per cent of business school adverts, whereas in the creative industries this rose to 82 per cent. Perhaps surprisingly, only 24.5 per cent of business school advertisements required experience of curriculum development and/or teaching, whereas the creative industries showed another incidence of 82 per cent. Clearly, while more research is needed, such indicators inform us that the issue is not only one of teaching style, but also one that has its roots in educator recruitment strategies. Creative industries recruiters are interested in practitioners who can teach; business school recruiters appear more interested in research capacity and status.

Our overview thus far has concerned itself primarily with the contexts within which art and design education takes place; we have looked at the sector and drawn parallels with aspirations in entrepreneurial education. We now consider what the sector does in the classroom and whether other parallels can be drawn.

CREATIVITY AND ASSOCIATED PEDAGOGICAL TOOLS IN AN ENTERPRISE CONTEXT

We acknowledge that creativity is not a new topic, yet it has only recently gained credibility as a legitimate subject for research (Gomez, 2007;

Petrowski, 2000) and, despite being acknowledged as integral to business, is 'slow to find its acknowledged place in the business world' (Hanna, 2008). Hamidi et al. (2008) claim themselves to be the 'first to investigate the importance of creativity in entrepreneurship education and theoretical models of entrepreneurial intentions' (Hamidi et al., 2008, p. 304). Writing for the UK newspaper the *Independent*, Wilce (2008) observed: 'Teaching creativity to the next generation of entrepreneurs is not as wacky as it sounds'. His article discusses the growing number of business schools that incorporate 'creativity' workshops into postgraduate programmes of study, though the foundations for these workshops and similar events are unclear, and links to established specialists from the creative industries are scant at best.

Let us first consider the view that teaching entrepreneurship is seen to involve both arts and science. The 'arts' includes creative and innovative thinking, and the 'sciences' the technicalities of business and management. Silver and MacLean (2007) conclude that the 'science' of entrepreneurship is teachable, typically including structured training with technical and personal entrepreneurial skills, such as financial management or marketing, but that the 'art' of entrepreneurship cannot be taught in the same way. They advocate: 'new ways of thinking skills and behaviours (arts) are required for the entrepreneurial businesses. The "art" of entrepreneurship can be learnt through the practical experience in the business environment rather than in the education setting' (Silver and MacLean, 2007, p. 7). While this sets the scene, it overlooks the potential journey toward the development of skill sets that could prepare the student for such creative engagements, leaping as it does straight into the workplace.

Observations such as these indicate the potential for more connectivity, yet overt links to the creative industries' educational systems and specialists are rare. As noted by Holzl (2005, p. 3): 'the importance of creativity and the interaction and contrast between competition and artistic objectives provides an interesting starting point for product innovation. Interestingly the link between creative industries and entrepreneurship is seldom made explicit'. As understanding potential links is central to our argument that pedagogical approaches within the creative disciplines align to emerging enterprise teaching and learning approaches, we will now outline potential parallels and aspects that we consider pertinent to both agendas.

- Experiential learning. Most classes are project-based and require hands-on approaches. Some classes are lecture-led, though theory can be offered after practical student experimentation.
- Problem-based learning. A brief or similar trigger for projects is

central to the active style of learning; the students are set a problem to solve. The educator becomes the coach or mentor, not the pre-disposed solution holder. Learning is context-driven, project briefs are issued that state scenarios, thus positioning the thinking skills required.

- Networking and interaction. Critiques and workshops encourage teamwork and open discussions in forum-based activities. These are most commonly found in formative assessment strategies. They lead and encourage further thinking through opportunities to prototype ideas. External engagement with clients and or partners is encouraged, thus new and pertinent perspectives can be brought to bear at appropriate stages.
- Personal engagement with studies. Portfolios, exhibitions and performances require the student to engage with an external and critical audience. The ownership of these events, through personal presentation, is implicit. Responsibilities that are associated with such overt connectivity with target audiences leads to improved levels of self-efficacy and broader stakeholder engagement.
- Assessment. Possibly the strongest contribution that the creative industries can offer is their assessment systems. These are constructively aligned (Biggs, 2003), so as to measure student performances that are directly related to the activity undertaken. Usually responding to a brief, there are few 'abstracted' assessments such as examinations or essays. For example, led by the Quality Assurance Agency subject benchmark statement on art and design (QAA, 2008), learning processes are often evaluated as much as the outcome. Peer review is integral during critiques. The nature of knowledge is explored and challenged by student-led investigations, techniques and skills are evaluated in context, redefining and challenging questions is rewarded. (See also Carey and Matlay, 2008; Penaluna and Penaluna, 2008b.)

We accept that within the confines of this chapter these are broad comparative observations, and we acknowledge that specialist areas also require closer investigation. For example, in the context of intellectual property management, an often overlooked yet important entrepreneurship skills and knowledge base, business owners are frequently unaware that disclosing information about their ideas may invalidate the opportunity to apply for patent protection (Gowers, 2006), yet product design students and graphic and advertising designers frequently find themselves tasked with explaining intellectual property procedures to clients who are 'logo-centric' and unaware of their potentially business-crippling misuse of material such as images, sounds and other copyrighted resources (see, for example, Penaluna et al., 2007).

Research that offers better insights is readily available. For example, the creative industries' use of visual narrative (Kellet, 2006b) to create fuller understanding of problems and situations is uncommon in traditional business studies, yet aligns well with 'entrepreneurial journeys' that embed emotional constructs into the learning process. Practical papers such as Vij and Ball's (2007) exploration into the relationship between impact and effect of entrepreneurship programmes in design computing have, despite winning international enterprise awards, not yet filtered into mainstream academic thinking. 'Emotion' and 'passion' are commonly used terms in creative disciplines; they are everyday occurrences. Despite this, there is a need for a more in-depth understanding of the important aspects and level of emotional engagement within creative industries education (Gibb, 2009).

THE DISCIPLINE OF DESIGN: PARALLELS AND CONSIDERATIONS

In his 2005 Treasury review of British industry's needs, Sir George Cox made a clear and unequivocal statement, providing 'compelling evidence of the impact creativity can have on business performance' (Cox, 2005, p. 4). At the 2006 UK 'Competitiveness Summit', Cox followed up on his findings; his comments are summarized below:

- Design, as a discipline, is an established approach to analysing developing and realizing business needs.
- Design does not limit its thinking to challenges as and when they appear; it 'sticks pins in them' and tests the questions being asked, often realizing new objectives and problems in the process.
- Responding to problems motivates designers. If design mentality can reach the boardroom of companies, then the current stagnation of business ideas might be addressed.

Design has been defined as 'working out a solution for any specific problem in diverse contexts' (Simon, 1981 in Lau, 2009, p. 154); hence design's relationship with problem-solving can be seen in terms of inter-dependent elements. Moreover, as 'the essence of design education is . . . to establish their (students') reservoirs of experience . . . fostering creative thinking processes for originality and novelty' (Simon, 1981 in Lau, 2009, p. 155), we can immediately draw many parallels with the aims of the entrepreneurship educator.

We must also consider a factor touched upon earlier: while art education is specifically interested in human interaction, the fine artist has primarily intrinsic desires to feed their creativity. They have a personal offering that they wish to explore and ultimately disseminate through presentations and gallery-style opportunities and environments. Conversely, the designer has to respond to problems that are primarily dictated by others. Motivation is derived from problem-solving, not pure 'blue sky' exploration; by challenge and curiosity, as opposed to the challenging of conformity to express personal perspectives. Memory and recollection are, therefore, important factors: the more diverse the recollection or observation, the more diverse the range of connections that can be drawn upon to solve a problem. Traditional education systems advance the conscious or 'ordinary memory'; design tests the 'intelligent memory' (Gordon and Berger, 2003) by considering what the subconscious has recorded, what assumptions have been made and what sensory perceptions have been involved. These are right-brain activities that take account of emotion and desire; they are inherently hermeneutical processes that require students to undertake considerable research in order to underpin their approaches (Kounios et al., 2006), less 'what I want', more 'what they want'.

Graphic design author Adrian Shaunessy (2005) considers the business environments that many designers enter; his text is as much about interpreting a business client's desires and wishes as it is about the profession itself. Perceived by many creatives to be a 'soulless' environment, he unpicks the motivational factors behind business imperatives and sets out ways to bridge the tensions and distrust that exist. Few graduates from studies outside of the design disciplines understand the basic principles of providing a constructive brief that the designer can work to in a creative manner (Penaluna and Penaluna, 2006; Shaughnessy, 2005). Moreover, once a brief is offered to a student or professional designer to consider, it is rare to find that embedded assumptions are not examined in some depth before the designer proceeds to any kind of response. They unpick the questions offered. For example, a manufacturer may want to sell high-performance power drills, whilst the designer knows that the consumer wishes to buy good-quality holes that are easy to make.

Thus, it can be argued that design has a particular role to play in entrepreneurship education; indeed, many of the above comments could easily substitute the word 'design' for 'entrepreneurship'. Design is the creative response to the needs, desires and ambitions of the consumer, so it maps almost seamlessly onto emergent pedagogical goals. Yet, despite the emergence of parallel observations in more commercially driven texts (Brown, 2009; Esslinger, 2009; Martin, 2009), the comparison remains almost non-existent in the academic entrepreneurship literature.

TRENDS AND FACTORS OF INFLUENCE: A DISCUSSION

There is a proliferation of courses in entrepreneurship; most of these are being developed in business schools. They are able to attract a high level of interest from students (Shane, 2003), so at first all seems well. However, when we dig a little deeper and unpick the provisions being offered, some new perspectives are revealed. Matlay (2006, p. 705) observes that: 'Despite such widespread acknowledgement of supply and demand, there exists a disparity in the content and quality of entrepreneurship education programmes on offer, including curricula design, delivery methods and forms of assessment'. Other criticism is extensive and well documented; for example, in 2003 Kirby asked: 'Entrepreneurship education: can Business schools meet the challenge?' Gibb (2005, p. 2) subsequently observed the silo mentality of our business schools which he felt can 'compartmentalise knowledge into functional boxes. Those boxes dictate the organisation . . . and consequently the delivery of knowledge and the value they give to it'. In a similar vein, Carey et al. (2007) note that: 'Recent research suggests that business schools are not always the best placed to deliver or encourage enterprise'; while Jones observes: 'If we accept that entrepreneurial types are merely those with a deposition towards challenging the norms of society (Aldrich and Kenworthy, 2001), then the advent of entrepreneurship education (located in business schools) is problematic' (Jones, 2008, p. 3).

It has often been assumed that leadership courses can help to develop enterprising mindsets, yet as noted previously, recent research by the Chartered Institute of Management (Patterson and Kerrin, 2009) refutes this assumption; while traditional leadership skills can help to develop ideas, they rarely help to initiate them. Further analysis allows us to develop the argument that business schools alone may not be best placed to deliver entrepreneurship education. For example, the literature consistently advocates that action learning, such as that consistently found in the creative disciplines, is a key component in delivering enterprise programmes (Brodie and Laing, 2007; Edwards and Muir, 2006; Pittaway and Cope, 2006), with a requirement to provide: 'a more enterprising approach to learning which is student centred and both action and process-orientated to support effective learning' (McKeown et al., 2006, p. 597). Important to this discussion, McKeown et al.'s (2006) study of the UK's business school provision identified that while respondents stressed the practical elements of their programmes, this was not borne out by the teaching methods they encountered. Referencing a course director's comments: 'We believe strongly in the practical nature of business creation' – this actually meant 'lectures, some workshops, some tutorials, with assessment 100 per cent exam-based' (McKeown, et al., 2006, p. 607). Recent discussions within the Higher Education Academy's Subject Centre for Business Management Accountancy and Finance (HEA-BMAF) confirm these perspectives, and the Subject Centre recently addressed the issue head-on by devoting an entire conference to the dilemmas of attempting to develop more appropriate assessment strategies (HEA-BMAF, 2010).

These findings contrast starkly with art, design and media programmes, where 70 per cent of courses surveyed by HEA-ADM/NESTA (2007, p. 41) were found to assess entrepreneurship learning outcomes, using a wide range of assessment instruments: 'the most common is a critical report, relating to either the students' project work in an academic context or on crucial, work-based log books focused on some form of reflection on work-based learning experiences'.

Business school programmes, or 'electives' providing entrepreneurship or business acumen, run for non-business school environments are missing significant findings, and the knowledge flow is extensively from the business school, with very little by return. For example, left-brain–right-brain cognition strategies are almost completely ignored (Bragg, 2005; Claxton, 1998; Niewenhuizen and Groenewald, 2004), and advances in cognitive neurology (Kounios et al., 2006) that underpin problem-solving strategies have yet to surface in their discussions (see Penaluna et al., 2010). Hence, the literature base offers minimal guidance to academics from the creative industries when they wish to engage more fully in the research agenda.

According to Kellet (2006a) these educators already develop their 'core' curriculum by integrating entrepreneurship and business elements that motivate students to engage with a topic outside of their core 'creative' discipline. While there is no apparent consistency in the offering between institutions and schools within them, the creative industries sector is seen to be responding to the call for integrating business acumen and entrepreneurship in its many guises into their programmes. While, within the business school environs, there is an urgent need for 'empirically rigorous research to bridge the knowledge gap that persists between the interests of various stakeholders in this area of policy intervention and actual entrepreneurial outcomes' (Matlay, 2006, p. 712), the very 'embeddedness' that is seen as successful integration within art and design may actually be hiding the existing good practice.

Although the entrepreneurship literature base for the creative industries is emerging slowly at best, there is evidence such as awards made at international conferences that suggest that the international academic entrepreneurship community is beginning to understand and embrace creative industries approaches. Other arguments are surfacing that indicate change may be afoot. For example, Starkey and Tempest (2009) note the growing awareness that the recent economic crisis was led by managers who were educated in large numbers in business schools. They suggest an alternative perspective, one that views 'management as an art, rather than a science'. Their paper proposes that we should rethink the business school and 'reinvent what they can do by an engagement with history and the design sciences' (Starkey and Tempest, 2009, p. 700).

There are other indicators of an emerging paradigm shift. For example, the HEA-BMAF recognized some of the issues discussed at its 2007 National Conference, and appointed a specialist in design, not business, to chair its newly formed Special Interest Group in Entrepreneurial Learning (see www.heacademy.ac.uk/business). Moreover, the New Deal of the Mind (NDotM) initiative is indicative of the creative industries' prompt response and enterprising approach to addressing the global financial downturn. It was critical of the lack of provision in the UK government's Flexible New Deal and Future Jobs Fund for the self-employed and free-lancers who 'are the lifeblood of the creative industries' (NDotM, 2009, p. 4), and advocated a return to the 1980s Enterprise Allowance Scheme. With support from the Federation of Small Businesses, juxtaposed with the general lack of understanding and support from Jobcentres, initiatives such as this might well determine the levels of success and recovery, not only for the creative industries, but also for those who wish to be independent in creative business development.

Capturing this expertise in a sustainable manner has, thus far, eluded the academic entrepreneurship community, as exemplified for example by Danko (2005), who is an international award-winning author on entrepreneurship; while she continues to author scholarly publications and provide presentations, they are no longer under the umbrella of 'entrepreneurship' but on the role of design as a tool for leadership. Similarly, Kellet, a significant contributor who provided evidence that led the HEA-ADM/NESTA review, has not contributed to an enterprise conference since 2006. Moving away from academic debates, she is developing 'creative warriors', an online tool to develop enterprise skills. Most notably, the National Council for Graduate Entrepreneurship's investigation into assessment strategies (Pittaway et al., 2009) omitted any creative industries contributions; in consequence, many perspectives on the development of innovation and creative skills were missed (Penaluna and Penaluna, 2009).

In 2009, NESTA launched its business planning 'toolkit' for creative industries educators; NESTA not only recognized the need for a more creative approach to teaching the creative student, but effectively bypassed traditional business language and approaches in order to deliver its innovative new strategies (see IEEC, 2009; NESTA, 2009).

Finally, it should also be noted that creative enterprise conferences, symposia and similar types of events can help to develop important independent discussions within the creative community (see, for example, www. enterprise.ac.uk/events/58). However, such events may also represent a potential 'disconnect' with more established business approaches, and could initiate a trend that might not be in the best interests of those who wish to see a broader acceptance of the creative industries approaches. However, as entrepreneurship continues to be developed as an adjunct to the business school, and the extensive literature that is critical of traditional business schools appears to be going largely ignored, these types of events provide excellent forums for debate. Thus, in terms of trends and factors of influence, this chapter has evidenced that, to some extent, the creative industries have already turned their back on more traditional discussions and debates.

CONCLUSION

This chapter has considered creativity in a business education context and concluded that there is a clear cultural deficiency. Calls by the European Commission's Directorate-General for Education and Culture exemplify this perspective; they advocate structured exchanges between art and other disciplines, especially between business and design specialists.

The chapter also investigated the business of creativity, offering perspectives that illustrate the view that these new and dynamic businesses are not attempting to catch up with mainstream industries; they are creating new goals and developing templates that lead the field (FOCI, 2009, p. 1). We note that 'design thinking' has recently emerged in general business literature, though this has yet to permeate academic discourse in any serious way. Design and business competitiveness have been interlinked in terms of 'broad economic competitiveness', not only by the World Economic Forum's global competitiveness report (WEF, 2009), but also by the earlier UK Treasury-led Cox Review (Cox, 2005) and Department of Trade and Industry research (DTI, 2005). The UK design industry has not only weathered the recent economic downturn, it has thrived on it.

We also looked at the educational context that has led to this level of success, asking questions as to how the creative sector has developed its educational provision and embedded enterprise and entrepreneurship. Understanding differences, such as the motivational constructs behind fine art and design, and seeing them as independent disciplines, helps to clarify some of the misunderstanding that may arise by viewing them within a single category. This discussion led us into a more focused investigation into well-established pedagogical tools that not only parallel emergent calls from enterprise educators, but also offer insights into methods of assessment, an area that is causing considerable concern within the business-based entrepreneurship community. There have been numerous calls for the development of more whole-brain or right- and left-brain thinking in entrepreneurship education, so we highlighted the extensive experience of design educators who work with emotional constructs as well as analytical ones in their day-to-day educational environments.

Through looking at trends and influences, we illustrated that, despite gaining some momentum, the creative industries have been practically invisible to the academic enterprise community, which has located much of its thinking in business school environments. Yet, creative industries educators, especially those from the design disciplines, deliver to a broad audience, from those in crafts-based disciplines through to those in inter-active digital media and the fast-evolving landscape associated with these kinds of business models. A commonality is their focus on the creation and exploitation of intellectual property (Henry, 2007; Penaluna et al., 2007). They inherently care about ideas and problem-solving; they readily challenge accepted norms and distrust conventions.

Interdisciplinary, multidisciplinary, transdisciplinary or however we wish to describe such approaches, presuppose collaboration. The business of creativity, or creativity in business, requires us to extend our thinking beyond traditional silos of experience (Penaluna and Penaluna, 2009). Wilson and Stokes (2005) recommend that art, music and design courses follow the emphasis in science degrees to underpin technology by business training to develop entrepreneurship skills in creative disciplines. Perhaps the depth of embeddedness eluded them, especially if they were seeking out traditional business terminologies. Importantly, they also observe that: 'it is equally important to encourage and support opportunities for creativity and flair in business and management education' (Wilson and Stokes, 2005, p. 375). They describe a 'leap of faith on both sides' for business students and art, music and design students to collaborate on projects and business plans.

In light of our discussion, we suggest that the creative entrepreneurial or entrepreneurship educator and academic author is charged with remits that seek to close the gaps identified. Specifically, we suggest that educators need to:

1. Enhance the propensity for individuals from all disciplines and professions to utilize 'creative thinking skills' so that they might improve the competitive capacity of their organizations. Problem-solving is

a skill-for-life competency, one that is embedded in design-based thinking.

2. Provide an understanding of the impact of design from micro- to macro-businesses, so that students and graduates are better equipped to liaise with or mimic creatives and other design professionals who can positively influence their business ventures.

3. Provide an enhanced understanding of the value of intangible assets, such as intellectual property rights, generated from creativity and associated outputs.

4. Seek out and consider more appropriately aligned assessment strategies. If creativity and predictability are anathema to one another, then assessment strategies that value the creative process need to be put in place (Carey and Matlay, 2008; Penaluna and Penaluna, 2008b). Examinations and other traditional assessment procedures cannot wholly achieve this, as they predict solutions to measure against, denying creative unknowns that lead to innovation.

When contextualizing our closing discussions, we remain mindful that most entrepreneurship conferences employ terminology that engenders a more business-focused dialogue. Therefore, it is perhaps not surprising that 'creatives' have not been more prevalent. Moreover, the business and creative mindsets may be perceived to be uncomfortable bedfellows. Thus far, most movement has seen the creative industries' attempts to contribute to the debate set against a strong perception that the business community has much more to offer them by return. But is that really the case? (See Penaluna and Penaluna, 2009.)

The reoccurring theme in this chapter is that the discipline of design has already been a significant contributor to economic development and offers considerable insights into the intersection between business and creativity. If we consider that design, as a function, infers creative use of resources and ideas in the creation of a new or improved product or service, it has much in common with the term 'entrepreneur' (Kellet, 2006a; Penaluna and Penaluna, 2006, 2008a, 2009; Rae, 2004). Business communication and promotion rely on sound business understanding; they are what design is all about. Yet despite every business and organization requiring such support, it has rarely featured in enterprise-related literature. As this discourse evidences, design education bridges the gap between business and creativity, and manages a tension that entrepreneurship and enterprise appears, through conferences and literature, still to be grappling with.

We have argued in this chapter that the creative industries have much to offer the enterprise agenda, and that a continuing and evolving dialogue is essential if we are to maximize creativity-related objectives. We also suggest that the UK's creative industries may well be at the forefront of pedagogical development, with the potential to enhance entrepreneurial capacity; yet thus far, they have not been fully engaged and few champions have emerged. Moreover, those with acknowledged expertise have often disengaged. There are clearly problems of perception, language and value; hence the connective tissue between the business school environment and its (potentially) creative partners is a thin strand at best; it is also a very unbalanced relationship. Future research in this area would clearly be of value.

In closing, we ask the reader to consider removing creativity and innovation from the enterprise agenda and questioning what would remain. Would it not be traditional business studies? Yet, in terms of educational expertise, we have evidenced here that in many ways this has been the case. This simple deduction has led the thinking behind our chapter's call for creative industries engagement with entrepreneurship education policy and development.

REFERENCES

Abrams, R. (2008), 'White collar or no collar: the choice for designers', *Design Council Magazine*, **4**, 52–57.

Amabile, T. (1998), 'How to kill creativity, *Harvard Business Review*, September–October, 77–87.

Anderson, S. and P. Ray (2001), *The Cultural Creatives: How 50 Million People are Changing the World*, New York: Three Rivers Press.

Biggs, J. (2003), *Teaching for Quality Learning at University*, Buckingham: Open University Press.

Björkegren, D. (1996), *The Culture Business: Management Strategies for the Arts Related Business*, London: Routledge.

Blackwell, A. and L. Harvey (1999), 'Destinations and reflections: careers of British art craft and design graduates', Birmingham: University of Central England Centre of Research into Quality.

Bragg, M. (2005), 'Educating for, about, and through entrepreneurship: a case study for whole-brain curriculum development', paper presented at Internationalizing Entrepreneurship Education and Training Conference, Guildford.

Brodie, J. and S. Laing (2007), 'Embracing innovative approaches to entrepreneurship teaching to support effective entrepreneurial learning', paper presented at Internationalizing Entrepreneurship Education and Training Conference, Gdansk, Poland.

Brown, G. (2005), speech by the Rt Hon. Gordon Brown MP, Chancellor of the Exchequer, at Advancing Enterprise 2005, accessed 22 October 2006 at www.hm-treasury.gov.uk/newsroom_and_speeches/press_15_5.cfm.

Brown, T. (2009), *Change by Design*, New York: Harper Collins.

Carey, C., L. Martin, H. Matlay and B. Jerrard (2007), 'Gender and entrepreneurship in the creative industries: what the literature tells us', paper presented at the Institute of Small Business and Entrepreneurship, Glasgow.

Carey, C. and H. Matlay (2007), 'Entrepreneurs as educators: the case of the creative industries in the UK', *Industry and Higher Education*, **21** (6), 435–43.

Carey, C. and H. Matlay (2008), 'Characteristics of creative disciplines education: a model for assessing enterprise?' paper presented at the Institute for Small Business and Entrepreneurship Conference, Belfast.

Carey, C. and A. Naudin (2006), 'Enterprise curriculum for creative industries students: an exploration of current attitudes and issues', *Education and Training*, **48** (7), 518–31.

Carey, C., K. Smith and L. Martin (2007), 'Supporting enterprise educators: how to promote enterprise in new areas', paper presented at the Institute for Small Business and Entrepreneurship Conference, Glasgow.

Caust, J. (2004), 'Which way to Nirvana? Unravelling the difference in discourse about art, culture and the meaning of life', paper presented at the 3rd International Conference on Cultural Policy Research, Montreal, QC.

Chia, R. (1996), 'Teaching paradigm shifting in management education: university business schools and the entrepreneurial imagination', *Journal of Management Studies*, **33** (4), 409–28.

Claxton, G. (1998), *Hare Brain Tortoise Mind: Why Intelligence Increases When You Think Less*, London: Fourth Estate.

Cox, G. (2005), *Cox Review of Creativity in Business: Building on the UK's Strengths*, London: HM Treasury.

Csikszentmihalyi, M. (2001), 'A systems perspective on creativity', in Jane Henry (ed.), Creative Management, 2nd edn, London: Sage, pp. 11–26.

Cunningham, S. (2005), 'Creative enterprises', in John Hartley (ed.), *Creative Industries*, Malden, MA: Blackwell Publishing, pp. 282–98, and at QUT Digital Repository, accessed 19 July 2009 at http://eprints.qut.edu.au.

Danko, S. (2005), 'Crossing educational boundaries: reframing entrepreneurship as a social change agent', paper presented at Internationalizing Entrepreneurship Education and Training Conference, Guildford.

Department for Culture, Media and Sport (DCMS) (2008a), 'From the margins to the mainstream: government unveils new action plan for the creative industries', press release, accessed 22 February at www.culture.gov.uk/Reference_library/Press_notices/archive_2008/dcms017_08.htm.

DCMS (2008b), 'Creative Britain: new talents for the new economy', London.

DCMS (2009), *Creative Industries Economic Estimates Statistical Bulletin*, January, accessed at www.culture.gov.uk/images/research/Creative_Industries_Economic_Estimates_Jan_o9.pdf.

Department of Trade and Industry (DTI) (2005), 'Creativity, design and business performance', DTI economics paper no 15, London.

Design Council (2005), 'The business of design: design industry research 2005', accessed at www.design-council.org.uk/en/Design-Council/3/Publications/The-Business-of-Design.

Design Council (2010), 'Design industry research 2010', accessed 17 May at www.designcouncil.org.uk/industryresearch?WT.dcsvid=NDA5OTYxMTY3MAS2&WT.mc_id=.

Edwards, L.J. and E. Muir (2006), 'Tell me and I'll forget; show me and I may remember; involve me and I'll understand: developing enterprise education through theory and practice', National Council for Graduate Entrepreneurship working paper, accessed 6 September 2009 at www.ncge.com/communities/research/reference/reports/Working%20paper/7/70.

Esslinger, H. (2009), *A Fine Line: How Design Strategies are Shaping the Future of Business*, San Francisco, CA: Jossey Bass.

European Commission (2009), 'The impact of culture on creativity', study prepared for the European Commission Directorate-General for Education and Culture, June.

Florida, R. (2002), *The Rise of the Creative Class: and How It's Transforming Work, Leisure, Community and Everyday Life*, New York: Basic Books.

Forum on Creative Industries (FOCI) (2009), accessed 14 July at www.foci.org.uk/index/php/Section1.html.

Fregetto, E. (2006), 'Do entrepreneurial inclined students learn more from simulations?', paper presented at Entrepreneurship Education Track, United States Association for Small Business and Entrepreneurship National Conference, Tuscon, AZ.

Gans, H.J. (1999), *Popular Culture and High Culture: An Analysis and Evaluation of Taste*, New York: Basic Books.

Gibb, A.A. (2005), 'Towards the entrepreneurial university: entrepreneurship education as a lever for change', National Council for Graduate Entrepreneurship policy paper 003.

Gibb, A.A. (2009), plenary presentation at the International Entrepreneurship Educators Conference, Heriot-Watt University.

Gomez, J.G. (2007), 'What do we know about creativity?', *Journal of Effective Teaching*, **7** (1), 31–43.

Goodman, M. (1995), *Creative Management*, London: Sage.

Gordon, B. and L. Berger (2003), *Intelligent Memory: Exercise Your Mind and Make Yourself Smarter*, London: Vermilion.

Gowers, A. (2006), *Gowers Review of Intellectual Property*, London: HM Treasury.

Hamidi, D.Y., K. Wennberg and H. Bergland (2008), 'Creativity in entrepreneurship education', *Journal of Small Business and Enterprise Development*, **15** (2), 304–20.

Handy, C. (1985), *Understanding Organisations*, Harmondsworth: Penquin.

Hanna, J. (2008), 'Getting down to the business of creativity', Harvard Business School Working Knowledge, accessed 15 April 2009 at http://hbswk.hbs.edu/item/5902.html.

HEA-ADM/NESTA (2007), 'Creating entrepreneurship: entrepreneurship for the creative industries', Brighton: Higher Education Academy, Art Design and Media Subject Centre/NESTA.

HEA-BMAF (2010), 'Assessment and assessment standards: challenges for business education', annual conference, Newcastle, 20–21 April, accessed 5 April at www.heacademy.ac.uk/business/.

Henry, C. (ed.) (2007), *Entrepreneurship in the Creative Industries: An International Perspective*, Cheltenham, UK and Northampton, MA, USA: Edward Elgar.

Henry, C. (2009), 'Let's hear it for the girls: women in the creative industries', Institute for Small Business and Entrepreneurship, Enterprise Matters, accessed 17 May at www.isbe.org.uk/pagebuild.php?texttype=EMPresPiece.

Henry, J. (ed.) (2001), *Creative Management*, 2nd edn, London: Sage.

Hesmondhalgh, D. (2002), *Cultural Industries*, London: Sage.

Higher Education Academy and Council for Industry and Higher Education (2006), 'Student employment profiles', York: Higher Education Academy.

Holzl, W. (2005), 'Entrepreneurship, entry and exit in creative industries: an exploratory survey', Creative Industries in Vienna: Development, Dynamics and Potentials working paper no. 1, www.wu-wien.ac.at/inst/geschichte/Projekt_Homepage/frameset.html, accessed 3 June 2009.

International Entrepreneurship Educators Conference (IEEC) (2009), Heriot-Watt University, EEUK & NCGE, September, accessed 10 September at www.ieec.co.uk/index.php?page=parallel-sessions.

Jones, C. (2008), 'Disconnected and dysfunctional business schools: reflections of a serial troublemaker', unpublished, personal communication with the authors.

Kellet, S. (2006a), *Emergent Practices in Entrepreneurship Education for Creatives*, Brighton: University of Brighton Higher Education Academy.

Kellet, S. (2006b), 'A picture of creative entrepreneurship: visual narrative in creative enterprise education', paper presentation at Internationalizing Entrepreneurship Education and Training Conference, Sao Paulo, Brazil.

Kets de Vries, M. (1977), 'The entrepreneurial personality: a person at the cross-roads', *Journal of Management Studies*, **14** (1), 34–57.

Kirby, D.A. (2003), 'Entrepreneurship education: can business schools meet the challenge?', *Education and Training*, **46** (8–9), 510–19.

Kounios, J., J.L. Frymiare, E.M. Bowden, I. Fleck, K. Subramaniam, Y.B. Parrish and M. Jung-Beeman (2006), 'The prepared mind: neutral activity prior to problem presentation predicts subsequent solution by sudden insight', *Psychological Science*, **17** (10), 882–90.

Kunzmann, K.P. (1995), 'Developing the regional potential for creative response to structural change', in J. Brotchie, M. Batty and E. Blakely (eds), *Cities in Competition: Productive and Sustainable Cities for the 21st Century*, Melbourne, NSW: Longman, pp. 286–94.

Lau, K.W. (2009), 'Creativity training in higher design education', *Design Journal*, **12** (2), 153–69.

Leadbeater, C. (2000), *The Weightless Society: Living in the New Economic Bubble*, New York: Texare.

Leadbeater, C. and K. Oakley (2001), *Surfing the Long Wave: Knowledge Entrepreneurship in Britain*, London: Demos.

Lumsdaine, E. and M. Binks (2006), *Entrepreneurship from Creativity to Innovation: Effective Thinking for a Changing World*, Oxford: Trafford.

Martin, R. (2007), *The Opposable Mind*, Cambridge, MA: Harvard Business School Press.

Martin, R. (2009), *The Design of Business: Why Design Thinking is the Next Competitive Advantage*, Cambridge, MA: Harvard Business School Press.

Matheson, B. (2006), 'A culture of creativity: design education and the creative industries', *Journal of Management Development*, **25** (1), 55–64.

Matlay, H. (2006), 'Viewpoint, researching entrepreneurship and education, part 2: what is entrepreneurship education and does it matter?', *Education and Training*, **48** (8–9), 704–18.

McKeown, J., C. Millman, S.R. Sursani, K. Smith and L. Martin (2006), 'Graduate entrepreneurship education in the United Kingdom', *Education and Training*, **48** (8–9) 597–613.

McWilliam, E. (2008), 'Unlearning how to teach', *Innovations in Education and Teaching International*, **45** (3), 263–9.

Meredith, G.G., R.E. Nelson and P.A. Neck (1982), *The Practice of Entrepreneurship*, Geneva: International Labour Office.

National Endowment for Science, Technology and the Arts (NESTA) (2003), 'Forward thinking – new solutions to old problems: investing in the creative industries', London: NESTA.

NESTA (2009), 'Enterprise Toolkit', accessed 8 September at http://nesta.org.uk/ enterprise-toolkit/.

New Deal of the Mind (NDotM) (2009), 'Do it yourself; cultural and creative self-employment in hard times', report for the Arts Council (England), accessed 25 September at www.newdealofthemind.com/?page_id=1329.

Nicholson, L. and A.R. Anderson (2005), 'News and nuances of the entrepreneurial myth and metaphor: linguistic games in entrepreneurial sense-making and sense-giving', *Entrepreneurship: Theory and Practice*, **29** (2), 153–72.

Nieuwenhuizen, C. and D. Groenewald (2004), 'Entrepreneurship training and education needs as determined by the brain preference profiles of successful, established entrepreneurs', paper presented at the Internationalizing Entrepreneurship Education and Training Conference, Naples, Italy.

Patterson, F. and M. Kerrin (2009), *Innovation for the Recovery: Enhancing Innovative Working Practices*, London: CMI/National Endowment for Science, Technology and the Arts.

Penaluna, A., J. Coates and K. Penaluna (2010), 'Creativity-based assessment and neural understandings: a discussion and case study analysis', *Education + Training*, **52** (8–9), 660–78.

Penaluna, A. and K. Penaluna (2005), 'Entrepreneurship for artists and designers in higher education', paper presented at Internationalizing Entrepreneurship Education and Training Conference, Guildford.

Penaluna, A. and K. Penaluna (2006), '*Cox Review of Creativity in Business*: implications for entrepreneurship educators', paper presentation at the Institute for Small Business and Entrepreneurship Conference, Cardiff.

Penaluna, A. and K. Penaluna (2008a), 'Business paradigms in Einstellung: harnessing creative mindsets, a creative industries perspective', *Journal of Small Business and Entrepreneurship*, **21** (2), 231–50.

Penaluna, A. and K. Penaluna (2008b), 'Entrepreneurial capacity? Entrepreneurial intent? Assessing creativity: drawing on the experience of the UK's creative industries', paper presented at the Internationalizing Entrepreneurship Education and Training Conference, Oxford, OH, USA.

Penaluna, A. and K. Penaluna (2009), 'Creativity in business/business in creativity: transdisciplinary curricula as an enabling strategy in enterprise education', *Industry and Higher Education*, **23** (3), 209–19.

Penaluna, A., K. Penaluna and D. Morgan (2007) 'I love IP: designing the student experience to exploit creative endeavour', paper presented at the Institute for Small Business and Entrepreneurship Conference, Glasgow.

Petrowski, M.J. (2000), 'Creativity research: implications for teaching, learning and thinking', keynote address at the ODEX of the West 2000 conference', *Reference Services Review*, **28** (4), 304–12.

Pink, D. (2008), *A Whole New Mind: Why Right-Brainers Will Rule the Future*, new edn, London: Marshall Cavendish.

Pittaway, L. and J. Cope (2006), 'Simulating entrepreneurial learning: integrating experiential and collaborative approaches to learning', National Council for Graduate Entrepreneurship working paper, accessed 25 September 2009 at www. ncge.com/communities/research/reference/reports/Working%20paper/7/60.

Pittaway, L., P. Hannon, A.A. Gibb and J. Thompson (2009), 'Assessment practice in enterprise education', *International Journal of Entrepreneurial Behaviour and Research*, **15** (1), 71–93.

Quality Assurance Agency (QAA) (2008), 'Art and design: subject benchmarks statements', Gloucester: Quality Assurance Agency for Higher Education.

Rae, D. (2004), 'Entrepreneurial learning: a practical model from the creative industries', *Education and Training*, **46** (8–9), 492–500.

Rae, D. (2005), 'Cultural diffusion: a formative process in creative entrepreneurship?', *International Journal of Entrepreneurship and Innovation*, **6** (3), 185–92.

Rae, D. (2007), *Entrepreneurship: From Opportunity to Action*, Basingstoke: Palgrave Macmillan.

Raffo, C., J. O'Connor, A. Lovatt and M. Banks (2000), 'Attitudes to formal business training and learning amongst entrepreneurs in the cultural industries: situated business learning through "doing with others"', *Journal of Education and Work*, **13** (2), 215–30.

Ramsden, P. (2008), 'The future of higher education: teaching and the student experience', report commissioned by John Denham, Secretary of State, accessed 29 January 2009 at www.heacademy.ac.uk/resources/detail/ourwork/policy/paulramsden_teaching_and_learning_and_student_experience.

Routamaa, V. and A. Miettinen (2007), 'Awareness of entrepreneurial personalities: a prerequiste for entrepreneurial education', National Council for Graduate Entrepreneurship working paper, accessed 25 September 2009 at http://www.ncge.com/communities/research/reference/reports/Working%20paper/7/.

Schumpeter, J. (1934), *The Theory of Economic Development*, Cambridge, MA: Harvard University Press.

Shane, S. (2003), *A General Theory of Entrepreneurship: The Individual-Opportunity Nexus*, Cheltenham, UK and Northampton, MA, USA: Edward Elgar.

Shaunessy, A. (2005), *How to be a Graphic Designer without Losing Your Soul*, London: Lawrence King Publishing.

Silver, J.A.K and C. MacLean (2007), 'Fostering an entrepreneurial mindset: a pan university holistic approach', paper presented at Internationalizing Entrepreneurship and Education Conference, Gdansk, Poland.

Smith, A.J., L.A. Collins and P.D. Hannon (2006), 'Embedding new entrepreneurship programmes in UK higher education institutions: challenges and considerations', *Education and Training*, **48** (8–9), 555–67.

Starkey, K. and S. Tempest (2009), 'From crisis to purpose', *Journal of Management Development*, **28** (8), 700–10.

Timmons, J.A. (1998), *New Venture Creation: Entrepreneurship for the 21st Century*, 5th edn, Homewood, IL: Irwin.

Vidal, R.V.V. (2004), 'Creativity for operational researchers, informatics and mathematical modelling', Technical University of Denmark.

Vij, V. and S. Ball (2007), 'Exploring the impact and effect of entrepreneurship programmes on university undergraduates', paper presented at the Internationalising Entrepreneurship Education and Training Conference, Gdansk, Poland.

Volkerling, M. (2000), 'From Cool Britannia to hot nation: creative industries policies in Europe, Canada and New Zealand', *International Journal of Cultural Policy*, **7** (3), 2–11.

Walker, A. (2008), 'The teacher practitioner: "Preparation for Discover", an exercise in determining the attributes of an entrepreneurial educator through the production of job specifications', presentation to Artswork, Bath Spa University Centre for Teaching and Excellence, 19 February.

Wilce, H. (2008), 'Teaching creativity to the next generation of entrepreneurs is not as wacky as it sounds', *Independent*, 9 October.

Wilson, K.E. (2009), 'Educating the next wave of entrepreneurs: unlocking entrepreneurial capabilities to meet the global challenges of the 21st century', introduction to a report of the Global Education Initiative, World Economic Forum, Switzerland, accessed 8 July at www.weforum/org/en/initiatives/gei/ EntrepreneurshipEducation/index.htm.

Wilson, N.C. and D. Stokes (2005) 'Managing creativity and innovation: the challenge for cultural entrepreneurs', *Journal of Small Business and Enterprise Development*, **12** (3), 366–78.

World Economic Forum (WEF) (2009), 'Educating the next wave of entrepreneurs: unlocking entrepreneurial capabilities to meet the global challenges of the 21st century', a report of the Global Education Initiative, Switzerland, accessed 8 July 2009 at www.weforum/org/en/initiatives/gei/EntrepreneurshipEducation/ index.htm.

5. Creative methodologies for understanding a creative industry

Ted Fuller, Lorraine Warren and Sally Jane Norman

INTRODUCTION

We have previously undertaken a stream of research that utilizes the field of entrepreneurship to study the emergence of novelty, that is, the processes by which new products, services, business models and patterns of behaviour arise through creative acts (Fuller et al., 2007; Fuller et al., 2004; Fuller and Warren, 2006a, 2006b; Fuller and Moran, 2000, 2001; Lichtenstein 2000a, 2000b, 2000c; McKelvey, 2004). As we summarize briefly below, this has been informed by entrepreneurship theories (for example effectuation), constructionist theory (for example patterning and identity formation), critical realism (morphological perspectives) and theories of social change (for example structuration). In particular, we have demonstrated the value of complexity theory (notably 'processes of emergence') in conceptualizing the practice of agility and foresight in the entrepreneurial firms we have studied.

In this chapter, we seek to extend previous conceptual work by articulating the development of a conceptually grounded framework that we suggest can capture the emergence of novelty in the creative industries, particularly those in the so-called digital economy. As we indicate below, the digital economy, through the Internet, improved communications and a range of Web 2.0 platforms, provides enormous potential for the creation of novelty as defined above, in ways that are hard to predict given the unexplored potential of many new technologies and the ongoing pace of technological change. Unexpected new ways of creating value have arisen on a system-wide basis, albeit that revenue streams for many new activities are not well understood or established. Better understanding of how new value-creating systems emerge in such landscapes can give us a better understanding of how such processes can be managed and supported, thereby contributing, in a small way, to better understanding of the sustainability of the industries overall.

This is important economically, as the UK is renowned for its creative industries in areas as diverse as music, animation, design, gaming, and the visual and creative arts. It has been estimated that the creative industries account for 7.3 per cent of the UK economy, parallel in size therefore to the financial services industry (DCMS, 2007). The livelihood of a growing proportion of UK citizens therefore depends upon the sector maintaining its growth trajectory, particularly in the South East. Together with London and parts of the East of England and South West, the South East region forms a 'mega region' of world-class significance in relation to the creative economy. The David Powell report (2002) suggests that the creative industries employ more than half a million people in the South East and contribute more than €40 billion to the regional economy. Creative and cultural industries represent around 30 per cent of its gross domestic product (GDP), making it the region's fastest-growing sector. Good understanding of the challenges and opportunities presented by the sector is, therefore, important from a regional development point of view. Yet studying the sector presents challenges.

Firstly, the 'creative industries' are very diverse, spanning a range of interlocking industries, including arts, culture, heritage, media, gaming, performance and occasionally sports; the production of both (aesthetic) artefacts and also surrounding services must also be considered.

Secondly, developments in digital technology have stimulated new impetus for rapid change since the start of the twenty-first century, presenting unlimited possibilities for new resonances between social practices and values and the techno-creative milieu. For example, disintermediation in the music industry has been made possible through the Internet, which allows new experiences anywhere, at any time, resulting in new behaviours in respect of the production and consumption of artistic output. Of course, this has had a profound effect on the power base in the industry, as old business models have been swept aside – at times, before new revenue streams have been established.

Thirdly, the creative industries have a distinctive character that challenges traditional models of research into business innovation and entrepreneurship. Specifically, the creative industries revolve around entrepreneurial, innovative and often unorthodox collaborations, whereby numerous large, small and micro-businesses come together for the duration of a single project, then disband and form new partnerships for the next project. This diversity, fluidity, interconnectedness and potential range of novel new combinations for which there may be currently no precedent presents a challenge for researchers, educators and policy-makers who want not only to know, but also to explain and, further, to anticipate what is going on, so that appropriate development and support mechanisms might be put in place. Inevitably, then, our research designs must address multiple contexts and levels presenting an analytical challenge to management researchers (Pettigrew et al., 2001).

The vehicle that is allowing us to test our central argument further is www.creatorproject.org. The Creator project is a research cluster funded by the Engineering and Physical Research Council (EPSRC) (EP/G002088/1) as part of the 'Connecting Communities for the Digital Economy initiative. Our approach was to work with actors in live projects in order to examine how novelty emerges over time in dynamic fluid domains where uncertainty is high and outcomes are indeterminate. Firstly, we carried out an Internet-based case study of Blast Theory/*Rider Spoke* (http://www. blasttheory.co.uk/bt/work_rider_spoke.html) to generate understanding of concepts such as pervasive computing, ubiquitous computing, urban sensing and the ecosystems surrounding them. Secondly, we carried out interviews and discussions with staff at IT-Innovation, a company involved in developing a new business model for a portal in the post-production rendering industries in Soho (http://www.it-innovation.soton. ac.uk/). Thirdly, we carried out participant observations of interactions in Proboscis's Sensory Threads project (http://proboscis.org.uk/projects/ sensory-threads/) and the Gesture and Embodied Interaction workshops at Newcastle and Cambridge (http://www.ncl.ac.uk/culturelab/assets/pdfs/ Gesture_and_Embodied_Interaction_Article_Jan09.pdf). We explored how novelty emerged through interactions between the actors in the projects, and how novelty was related to value creation and the possible engagement of (new) external stakeholders.

THEORETICAL DEVELOPMENT

Thus far in our work, our overarching research question has been: how do processes of entrepreneurship result in the emergence of new phenomena (new products, services, value-creating systems) in particular social or industry contexts? While the agential dimension of entrepreneurship suggests that acts of creativity are significant in initiating change, the emphasis on context too is very significant. We argue that to remain fit over time in the dynamic, fluid landscape of the creative industries, it will be essential that creative firms constantly organize for novelty in anticipation of new collaborations, new networks and new patterns of consumer behaviour. This need is heightened by desirable heterogeneity of actors engaged in the creative landscape, since innovation tends to spring from the fertile boundaries of previously dissociated areas of activity. Sustaining creative diversity through broad-based satisficing (Simon, 1957) rather than quick-win optimization approaches is likely to enhance more effectively the dynamics of such communities. Those seeking to engage will have to act on contingency, where strategy is what is possible in an environment where the future is unpredictable (for example Sarasvathy, 2001), fast-moving and contains many actors, artefacts and potential collaborators that may co-evolve in complex non-linear ways.

Yet, as Lichtenstein et al. (2006) discuss, the study of system-wide dynamics is challenging, as the process can span long periods of time and many modes of activity take place across different contexts (Low and MacMillan, 1988). An obvious approach to dealing with this fluidity is to simplify research designs by focusing on one level of analysis, in most cases the individual, the firm or the industry. Yet this can only lead to partial, impoverished pictures of what is surely a far more rich and vibrant milieu. Hence, we have turned to complexity theory for a more integrated approach.

Management theorists' interest in complexity theory is based, firstly, on complexity's emphasis on order creation in open, non-linear, dynamic systems, a view that resonates with similar themes in organizational theory; and secondly, on the potential to theorize (through the notion of emergence) across multiple levels of analysis, such as individuals, firms and the broader environment. Using a metaphorical language for change and development (Lissack, 1997), complexity theory has been used in the design of organizational strategies (Burnes, 2005; Houchin and MacLean, 2005; Lichtenstein et al., 2006; Lichtenstein, 2000a; Stacey et al., 2002; Stacey, 2003). Concomitantly, the value of complexity theory in theorizing entrepreneurship has been recognized (Fuller et al., 2007; Fuller et al., 2004; Fuller and Warren, 2006a, 2006b; Fuller and Moran, 2000, 2001; Lichtenstein, 2000a, 2000b, 2000c; McKelvey, 2004). McKelvey (2004) contends that this approach is relevant because at a deep theoretical level it is consonant with the creative destruction of Schumpeterian entrepreneurship (Schumpeter, 1934), where entrepreneurship is defined as discontinuous change that destroys economic equilibria. Old orders are destroyed, new economic 'orders' are created in contexts that are far from equilibrium. In this vein, 'emergence' is a powerful trope that can capture the way novel structures come into being; in general terms, conjunctions of forces can produce an outcome that is more than, or at least behaves differently from, the sum of its constituent parts.

While the mainstream literature on entrepreneurship includes notions of emergence, in particular the emergence of new enterprises and products (for example, Busenitz et al., 2003; Fischer et al., 1997; Fleming and Sorenson, 2001; Gartner, 1993; Garud and Karnoe, 2003), complexity theory suggests that there are some gaps that merit further study (Fuller et al., 2008). Lichtenstein et al. (2007, pp. 238–40) argue that there should be more focus on the dynamic processes and conditions that lead to the emergence of novelty, rather than what emerges and when. They argue that interdependent patterns of wide-ranging entrepreneurial activities, rather than individual acts such as creating business plans, are significant in initiating processes of emergence towards novelty. This implies that entrepreneurs must combine advanced thinking processes and time- and life-management skills, sustaining a multidimensional focus for many months at a time and, by implication, a high degree of entrepreneurial competence, agility and foresight. In the creative industries, they must also maintain high artistic and cultural acumen.

Further, although Fuller and Moran (2001) suggest that these patterns of behaviour operate through multiple hierarchical structural levels, there has also been a tendency to reify entrepreneurship as the activities of individuals (entrepreneurs) within the process. Even where a broader 'system-wide' view is taken, as in Lichtenstein et al. (2007), the scope is limited, still largely centring on the individual. Yet, as Low and McMillan (1988) and Aldrich and Martinez (2001) point out, to understand entrepreneurship, one needs to understand the interaction between process and context, strategies and outcomes. There are a few studies that analyse organizational emergence and entrepreneurial behaviour related to the embeddedness of entrepreneurship, drawing on sociological theory such as Giddens' structuration theory (for example Jack and Anderson, 2002), the concept of structural embeddedness (for example Simsek et al., 2003), or institutional approaches (for example Smallbone and Welter, 2006) and social constructionist approaches (Fletcher, 2006; Down, 2006), and in doing so they add different contextual viewpoints, albeit implicitly. However, this question of multiple levels of analysis and multilevel theory-building is still a key issue for entrepreneurship research (Davidsson and Wiklund, 2001; Phan, 2004), in particular because of the widening contexts in which both the discourse and the practice of entrepreneurship are engaged, for example in corporate and public contexts as well as individually founded firms. Given the economic and political significance of the creative industries agenda, the need to develop entrepreneurial competence and improve outcomes is clear.

The above discussion suggests that it may be useful to research how patterns of behaviour that span process and context arise, leading to better understanding of how novelty emerges in entrepreneurial firms. While complexity theory suggests that it is not possible to predict or determine outcomes in advance, Snowden (2002), Stacey (2003) and Lichtenstein et al. (2007) suggest that understanding how meaningful patterns of behaviour emerge over time in a system-wide manner can enhance the likelihood of desirable outcomes through increasing performance generally. These patterns impact systemically at the firm level and beyond, through a wider network of stakeholder relationships that are mediated by the social and cultural relations in and surrounding the firm. For the creative industries, there can be tensions around the notion of realizing economic value from artistic, cultural or creative endeavour, particularly where the content is seen as subversive, or critical of the financial or political establishment.

Of course, the power to achieve a particular stated goal is limited for any small firm or collaboration, particularly in dynamic industries dominated by influential incumbents (unless it controls the market entrance of a disruptive innovation; Christensen, 1997). Entrepreneurs have to act on contingency, where strategy is what is possible in an environment where the future is unpredictable (for example Sarasvathy, 2001), and often dominated by large firms and fast-moving technological and industrial standards that co-evolve in complex non-linear ways (Garnsey and Heffernan, 2005). Yet to remain fit over time, it is essential that the entrepreneurial small firm constantly organizes for novelty in anticipation of industry change, particularly in high-velocity industries where uncertainty is high. Lichtenstein (2000b) shows how in each of four high-technology business start-ups the business model had to be changed several times before becoming stable, relative to an unstable and unpredictable environment.

Furthermore, if it is to be successfully sustained, not only does the creative output of entrepreneurship need to be 'novel', but it also has to be perceived as valuable in use or in exchange; by being 'novel and appropriate, useful, correct or a valuable response to the task at hand' (Amabile, 1996, p. 35, quoted in Lepak et al., 2007). This is of particular sensitivity in the field of creative industries, given the unpredictability of the perceived value of many artistic and creative endeavours, which we discuss later in the chapter. Hearn and Pace (2006) suggest that it would be unwise to adopt uncritically models derived from other industry sectors without considering the particular dynamic of the creative industries. They argue for 'value-creating ecologies', where value creation is not a readily understood one-way process, as implied by the value chain, but instead involves systemic processes of reiteration, feedback and co-creation on the part of consumers as well as producers, where the lines between production and consumption are increasingly blurred.

We found Chesbrough's distinction between value creation and value capture to be a helpful analytical difference when considering some of the cases in this research. (Chesbrough et al., 2006, p. 2). However, it is clear from the body of knowledge on value creation and value capture

Table 5.1   EROS processes of emergence

Process	Behaviour
Experimenting	Diverse exploratory behaviours that might (or might not) become part of the firm over time; new things tried out in often very informal ways, small scale; often developed through exploration of social interactions; shared experiential learning across project teams and stakeholders; 'what works'
Reflexivity	Continuous reflection on the identity of the firm and the self-identity of its owner(s) through the discourses within the business and with stakeholders; vision setting through narratives of self and firm; 'who we are'
Organizing	Organizing around a dominant logic (or project); patterns established through negotiated practice; pattern-making and pattern-breaking; 'what needs to be done now'
Sensitivity	Interpretation of shifts in industry landscape; detection of difference; weak signals; triggers and thresholds for change; 'what we might do'

(for example Lepak et al., 2007) that these concepts are contestable and open to multiple interpretations. Significantly, as Lepak et al. assert, value creation and capture (and, we suggest, intermediate processes), operate at multiple levels. The relationship between value creation and its capture and the systems in which value is produced and enjoyed is a continuing field of study, to which this chapter contributes.

Fuller et al. (2004), Fuller and Warren (2006a, 2006b) and Fuller et al. (2007) have reported four interrelated behaviour patterns, or 'processes of emergence', that lead to the emergence of novelty in entrepreneurial settings in different industries: new business models, new products, new careers. These processes of emergence, set out in Table 5.1, have been characterized as the 'EROS' model – experiments, reflexivity, organizing and sensitivity.

The processes in Table 5.1 should be seen as interconnected, not separate, and we argue that it is the multidimensional concentration on these patterns of behaviour that is at the heart of entrepreneurial competence through effective strategizing over time to produce a sustainable endeavour. The four EROS processes interact to produce new emergent structures over time. Each process interrelates with the others through multiple layers of cognition, language, performance and relationships, albeit strongly influenced by the entrepreneur. Further, on examining the 'stability' of a firm that had been in existence for about 20 years in a fast-moving environment, we concluded that its ontology at periods in that

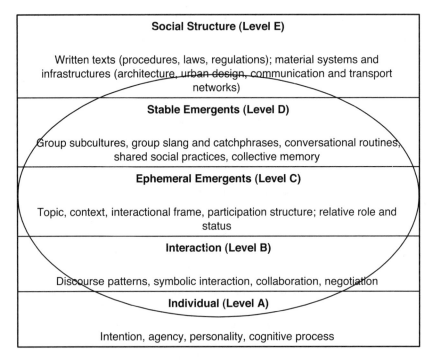

Source: The emergence paradigm (Sawyer, 2005, p. 211), showing the 'circle of emergence' (p. 220), i.e. that area which is subject to social emergence.

Figure 5.1   The emergence paradigm

history was manifest in an ongoing set of temporary stable emergents and ephemeral structures, reflecting Sawyer's (2005) 'emergence paradigm' of social structures that (influenced by Archer's work, 1995) posits a hierarchical model of individual, interaction, ephemeral emergents, stable emergents, and social structures (see Figure 5.1).

We have identified such temporary structures in our early empirical work in this domain. They seem to include particular business models, particular identities, particular dominant logics, particular triggers for change, and so on. Within that milieu, some were more stable than others and became part of the business; others initially commanded intensive resource and attention, but were not developed through to fruition. Nonetheless, even ephemeral and unstable structures that did not persist, exhibited ontological status and considerable causal power – at least for a time, as the firm sought to make its way forward in a highly uncertain environment. There was a dynamic tension between the self-identity of the entrepreneur and the identity of the firm which was highly stable and causal to the dynamics and direction of the firm. Similarly, the 'stable' structural nature of economic systems provided a constraining framework (you have to make profits, pay staff and so on). However the instability of the industry, created mainly by new technology, deregulation and therefore greater competition, provided a downward causation on the (in)stability of the emergents of the firm, for example on their everyday practices, everyday discourse patterns, types of collaboration, potential new projects and the intentions of the entrepreneurs involve.

The relation suggested in our research between the entrepreneurial mechanism provided by the EROS processes and the ontological emergence of novel structures led us to propose the model combining the two, which is set out in Table 5.2. We suggest that this model has considerable analytical power with regards to understanding the production of order at multiple levels and the articulation of types of proactive processes that are associated with the construction of order in practice. This approach, we argue, may benefit the study of entrepreneurship as a class rather than as a set of subdisciplines (Thornton, 1999), not only in a conceptual sense based on a rigorous treatment of emergence, but also by providing a methodological framework. As stated earlier, there are few empirical studies which have explored facets of entrepreneurial embeddedness in the wider context of society – in part because of the methodological challenge.

If we are to study the dynamics of volatile new industries, we need to address the problem of making sense of multiple observations across different levels and showing linkages between levels as new structures (products, services, business models, value-creating systems) emerge over time: an issue not just for the practicalities of our project, but also for entrepreneurship researchers generally. Such research is open to the development of congruent methodologies, that is, in the words of the title of the chapter, examining creativity requires creativity in methodological approach. Growing awareness of processual theories of entrepreneurship (Steyaert, 2007) have resulted in more sophisticated methodological approaches that relate the activities and behaviours of individuals over time to the firm and other contextual factors. Yet, so far there has not been a methodological approach that has taken advantage of the possibilities offered by rigorous theoretical conceptualizations of emergence. We are thus experimenting creatively with data capture methods and analysis guided by this methodological conceptualization. Pettigrew et al. (2001, p. 698) have highlighted that the issues of multiple contexts and levels from a major analytical challenge for the study of organizational change: a key issue is, however, how many levels of context should be considered, and how many multiple processes do we include in our analyses? While we would not claim that our

Table 5.2   Entrepreneurial mechanisms in the context of Sawyer's emergence paradigm

	Experiments	Reflexive identity	Organizing domains	Sensitivity to (changes in) conditions
Social Structure (Level E)	The stability of social structures enables relative experiments to take place	Stable structures will provide grounding to self-identity. Also will create tension as between structures	Much will be 'taken for granted', such that stable emergents are seen as innovative and/or threatening	By definition, stable social structures will be resilient to change
Stable Emergents (Level D)	The results of 'successful' experiments, are ones supported by social action	Sense of self in context, both personal and at the level of the firm	Dominant logic clear through regular discourses and habitual actions	Perhaps identified as challenges or threats to stability
Ephemeral Emergents (Level C)	Whether as thought experiments, discussions or as short-term practice, the transient nature of these emergents are a key part of ascertaining the legitimacy of particular sets of actions	The shaping of the individuals' sense of self and the (new) ventures sense of self within the context of existing markets, etc.	The salient organizing domain is that of 'experiment', i.e. an overt reflexivity that links stability with instability	The ephemeral emergents are the manifestation of the sensitivity of the individual and organization
Interaction (Level B)	Interactions in experiments are constrained by existing emergents and struc- tures. The introduction of new discourses	Discourse patterns, for example, are a part of both the maintenance of identity and the renewing of	Discourse has been used to identify ephemeral and stable emergents in entrepre- neurial practice	Interactions provide a mechanism of sensitivity to external conditions

Table 5.2 (*continued*)

	Experiments	Reflexive identity	Organizing domains	Sensitivity to (changes in) conditions
	and meaning into the firm from external structures (e.g. new industries or new technologies) produces changes in interactions and emergents	expressed identity	Discourse has been used to identify ephemeral and stable emergents in entrepreneurial practice	Interactions provide a mechanism of sensitivity to external conditions
Individual (Level A)	Entrepreneurial intention is seen as an important motivating reason for entrepreneurial action	Self-identity can form a stable emergent and in this model provide bottom-up causality of emergence	Intention and personality have causal influence on emergence in entrepreneurial settings	The individual's cognitive awareness and openness to change/ resilience will be causal to emergents

model (Table 5.2) solves the problems of the social sciences that Pettigrew et al. are addressing, the four processes that we have identified (Fuller and Warren, 2006a, 2006b; Fuller and Fewster, 2006) are grounded in empirical observations of entrepreneurial firms. This suggests that we have gone some way towards capturing an entrepreneurial mechanism in the cases considered, that spans the individual, firm and industry network levels of analysis. It is therefore attractive to consider whether the model could be used as a framework to capture data concerning multiple observations at multiple levels of analysis over time, thus adding methodological value, as well as theoretical explanatory power (Fuller et al., 2008).

DEVELOPING AN EMPIRICAL TESTBED IN THE CREATIVE INDUSTRIES SECTOR

Acts of individual creativity that result in artistic, social or cultural capital may not, in themselves, realize economic value, or be widely available, reproducible or disseminated as products or services outside the initial act of creation. In this case, the 'value-creating system' that has emerged may be of enormous artistic significance, but the economic potential remains – perhaps intentionally so – untapped (indeed, some might claim this ostensible gratuitousness to be a qualifier of artistic acts). Thelwall (2007) refers to such 'first-order' activities, where endeavour is intrinsically linked to the human labour involved, and is therefore inherently non-scalable. Here, the expertise of individuals is the core asset upon which success is based; it is unlikely that such resources as these can be replicated in line with the requirements of further growth within the sector. This is in contrast to 'second-order' activities, such as buying the CD of a music performance where scalability has been achieved through removal of the expert skills through reproduction to meet consumer demand and spread appreciation.

In moving from first-order to second-order activities, the value-creating system is inevitably extended to include more actors with different sets of values, vocabularies and discourses, as the dynamic between converting artistic, cultural and intellectual capitals to economic capital is explored. Of course, this transition from first-order to second-order activities is not necessarily innovative, or entrepreneurial, if 'traditional' business models are at the heart of the process: discussions tend to focus on contractual arrangements around established costs and revenues in accordance with likely consumer demand (Caves, 2000). Such systems are well understood, stable, with relatively predictable inputs and outputs. However, as we have stated earlier, new digital technologies have thrown up innovative new possibilities that can challenge, disrupt and even overthrow existing revenue streams and industry patterns. It is this indeterminacy of outcome, the dynamic and unpredictable, the unknown shape or character of scalability in new industries, and how it will be achieved, that resonates with the tenets and underpinning assumptions of complexity theory. And it is here that we believe our framework has the methodological potential to capture and make sense of multiple observations across different levels of analysis and show linkages between levels as new phenomena (products, services, business models) emerge over time. We argue that in identifying and linking the unstable and ephemeral emergents that inevitably arise during creative collaborations – the twists and turns, unformed explorations, failed experiments, discarded and retained ideas – to entrepreneurial processes that preserve artistic and creative value, we can gain much improved insight into how creative individuals operate and achieve sustainability in conditions of high uncertainty.

OBSERVATIONS FROM THE RESEARCH DATA

The purpose of a methodology is to give theoretical and conceptual sense to observed data. Our gaze is towards empirical emergent ontological properties that have an influential effect on the shape and sustainability of the system we are observing. In practice, this means keeping an eye on the group of actors foregrounded in the study and on the artefacts, discourses and exchanges produced. Our analytical perspective is value creation, as this is the instrumental goal of the research: how is value created and captured? Thus, our analytical question is the relationship between the production of (ephemeral) emergent properties and their stability in relation to 'value'.

Exposure to the projects (Sensory Threads, Gesture and Embodied Interaction, and IT-Innovation) has afforded us a rich stream of data and connections that will take many months to analyse. In this limited space, it is only possible to identify some preliminary outcomes that are nonetheless highly promising. Using our conceptualization and our framework, we were able to identify and track the emergence of 'stable emergents':

- Sensory Threads: the 'Rumbler', a novel interactive soundscape device.
- Gesture: a unique combination of skill-sets in the sound-and-motion-capture domain, supported by robust and reusable (computer program) code.
- IT-Innovation: a potential business model as yet untested.

What was particularly interesting in observing the interactivity between agents was the way that values associated with creativity or technicality interacted with economic value capture. These 'stable emergents' arose during the period of the projects from very early stage ideas that were not well articulated at the outset of Creator. As discussions in the rich interdisciplinary milieu progressed, possible trajectories were identified and tested out, either as thought experiments or shared metal models, or sometimes as rough working prototypes. At some point, these 'ephemeral emergents' were narrowed down to the most promising variant; at this point the transition from ephemeral to stable occurs. We would moot that this is the point at which discussions shift from value creation to value capture. We will develop this significant outcome further as a contribution to the entrepreneurship and innovation literatures.

We would also moot that what sustained the dynamics of the interactions was the anticipation of value. Rosen (1985) suggested that the ability of a system to anticipate its own future ('anticipatory systems') distinguishes living (evolutionary) systems from non-living, non-evolving systems (we paraphrase Rosen). Given our keen interest in value creation, the question 'What value is anticipated by the actors in the system, and how does this sustain the dynamics?', is a continuing part of the analysis. However, it is clear from our initial analysis that technical solutions, artistic experiences, reputations, fun, public credibility (that is, a mix of human, social and cultural capitals) are as powerful in the sustainability of the dynamics as the anticipation of economic rents in the cases we are observing. We would posit that the dynamics of emergence in creative industries require anticipations of multiple forms of value, and that these can be linked to individual, organizational and sector-level ontologies, that is, what meaningfully exists at a recognizable unit of analysis. The nature of values anticipated guides sensitivity to environment, organizing domains, reflexive identity and the emergent evaluation and purpose of experimental practice.

The interrelationships between agents, consolidated by trust grounded in shared creative practice, which in turn motivates the anticipation of mutually recognized value, can be theorized as a 'value-creating system'. In an active value-creating system, value is created by transformation or conversion of capitals. Activity therefore involves some form of conversion process involving interaction between agents. If what is produced has sustainable value, then it will have changed or shaped structure (for example habits, patterns of behaviour, power relationships, anticipations, resource flows). The nature of structural change is unpredictable and is emergent from the interactions. It may be ephemeral (short-lived), but during its existence it exerts causal power, as part of structure, that is, it influences (empowers, or constrains, or guides) the interactions between agents.

Such insights help us to understanding the nature of the economic structures in which creative activities within the digital economy will produce economic value. Put simply, a narrow focus on value capture (property rights, business model, market exchanges), does not explain how value is produced, for example as social, cultural and human capital (Bourdieu, 1986); nor how changes in social patterns and habits (consumption, desires, practices), whose stability creates the possibility of value capture, are caused through the presence of value-creating systems.

CONCLUSION

This chapter presents work in progress to test and demonstrate a methodological approach that takes advantage of possibilities offered by a theoretical conceptualization of emergence. We present to what extent we have been able to resolve at least some of the methodological concerns raised at the outset of this discussion. Through testing our framework, we will be able to assess to what extent there is the potential to capture, in principle, the emergence of any novel form, be it product, service, new business model, firm or behaviour in the creative industries sector.

In doing so, we hope to gain insight into how creative individuals and groups achieve sustainability, that will be valuable to policy-makers, practitioners and educators. Our immediate findings are that it is possible to conceive of emergence through interactions of multiple levels and to narrow down the salient aspects of a whole system of value creation and value capture, reducing the risk of failing to recognize causes outside the immediate gaze of those interested in value capture, which are of public and national interest.

REFERENCES

Aldrich, H.E. and M.A. Martinez (2001), 'Many are called, but few are chosen: an evolutionary perspective for the study of entrepreneurship', *Entrepreneurship: Theory and Practice*, **25** (4), 41–57.

Amabile, T.M. (1996), *Creativity in Context* (update to *The Social Psychology of Creativity*), Boulder, CO: Westview Press.

Archer, M. (1995), *Realist Social Theory: The Morphogenetic Approach*, Cambridge: Cambridge University Press.

Bourdieu, P. (1986), 'The forms of capital', in J.E.E. Richardson (ed.), *Handbook of Theory of Research for the Sociology of Education*, New York: Greenwood, pp. 241–58.

Burnes, B. (2005), 'Complexity theories and organisational change', *International Journal of Management Reviews*, **7** (2), 73–90.

Busenitz, L.W., I. West, G. Page, D. Shepherd, T. Nelson, G.N. Chandler and A. Zacharakis (2003), 'Entrepreneurship research in emergence: past trends and future directions', *Journal of Management*, **29** (33), 285–308.

Caves, R.E. (2000), *Creative Industries, Contracts between Arts and Commerce*, Cambridge, MA, USA and London: Harvard University Press.

Chesbrough, H.W., W. Vanhaverbeke and J. West (2006), *Open Innovation: Researching a New Paradigm*, Oxford: Oxford University Press.

Christensen, C.M. (1997), *The Innovator's Dilemma: When New Technologies Cause Great Firms to Fail*, Boston, MA: Harvard Business School Press.

Davidsson, P. and J. Wiklund (2001), 'Levels of analysis in entrepreneurship research: current research practice and suggestions for the future', *Entrepreneurship: Theory and Practice*, **25** (4), 81–99.

Department for Culture, Media and Sport (DCMS) (2007), 'Staying ahead: the economic performance of the UK's creative industries',

Down, S. (2006), *Narratives of Enterprise: Crafting Entrepreneurial Self-Identity in a Small Firm*, Cheltenham, UK and Northampton, MA, USA: Edward Elgar.

Fischer, E., A.R. Reuber, M. Hababou, W. Johnson and S. Lee (1997), 'The role of socially constructed temporal perspectives in the emergence of rapid growth firms', *Entrepreneurship: Theory and Practice*, **22** (2), 13–30.

Fleming, L. and O. Sorenson (2001), 'Technology as a complex adaptive system', *Research Policy*, **30**, 1019–39.

Fletcher, D. (2006), 'Entrepreneurial processes and the social construction of opportunity', *Entrepreneurship and Regional Development*, **18** (5), 421–40.

Fuller, T. and R. Fewster (2006), 'The emergence of Tesco.com: a study of corporate entrepreneurship', paper presented at Babson–Kauffman Entrepreneurship Research Conference, Kelley Business School, University of Indiana, Bloomington, IN.

Fuller, T. and P. Moran (2000), 'Moving beyond metaphor: towards a methodology for grounding complexity in small business and entrepreneurship research', *Emergence: A Journal of Complexity Issues in Organizations and Management*, **2** (1), 50–71.

Fuller, T. and P. Moran (2001), 'Small enterprises as complex adaptive systems: a methodological question?', *Entrepreneurship and Regional Development*, **13** (1), 47–63.

Fuller, T., P. Moran and P. Argyle (2004), 'Entrepreneurial foresight: a case study in reflexivity, experiments, sensitivity and reorganisation', in H. Tsoukas and J. Shepherd (eds), *Managing The Future: Foresight in the Knowledge Economy*, Oxford: Blackwell Publishing, 171–8.

Fuller, T. and L. Warren (2006a), 'Entrepreneurship as foresight: a complex social network perspective on organisational foresight', *Futures, Journal of Policy, Planning and Futures Studies*, **38** (7), 956–71.

Fuller, T. and L. Warren (2006b), 'Complex explanations of order creation, emergence and sustainability as situated entrepreneurship', in P.R. Christensen and F. Poulfelt (eds), *RENT XVIII Anthology 2005: Managing Complexity and Change in SMEs: Frontiers in European Research*, Cheltenham, UK and Northampton, MA, USA: Edward Elgar, pp. 136–55.

Fuller, T., L. Warren and P. Argyle (2007), 'Sustaining entrepreneurial business: a complexity perspective on processes that produce emergent practice', *International Entrepreneurship and Management Journal*, **4** (1), 1–17.

Fuller, T., L. Warren, P. Argyle and F. Welter (2008), 'A complexity perspective on entrepreneurship: a new methodology for research in high velocity environments', paper accepted for British Academy of Management conference, November.

Garnsey, E. and P. Heffernan (2005), 'High technology clustering through spinout and attraction: the Cambridge case', *Regional Studies*, **39** (8), 1127–44.

Gartner, W.B. (1993), 'Words lead to deeds: towards an organizational emergence vocabulary', *Journal of Business Venturing*, **8**, 231–9.

Garud, R. and P. Karnoe (2003), 'Bricolage versus breakthrough: distributed and embedded agency in technology entrepreneurship', *Research Policy*, **32**, 277–301.

Hearn, G. and C. Pace (2006), 'Value-creating ecologies: understanding next generation business systems', *Foresight*, **8** (1), p. 55–65.

Houchin, K. and D. MacLean (2005), 'Complexity theory and strategic change: an empirically informed critique', *British Journal of Management*, **16** (2), 149–66.

Jack, S.L. and A.R. Anderson (2002), 'The effects of embeddedness on the entrepreneurial process', *Journal of Business Venturing*, **17**, 467–87.

Lepak, D.P., K.G. Smith and M.S. Taylor (2007), 'Value creation and value capture: a multilevel perspective', *Academy of Management Review*, **32** (1), 180–94.

Lichtenstein, B.B., N.M. Carter, K.J. Dooley and W.B. Gartner (2007), 'Complexity dynamics of nascent entrepreneurship', *Journal of Business Venturing*, **22**, 236–61.

Lichtenstein, B.B., K.J. Dooley and G.T. Lumpkin (2006), 'Measuring emergence in the dynamics of new venture creation', *Journal of Business Venturing*, **21** (2), 153–75.

Lichtenstein, B.M.B. (2000a), 'Emergence as a process of self-organizing: new assumptions and insights from the study of non-linear dynamic systems', *Journal of Organizational Change Management*, **13** (6), 526–44.

Lichtenstein, B.M.B. (2000b), 'Generative knowledge and self-organized learning reflecting on Don Schön's research', *Journal of Management Inquiry*, **9** (1), 47–55.

Lichtenstein, B.M.B. (2000c), 'Self-organized transitions: a pattern amid the chaos of transformative change', *Academy of Management Executive*, **14** (4), 128–41.

Lissack, M. (1997), 'Of chaos and complexity: managerial insights from a new science', *Management Decision*, **35** (3), 205–18.

Low, M.B. and I.C. MacMillan (1988), 'Entrepreneurship: past research and future challenges', *Journal of Management*, **14** (2), 139–61.

McKelvey, B. (2004), 'Towards a complexity science of entrepreneurship', *Journal of Business Venturing*, **19** (3), 313–29.

Pettigrew, A.M., R.W. Woodman, K.S. Cameron (2001), 'Studying organisational change and development: challenges for future research', *Academy of Management Journal*, **44** (4), 697–713.

Phan, P. (2004), 'Introduction: entrepreneurship theory: possibilities and future directions', *Journal of Business Venturing*, **19**, 617–620.

Powell, D. (2002), 'Creative and cultural industries: an economic impact study for South East England', research report by David Powell Associates Ltd, for South East England Cultural Consortium and the South East England Development Agency.

Rosen, R. (1985). *Anticipatory Systems: Philosophical, Mathematical and Methodological Foundations*, Oxford: Pergamon.

Sarasvathy, S.D. (2001), 'Causation and effectuation: toward a theoretical shift from economic inevitability to entrepreneurial contingency', *Academy of Management Review*, **26** (2), 243–63.

Sawyer, R.K. (2005), *Social Emergence: Societies as Complex Systems*, Cambridge: Cambridge University Press.

Schumpeter, J.A. (1934), *The Theory of Economic Development: An Inquiry into Profits, Capital, Credit, Interest and the Business Cycle*, Cambridge, MA: Harvard University Press.

Simon, H.A. (1957), *Models of Man: Social and Rational*, New York: Wiley.

Simsek, Z., M.H. Lubatkin and S.W. Floyd (2003), 'Inter-firm networks and entrepreneurial behavior: a structural embeddedness perspective', *Journal of Management*, **29** (3), 427–42.

Smallbone, D. and F. Welter (2006), 'Conceptualising entrepreneurship in a transition context', *International Journal of Entrepreneurship and Small Business*, **3** (2), 190–206.

Snowden, D. (2002), 'Complex acts of knowing: paradox and descriptive self awareness', *Journal of Knowledge Management*, **6** (2), 100–11.

Stacey, R.D. (2003), *Strategic Management and Organisational Dynamics, the Challenge of Complexity*, London: FT Prentice Hall.
Stacey, R.D., D. Griffin and P. Shaw (2002), *Complexity and Management, Fad or Radical Challenge to Systems Thinking?*, London: Routledge.
Steyaert, C. (2007), '"Entrepreneuring" as a conceptual attractor? A review of process theories in 20 years of entrepreneurship studies', *Entrepreneurship and Regional Development*, **19** (6), 453–77.
Thelwall, S. (2007), 'Capitalising creativity: developing earned income streams in cultural industries organisations', cultural snapshot no 14, accessed 30 August 2008 at http://proboscis.org.uk/publications/SNAPSHOTS_capitalcreativity. pdf,
Thornton, P.H. (1999), 'The sociology of entrepreneurship', *Annual Review of Sociology*, **25**, 19–46.

6. Action learning in new creative ventures: the case of SPEED

David Rae

INTRODUCTION

SPEED (Student Placements for Entrepreneurs in Education) was a project funded by the Higher Education Funding Council for England (HEFCE) under the Higher Education Innovation Fund (HEIF round 3). It ran in 13 higher education institutes (HEIs) in the United Kingdom between 2006 and 2008, and has led to several successor projects. SPEED is of wider interest for pioneering action learning in student entrepreneurship for several reasons. Firstly, as a national project, it brought together a diverse group of HEIs and educator-practitioners who themselves engaged in an action learning process to enact the project, in which their learning overlapped and connected with the student entrepreneurs' learning. Secondly, it was significant in its scale, with the target of supporting 750 student ventures over two years, a target which was exceeded with 770 ventures being created. Thirdly, some 43 per cent (or 330) of these new ventures were in the creative and related industry sectors, forming the most numerous segment of the programme. Many more ventures applied creative approaches in their development.

This chapter summarizes the experiences gained from the SPEED programme, which set out to enable university students to establish their own business ventures as work experience projects. In so doing, SPEED created a significant and innovative example of action learning applied to new venture formation and entrepreneurial development. The chapter explores what is known about action learning and entrepreneurial learning in relation to new venture creation. It discusses the types of creative businesses that were developed by the students participating in the SPEED programme, and considers what conceptual and practical learning can be applied and transferred more generally.

Following this introductory section, a critical review of the literature in relation to action learning, new venture creation and creative enterprise is presented. A summary of the development and delivery of the SPEED programme is then provided, highlighting and conceptualizing the action learning process of new venture creation. The author discusses the range of creative enterprises established by the participating students and the sustainability of their business models. Finally, suggestions are made as to how the experiences and learning gained can be embedded into more general practices to support creative entrepreneurship in the challenging economic and employment conditions following the 2008–09 recession.

REVIEW OF PRIOR WORK

The genesis of action learning as an approach is well documented in the literature (Revans, 1980, 1982), but the emphasis in much of the earlier work places the application on learning at a generic level, particularly within larger, public sector and corporate organizations (Pedler, 1991; Pedler et al., 1997). While the approach of action learning as connecting practice and theory through reflection, learning by doing and generating social rather than individual cognition has immediate connections with the challenges of managing small businesses, much of the practice and literature of action learning has placed it in the context of management development within larger organizations. For example, Revans (1982) instigated the principle of managers taking responsibility for their work unit and viewing it essentially as a small organization with a degree of autonomy for improving performance, even when the context was within a department of a large organization.

There have been many developments of the basic notion of action learning. Marsick and Watkins (1990, 1997), for example, developed four types of experiential, workplace, informal and incidental learning. Following Kolb's theory of experiential learning (1984), Honey and Mumford (1992) and Mumford (1995) also developed fourfold notions of behavioural learning. In reviewing a number of such learning theories there is a duality between expected, incremental learning and deeper, transformative, unexpected learning (Rae, 2003). This has emerged in the literature around small business management, for example through Matlay (2000), who noted that the prevalent learning mode of small business owner-managers was in single-loop learning, with a small minority practicing double-loop learning as a competitive strategy; and by Devins et al. (2005), who highlighted the 'informal or incidental' nature of learning in small businesses in developing a conceptual model of learning in the micro-business world.

Gibb recognized the virtues of 'smallness', initially in arguing for the need for business schools to address small business management (Gibb, 1996), but then challenging their effectiveness (Gibb, 2002), seeing the smaller firm as a learning organization (Gibb, 1997) and creating condu-cive environments for learning and entrepreneurship (Gibb, 2001); making educational, conceptual and policy connections between highly practice-based and active forms of learning with both small firm management and entrepreneurship. Gibb and Ritchie's (1982) model of new venture creation conceptualized the stages of starting a business and the develop-mental factors involved, while Gibb's later (2002) model linked personal learning to new business process development. From these foundations, both practical and conceptual development took place.

The period from the mid-1990s saw increasing experimentation by educa-tors in running action learning-based programmes for managers of existing small firms and also in new venture creation. The author recalls that in setting up The Hive, a centre for entrepreneurship at Nottingham Trent University in 2000, the Headstart programme for new venture exploration was based on action learning approaches. There are many examples of inno-vative entrepreneurship programmes, which used some aspects of action learning. For example, Jones-Evans et al. (2000) described an action learn-ing approach to developing entrepreneurial graduates; Collins et al. (2006) piloted the use of 'synergistic learning' in a 'discovering entrepreneurship' programme and found four types of social participation used in the learning process: cooperation, co-learning, consultation and collective action.

In Canada, Vincett and Farlow (2008) ran a course in which they found that: 'by allowing students with real business ideas to actually be entre-preneurs, rather than pretending to be, a large part of the entrepreneurial life is experienced directly'. Their approach required students to validate business ideas by speaking to customers, and by extensive contact with the outside community. Munro and Cook (2008) used the small enterprise as the authentic learning environment (SEALO), as distinct from the tradi-tional learning environment. They characterize the SEALO as a student-controlled environment for active learning in which there is awareness of real business issues; the approach also expands personal networks, fosters entrepreneurial attitudes and increases confidence with small and medium-sized enterprise (SME) owners. Their entrepreneurial action learning cycle 'envisions, energises and expedites', and this results in a change in the envi-ronment. The SEALO approach was used in Thames Valley University as a facet of its enactment of SPEED.

Turning to the conceptual development of learning in entrepreneurship, from the late 1990s onwards the emerging literature on entrepreneurial learning made repeated connections with the notion of this learning as active, connected with individual emergence and the development of iden-tity and praxis, and deploying narratives as a means of articulating and theorizing from learning (for example Deakins and Freel, 1998; Rae, 2000,

2005; Cope and Watts, 2000: Cope, 2003, 2005). Taylor and Thorpe (2004) explored, through a problem-centred and socially constructed perspective, the social dimension to entrepreneurial decision-making, in which learning and influence emerge from ongoing negotiations within a network of actors. Heinonen and Poikkijoki (2006) set out a model of a four-stage entrepreneurial process, connected with behaviours, skills and attributes. They introduce an entrepreneurial-directed approach to education, based on circles of experiential learning, with new activity producing new experience and new thinking through reflection. In a similar vein, Atherton (2007) developed a five-stage pre-start framework preceding new venture creation, mapping the stages from awareness to engagement and identifying likely personal development thresholds and questions. However, Jones and Holt (2008) used an activity theory framework to analyse entrepreneurs engaged in creating new business ventures, and concluded that this resulted in more comprehensive understanding which undermined simplistic linear frameworks and revealed the inherent 'messiness' and 'richness' associated with the shift from conception to gestation.

The period since 1998 saw 'the creative industries' being repeatedly defined as an economic and policy concept (Leadbeater and Oakley, 1999; DCMS, 2001). There has been critique of the claims made for their significance, but it is also evident that regeneration in many urban areas has resulted from the growth of a creative economy, with greater policy support to encourage this (Shorthose, 2000, 2004; Heartfield, 2000). In parallel, a significant proportion of the increase in higher education provision and participation has been in arts, creative, media and associated subjects, thereby increasing the potential workforce in these sectors well beyond their actual absorptive capacity. Furthermore, there had long been a culture of self-employment and '*petit* entrepreneurship' in the arts and creative sectors (Baines and Robson, 2001). More recently, however, there has been both formal acceptance of and a significant increase in creative entrepreneurship as the nature of the economy has changed. Technological potential has increased with the advent of digital media, and the growth of a graduate population with creative skills and ambitions has given rise to widespread new opportunities for creative enterprise (Rae, 2007b). So, for example, the dynamics of situated creativity, in which consumers co-create cultural media though digital interfaces, is rapidly becoming a major force in transforming the balance of cultural production and consumption, and in the development of social network markets mediated by technology (Potts et al., 2008). It is increasingly demonstrable that creative entrepreneurship is an economic and cultural force for transformation well beyond what we can now see as the artificially limited scope of the administratively defined 'cultural industries' (Bilton, 2007; Potts and Cunningham, 2008).

Given these factors, together with declining prospects of creative employment in the UK 'corporate' media sector, such as ITV, Channel 4 and the regional press, it is increasingly the case that the most likely way for a graduate in a creative subject to find relevant employment may well be to create their own career through entrepreneurship or self-employment. Universities have responded to the need to prepare graduates for creative entrepreneurship (Henry, 2007), and the SPEED project can be seen as one such response, alongside specialized arts and creative enterprise programmes (Penaluna and Penaluna, 2006). However, an important factor is the nature of the person's motivation towards enterprise: do they aspire to make their creative output into a business, or are they primarily interested in furthering their creative practice, for which generating an income through business activity is a necessary, but not prime aim? This question is addressed later in this chapter.

In summary, there are increasing connections between the development of theories and practices in action learning, in enterprise education, entrepreneurial learning and new venture creation, which convey increasing critical awareness of educational practices and the contributions of the learning and external environment, social behaviour and other influences. Neither action learning nor entrepreneurial learning are fully accepted or adopted within higher education, as the values of practical and emergent learning challenge the 'bureaucratic control' culture of academia which privileges programmed knowledge (Gibb, 2002). However, learning for entrepreneurship in the context of higher education increasingly takes place in innovative ways beyond the formal environment of the classroom, through social, digital, experiential and discovery learning, which can challenge orthodox pedagogies. Action learning has been more widely applied in the context of larger organizations, although it has obvious conceptual and practical points of connection with entrepreneurial learning and management learning in the small business context. These include the scope for personal development, the shared social dimension of learning, the use of digital media including social networking tools, the emergent, contingent and transformational dynamics of learning, especially through the focus on resolving practical problems and investigating opportunities by applying systematic methods, through which new understanding is created. These aspects provide a useful pre-understanding for the study presented in this chapter.

METHODOLOGY

The research approach adopted for the study is consistent with the topic, and involved the author being engaged closely with the project from its inception through to completion. In this regard, the author acted as both an active participant and a reflective observer. He set up and managed a SPEED programme in which he selected participants and ran a monthly action learning group, gaining direct experience of the students' learning and development. This collaborative and reflexive approach to research has been influenced by a number of writers. For example, Lewin (1951) developed core principles of field theory in social science, which were developed further as action science (Argyris et al., 1987). Schon (1983) articulated the notion of the reflective practitioner, and Argyris (1982) highlighted theoretical stances on organizational intervention, while they jointly developed a theory-of-action perspective (Argyris and Schon, 1978). Lave and Wenger (1991) and Wenger (1998) developed essential insights into communities of practice, of which the SPEED practitioner community is an example, and of social cognition, which again apply to this experience. Murray and Lawrence (2000) developed principles for practitioner-based enquiry, which informed this research, while Heron (1996) developed influential philosophical and practical frameworks for cooperative enquiry. Watson (1994) directly influenced the craft skills and critical awareness of the researcher's judgement in undertaking research as an active participant.

In the course of this project, the author collated a log of field notes from his involvement with the originators of SPEED, the project partners, student entrepreneurs and others. These included notes from action learning group meetings, individual consultations and conversations with students, both during and following their completion of the programme. At each stage, practical and conceptual insights were developed. The work of other practitioners and researchers in the programme has also contributed, while the existence of a dataset of SPEED participants and websites constitutes a collective body of knowledge about the programme. The research has been validated by sharing and checking with other researchers and co-participants to ensure that the cases and models included are authentic and representative of those encountered in the programme.

THE SPEED PROGRAMME IN ACTION

The SPEED concept was developed by Birch (Staffordshire University) and Clements, (University of Wolverhampton) in 2005, who recognized the unrealized potential of enabling entrepreneurial students to start business ventures during their studies as work experience projects, forming an alternative to conventional work placements. This aimed to develop enterprise and creativity skills among students while supporting controlled risk-taking, enabling potential entrepreneurs to test out business concepts and produce new graduate enterprises. The idea was proposed at the 2005 Institute for Small Business and Entrepreneurship (ISBE) conference, attracting enterprising educators from other universities to develop a collaborative project application for HEIF Round 3 funding, led by Wolverhampton.

The stated purpose of SPEED was: 'to identify, nurture and convert potential and existing entrepreneurial spirit into business reality. To make it more possible for "would-be" entrepreneurs to convert their ideas, concepts and dreams into a sustainable business plan, giving them a genuine self-generated future career option' (Birch and Clements, 2006).

By enabling students to develop and run a business venture, SPEED would provide an experiential route to developing entrepreneurial and business management skills. This in turn would help establish sustainable ventures, driving cultural change within HEIs, embedding enterprise and entrepreneurship in the curriculum and aiding graduate retention in regional economies: 'to create a new body of entrepreneurs with real business start-up experience . . . one step closer to future business creation, either immediately, or following their graduation, or after an intervening period in employment' (Birch and Clements, 2006).

An ambitious funding proposal was prepared and approved by HEFCE in early summer 2006, the only collaborative project featuring student enterprise to succeed in a competitive process. SPEED required universities to make learning opportunities and physical resources, such as incubation and grow-on space, available to facilitate graduate entrepreneurship across all academic disciplines. The project started in August 2006 and ended in December 2008. It included 12 English universities and one in Northern Ireland, with a contract value of £5 million, each partner committing to a specific number of placements between ten and 120. It aimed to support 750 student ventures, although 770 were actually supported. Each venture attracted HEIF funding of £6000, of which £1500 was allocated to the partner institution for staffing and infrastructure. A bursary of £4500 was also made available to the student to cover business start-up costs, training, access to business incubation facilities and information technology (IT).

CREATIVE ENTERPRISES IN SPEED

Data collected by the project management team showed a gender distribution of 63 per cent male and 37 per cent female participants among the 770 participating students (IIE, 2008). In terms of subject areas, business (22 per cent) and art and design (28 per cent) together constituted half of the students, with engineering, computing/IT, and sports, performing arts and leisure being less well represented but still significant. Students generally participated in their second or third year of an undergraduate degree, either as a full placement year or part-time alongside taught modules. Partners had flexibility in the study modes supported by SPEED.

With regard to the types of business established, design and retail were the most popular, with 15 per cent each, and services, media and IT constituted 12–13 per cent each, with a wide distribution of other business types. Creative businesses, including photography, media, marketing design and product design, constituted 43 per cent overall. This relatively crude analysis does not reflect the creativity also used by many students in establishing ventures outside the 'creative industries'. For example, many students were creative in the area of retailing, the sale of creative products, or simply applied creativity to their businesses. An analysis of a sample of SPEED creative businesses registered on the project website showed some 32 different types of business activities. Box 6.1 groups these into four broad types, comparable with the Department for Culture, Media and Sport (DCMS, 2001) classification of creative industries, with examples of business activities included in each type.

It is important to note that some ventures were active in more than one of these types, such as crossing over between creative design, production and trading, which could either provide the scope for a more sustainable business model or, alternatively, stretch their resources and time too far. Examples of each type are cited below.

Entrepreneurs in the creative industries are a diverse population with a wide range of motivations, interests, skills and outlooks, and degrees of entrepreneurial and creative ability, which enable them to operate as multi-functional businesses. Björkegren (1996) proposed that both a creative and a business strategy are required for the successful development of a creative enterprise. People running creative enterprises often prioritize either the creative development or the business development of their enterprise, while a minority may do both (Rae, 2007a). Based on this logic, a simple conceptual framework, which builds on Ansoff's (1963) classic model of business strategy, is proposed in Figure 6.1 to provide a typology of creative entrepreneurs (McElwee and Rae, 2008). This model uses the definition of entrepreneur as: 'the person who acts in an enterprising way, by identifying or creating and acting on an opportunity, for example, by setting up a business venture' (Rae, 2007a). It suggests that there are different types of creative entrepreneurs, and that their interests, motivations and lifestyles play a fundamental role in orienting the enterprise either towards primarily creative or business achievement, or a combination of both.

This framework provides a means of characterizing the SPEED creative

---

BOX 6.1 TYPES AND SUBTYPES OF CREATIVE BUSINESS ACTIVITIES

1. Creative design and production
   - Fine arts – ceramics, glass, sculpture
   - Furniture and lighting design and production
   - Craft production
   - Fashion designer-maker
   - Landscape and garden design

2. Performance and experience
   - Event and festival promotion
   - Music promotion and staging
   - Firework display
   - Creative travel experiences

3. Digital, Media and promotion
   - Photography
   - Video production
   - Marketing and advertising
   - Magazine and book publishing
   - IT gaming
   - Graphic and web design

4. Trading
   - Online retailing
   - Art dealer and gallery management
   - Fashion retailing
   - Memorabilia sales

---

entrepreneurs, and each of the positions is further explained below in terms of its likely characteristics. However, it should be noted that there are clear dangers of oversimplifying creative enterprise through such frameworks. Bourdeau's (1977) theory of practice and 'habitas' introduces the notion that individuals' acquired dispositions or practices and assumptions influence their social participation, and this has been developed in the area of creative entrepreneurship (for example Pankaj and Conklin, 2009). The matrix should not infer a fixed classification, rather a preferred domain of operation for a person at a point in time with the potential for progression into another domain. The business growth orientation

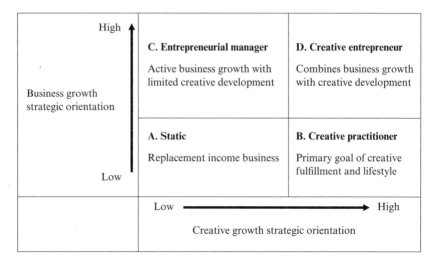

Figure 6.1   Conceptual framework for creative enterprises

suggests that creativity may be seen as a means for business performance, while the creative growth orientation suggests that enterprise is a means to creative fulfillment. But these should not be viewed as 'either/or' exclusive paths, since it is often the case that the balance is in preferring to do more of one than the other. As Bilton (2007, p. 174) argued: 'Management is a creative process and creativity is a managed process.'

Framework Explanation: A. Static

The static creative enterprise tends not to seek active creative or business development. It may meet an existing need and often operates as a hobby-based business, providing a sideline to other activity, including independent artisans and craftspeople running a studio on a part-time basis, and people who have started a business which has 'got stuck' and may be unlikely to survive unless they break out of the 'static' box. Such enterprises are numerous but tend to be low in entrepreneurial intent, capability and confidence. In order to develop, they need to progress in either business or creative performance or, ideally, in a combination of both, otherwise the business may not be sustainable.

Case: Creative design and production
Elspeth: jewellery design and production

Elspeth designed and made a selection of ceramic and glass jewellery to exhibit for her final degree show and had very positive feedback on the creative design, use of materials and quality of finish. She aimed to produce and sell her artefacts through independent craft, fashion and jewellery shows and shops. After participating in SPEED, she found that the time taken to produce and sell her work did not provide sufficient income to live on, and running the business did not give her the creative time to design new work, so she ceased trading and now works in fashion retailing.

Framework Explanation: B. Creative Practitioner

Creative practitioners are motivated primarily by the wish to practice their creative skills, and generating an income through an enterprise is a necessary means to fulfil this. They include freelance artists and designer-makers, who may be limited in business management and entrepreneurial skills and ambitions, and are likely to be self-employed or running micro-businesses that trade on their creative skills. However, they may need to develop entrepreneurial and business skills to create a business that is viable and sustainable for longer-term survival. They probably constitute the majority of creative enterprises.

Case: Creative practitioner – media and promotion
Gwyn and Dan: Warped Noise
Whilst studying for BSc (Hons) Film Production Technology degrees, the partners formed Warped Noise in 2006 to showcase their work. They focused on developing a business to unite the music and film industries by producing video projects for music bands and artists. Warped Noise Productions offers music videos, short films, promotional and educational videos production, and post-production services. Warped Noise Productions has filmed many bands and community projects, produced award-winning films and has a network of associates including specialists in 3D modelling, graphic design and illustration.

Framework Explanation: C. Entrepreneurial Manager

In this category, the development and growth of a successful business is the prime goal and motivation. Creative development is necessary but likely to be secondary. There is a well-defined creative activity, which is able to generate a sound income and profit stream, and the business strategy is to manage and grow this effectively. The creative origination and activity may be subcontracted or bought-in, while creative approaches may well be applied to marketing, customer relations and other aspects of the business. Examples include craft, retail, clothing and gallery centres, which attract visitors and buy in artefacts to resell, such as imported African crafts.

They may need to develop creative management and innovation skills to optimize the creative contribution to ensure innovation and renewal of the business.

Case: Entrepreneurial managers – trading
Rosanna and Robert: Electronic Pets

'It's pets . . . without the poop!' Electronic Petshop is a retailer with the widest range of interactive and electronic pets available on the Internet. This niche business has a lively website and offers fun pets for parents of young children (which they purchase before they get their own pet), people with learning difficulties or allergic to pet fur, as well as those looking for zany and unusual gifts. Rosanna and Robert won a series of business awards and have traded successfully since 2007. Their creative marketing flair and personalized approach differentiated them from other online retailers, but the approach did not change significantly over time.

Framework Explanation: D. Creative Entrepreneur

Creative development and business development are interdependent and equally important, in that creativity is the *raison d'être* for the business, but successful commercial performance is vital to fund ongoing creative activity and renewal. Creative entrepreneurs can be recognized by their creative and entrepreneurial proactivity. Examples can be found in digital media production, artists and designers who actively promote their own work online and via a distinctive personal branding, and those who push the boundaries of innovative spaces for successful creative activity, such as event production. In these businesses, creative activity is both entrepreneurial and sustained, creating market demand in new ways and representing the optimal balance between creative and commercial performance.

Case: Creative entrepreneurs – performance and experience
PJ, John and Paul: UXL

UXL is a melodic rock band formed by three brothers, who studied professional music production, and a friend. They joined SPEED in 2007 and subsequently established a music business fan base through touring as a support act and on the club circuit, releasing a well-received single and album CD, and gaining strong reviews in the guitar and music press. The band is promoted through a well-designed website and Myspace pages where fans can keep in touch and find out about the band.

The above cases illustrate the range of types of business activities and entrepreneurial dispositions of the creative ventures that developed from

SPEED, displaying, in quite different ways, their application of creative imagination, skills and enterprise. Cases B, C and D have continued to trade sustainably, having survived for over three years through a major recession. As remarked earlier, students have different motivations towards creative enterprise, some aspiring to make their creative output into a business, others primarily interested in furthering their creative practice, for which generating an income through business activity is necessary but not a prime aim. The students learned in different ways to negotiate the combinations of creative and entrepreneurial intent in the process of learning to become creative entrepreneurs.

EVALUATING SPEED

This section summarizes the evaluations that have been conducted for SPEED and reflects on their findings to inform the development of creative enterprise support programmes in higher education. Independent evaluation showed that SPEED had a positive effect in increasing students' self-efficacy, with a small negative effect on entrepreneurial intentions. It was successful in recruiting entrepreneurially inclined individuals, a high proportion of whom had at least one parent who had run their own business. Significantly, few students had experienced formal enterprise education prior to joining SPEED, meaning that it was their prime source of entrepreneurial learning (Good and Cooper, 2009).

Woodier (2008) conducted a longitudinal study of students in a participating HEI, addressing student readiness to make the transition to entrepreneurship through enterprise education. She found many students experienced balancing study, work and business to be challenging, and most continued with paid work alongside developing their business; only a few were running their businesses on a full-time basis, as the time required to research business ideas was longer than envisaged, and managing multiple time commitments was challenging.

Corcoran (2008) assessed students' developmental needs beyond the initial front-loaded skills training, finding after one year that 60 per cent of the current associates were actively trading, as were 28 per cent of those up to four months after completion, but this fell to only 5 per cent of students one year after completing SPEED. The businesses of those studying art, media, design, music and information and communication technology (ICT) were most likely to be sustainable beyond the second year of trading. The majority aspired to a portfolio career involving some aspect of entrepreneurship. Corcoran also discovered a high demand for 'download and keep' e-learning materials, and produced downloadable training videos through his independent media business to meet this demand. Students demonstrated a need for entrepreneurial skills even if their intention was not to start a new venture, while those commercially active expressed a need for skills development beyond the start-up phase of their business (Corcoran, 2008).

The SPEED management team summarized conclusions in their final report (Box 6.2), asserting that:

> we believe that the SPEED programme has been spectacularly successful. All of our students have gained considerably from their involvement. Some have demonstrated individual sustainability and are continuing their business activities post graduation. Others, while entering conventional employment, have gained the skills to become organisational intrapreneurs. (Clements and Moore, 2009)

The management team concluded that, where experiences were more difficult or the business unsustainable, these programmes were still educationally successful. Academic partners reported institutional benefits of encouraging entrepreneurial activity amongst academic staff in relation to curriculum and learning development. A legitimate question is how many of the ventures established have continued to trade. While complete information was not available, the author contacted a subset of 30 creative businesses that had been established and found that 15 had ceased trading, 14 continued to trade sustainably and some had established strong and distinctive business models. This represented a success rate of 47 per cent from a small sample, which is positive given the challenging economic climate and inevitable changes that graduates encounter in leaving university, but less 'spectacular' than the official report attests. However, the learning opportunity to experiment with entrepreneurship and to discover that either the chosen business venture or being an entrepreneur is not the preferred option may still be a positive one.

CONCEPTUALIZING THE SPEED ACTION LEARNING PROCESS

This section develops a model based on the entrepreneurial action learning in the SPEED programme and, perhaps more importantly, offers a more general conceptual framework for use in comparable action learning and venture creation programmes. The model conceptualizes the entrepreneurial action learning process experienced by the students on their journeys towards entrepreneurship. It builds on Gibb and Ritchie's (1982), Gibb's (2002) and Atherton's (2007) models of learning and new venture formation, in the context of action learning projects such as SPEED. This

---

BOX 6.2 CONCLUSIONS FROM THE SPEED PROJECT

Institutional learning:

1. Institutional collaboration is vital, especially where participants are drawn from institutions with different academic, research, geographical and historical profiles.
2. Collaboration develops synergies and bilateral corollary activities and stimulates interactions, which enhance educational development.
3. Programmes such as SPEED promote engagement of staff between individual campuses, subjects and partner institutions.
4. SPEED encouraged higher education (HE) engagement with local businesses and regional regeneration agenda in shaping policies in response to economic conditions.

The student learning experience:

1. Entrepreneurial learning should be a key element of the undergraduate experience irrespective of the nature of academic study or immediate individual aspirations.
2. For students with entrepreneurial potential, gaining early business awareness and interpersonal skills benefits progression beyond HE.
3. Entrepreneurship education teaching needs to be realistic. Students learn more from doing and from interacting with real entrepreneurs and businesses than from studying the processes.
4. Delivery programmes need to be flexible and adaptable to individual needs.
5. The substantial involvement of female students, from across the spectrum of social and cultural backgrounds and from creative and vocational subjects surpassed expectations.
6. The availability of seedcorn funding within enterprise programmes is important, but not 'mission critical' as students may be able to leverage additional post-start funding.

> 7.   Some participants were successfully involved in multidisci-
>   plinary teams, suggesting greater potential for peer-to-peer
>   development.
>
> *Source:*   Clements and Moore (2009).

represents the learning process within a programme where student learning occurs, and needs to be supported, in a range of ways that are often
unplanned, emergent, short-term and non-sequential; that is, entrepreneurial. It is quite detailed, yet only suggests the complexity and variability
of the individual learning experience.

At the top is the student journey to entrepreneurship, with seven interlinked phases indicating those that an entrepreneur establishing a new
venture would typically complete, although not necessarily in the sequence
shown. Indeed, it might be the case that not all of the phases will be com-
pleted: for example, not all students developed a product or service, and
not all progressed to early trading. The students' learning journeys are
individual, emergent and, while they might be planned to an extent, the
messiness of translating their aspirations into reality inevitably alters plans
and creates new needs. However, this trajectory is the most important
motivation and vehicle for learning because, unlike much other curricular
learning, it is based on the learner's goals.

In the centre are indicative 'triggers' suggesting 'why' students learned.
Within SPEED the only prescribed learning was a short induction programme. Most other learning was initiated by the student entrepreneurs
through their questions, corresponding to Revans's Q (questioning insight)
learning (Revans, 1982). Triggers for learning included, for example: individual interest or curiosity; intended learning; learning arising from a
perceived opportunity; a critical incident such as a need or problem, an
impending decision, or a gap in knowledge or resources. Learning was
contingent on the recognition of these triggers by the student and their
responses to them. As Corcoran (2008) suggested, curriculum-based or
'push' learning (Revans's learning, programmed knowledge) tended not to
be as timely, nor was it perceived as relevant or effective.

The prevailing mode of action learning on SPEED was 'pull' learning,
when a trigger prompted learning. In the lower-right corner of the model
(Figure 6.2) are indicative examples of the types of learning students would
experience, typically personal learning in such areas as managing time
and multiple priorities; interpersonal relationships with team members,
potential stakeholders and others; and self-efficacy; as well as many areas

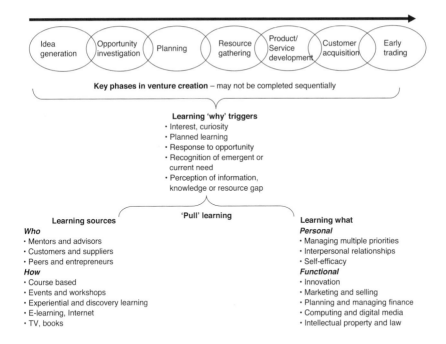

Figure 6.2   The student learning journey towards entrepreneurship

of functional learning which might be drawn on in the course of establishing the venture, such as innovating, developing a customer base, managing money, using digital media, and so on. In the lower-left corner is an indicative list of the sources and methods of learning they might use. The roles of social contact, from mentors and peer-based learning as well as experienced entrepreneurs, together with experiential discovery learning and digital learning media, typify the range of learning sources used. The response to the 'pull' for learning was a combination of what was learned together with how, and with or from whom, this was learned.

Student entrepreneurs may not know in advance what they need to learn in order to accomplish their goals, nor are they necessarily aware of what, when and how they are learning, but they need to be able to apply what they learn. Of greatest importance to the student is gaining the information, knowledge, capability or help to complete the task or solve the immediate problem. Therefore, entrepreneurship educators and facilitators need to ensure that the range of learning sources (who, how and what) is readily available to students when required, to enable them to work through the relevant phases of their venture creation. This involves supporting individuals with different needs, at differing stages, and in different sequences.

This seems a complex approach to learning because it involves both the provision of demand-led knowledge and other learning resources such as digital and web-enabled media, and personalized learning. The development of conscious, reflective and transferable learning-through-action needs to be encouraged by educators and mentors to assist ownership of learning for longer-term effectiveness. Action learning, supported by peer groups, mentoring and access to a 'pull' model of learning resources, are all increasingly valued and used by student entrepreneurs.

CONCLUSIONS AND IMPLICATIONS FROM THE SPEED EXPERIENCE

The SPEED programme exemplifies ways in which 'entrepreneurial universities' can work, in being enterprising, collaborative and effective in using external funding to achieve economic impact (Rae et al., 2009). It combined an enterprising, practitioner-driven approach to provide an innovative and largely effective programme. The relationship with research and theory was secondary, and such projects can benefit from a more robust research and conceptual design for which the knowledge exists, but the short-term nature of collaborative projects inevitably dissipates the shared human capital and the ownership of what has been learned, making its transfer to subsequent projects less effective. There is a significant danger with action learning that once the action has ceased, the learning is lost, and the role of research must ensure that it is shared, as in the case of the Lancaster Leading Enterprise and Development (LEAD) project (Smith and Robinson, 2006). This problem of sustainability frequently occurs when funded projects end and their networks with accumulated social knowledge are dispersed. In the case of SPEED, the documented research could at least be made available on a single website for easy access.

This reflection on the SPEED project suggests a number of avenues which merit further research. It enabled a significant number of students to develop a creative enterprise and to learn from this experience, with a range of outcomes. The scope for students and graduates to learn by doing in developing a creative business, or a business venture which applied creative thinking to its design and operation, is vital for growing the human capital of such skills which can be applied in the knowledge-based, creative and digital economy. However, we do not yet know enough about the medium-term survival of the ventures they established, which business models were sustainable, or what support beyond the initial programme they required to achieve this.

SPEED spawned successor projects, in both the East and West Midlands, into which many of its design characteristics were incorporated, with compromises to meet the constraints of European funding. The concept was also developed in Wales and with other European partners. These spin-offs require evaluation against the original concept. There was the potential for the approach to become a mainstream curricular option in all universities, where students would be able to start and run a business venture as part of their studies. However, public spending constraints appear to make this unlikely, yet investigation and experimentation with 'lean', minimal-cost options could be conducted through action research.

This experience builds on other innovative applications of action learning summarized earlier, which demonstrate that action learning, venture creation and entrepreneurial learning can be combined successfully to focus on student entrepreneurship in the creative industries. It demonstrated this distinctively through venture creation on a large-scale, multi-HEI basis, with a flexible approach, and powerful educator, institutional as well as student learning from the experience. The value of a 'pull' rather than 'push' approach to facilitating student action learning, and the development of ways of supporting this, were significant and represent a contribution to theory and practice. Such learning by doing, through action and experience, is important in enabling graduates to transfer and apply their skills in highly flexible ways, which they increasingly require.

The final issue is the economic context for educators, institutions and students. Enterprise educators face great challenges in enabling graduates to start their careers in an economic and employment environment characterized by post-recession uncertainty, high levels of debt and a scarcity of job opportunities (Rae, 2009). With growing prospects of graduate worklessness, there is an emerging crisis facing UK universities in graduate employment, with creative and arts graduates being severely affected. The nature of graduate careers has changed fundamentally, with the expectation of readily 'finding a graduate-level job' being unrealistic for many graduates, perhaps especially in the arts and humanities. HE and creative education raise aspirations that will not be readily met through employment for many. Creative entrepreneurship is an essential contribution to bridging the widening gap between HE and graduate participation, which is increasingly required in the new economy. Enterprising action learning is increasingly essential for more students, at different stages of the curriculum, because in many universities there is a real danger of enterprise learning remaining either optional or a minority activity (NCGE, 2007). Public spending cuts in HE are exacerbating this trend. The ability to undertake entrepreneurial action learning, therefore, needs to be part of the survival package for the transition from university to work for as many students as possible, giving them the option of creating their own business venture or availing themselves of enhanced employment prospects in small businesses.

REFERENCES

Ansoff, I. (1963), *Corporate Strategy*, Harmondsworth: Penguin.

Argyris, C. (1982), *Reasoning, Learning and Action: Individual and Organizational*, San Francisco, CA: Jossey-Bass.

Argyris, C., R. Putnam and D. Smith (1987), *Action Science*, San Francisco, CA: Jossey-Bass.

Argyris, C. and D.A. Schon (1978), *Organization Learning: A Theory of Action Perspective*, Reading, MA: Addison Wesley.

Atherton, A. (2007), 'Preparing for business start-up: "pre-start" activities in the new venture creation dynamic', *Journal of Small Business and Enterprise Development*, **14** (3), 404–17.

Baines, S. and L. Robson (2001), 'Being self-employed or being enterprising? The case of creative work for the media industries', *Journal of Small Business and Enterprise Development*, **8** (4), 349–62.

Bilton, C. (2007), *Management and Creativity: From Creative Industries to Creative Management*, Blackwell Publishing.

Birch, C. and B. Clements (2006), 'Creating graduate entrepreneurship through self-employed work placements – Project SPEED', paper presented at 29th Institute for Small Business Affairs Entrepreneurship and SME Development conference, Cardiff, November.

Björkegren, D. (1996), *The Culture Business: Management Strategies for the Arts Related Business*, London: Routledge.

Bourdieu, P. (1977), *Outline of a Theory of Practice*, Cambridge: Cambridge University Press.

Clements, B. and S. Moore (2009), 'SPEED final report by the lead institution', Institute for Innovation and Enterprise, University of Wolverhampton.

Collins, L., A. Smith and P. Hannon (2006), 'Discovering entrepreneurship: an exploration of a tripartite approach to developing entrepreneurial capacities', *Journal of European Industrial Training*, **30** (3), 188–205.

Cope, J. (2003), 'Entrepreneurial learning and critical reflection', *Management Learning*, **34** (4), 429–50.

Cope, J. (2005), 'Toward a dynamic learning perspective of entrepreneurship', *Entrepreneurship Theory and Practice*, **29** (4), 373.

Cope, J. and G. Watts (2000), 'Learning by doing: an exploration of critical incidents and reflection in entrepreneurial learning', *International Journal of Entrepreneurial Behaviour and Research*, **6** (3), 104–24.

Corcoran, A. (2008), 'Enterprise education in an Olympic year: sprint or decathlon?', paper presented at 31st ISBE Conference, Belfast, November.

Deakins, D. and M. Freel (1998), 'Entrepreneurial learning and the growth process in SMEs', *Learning Organization*, **5** (3), 144–55.

Department for Culture, Media and Sport (DCMS) (2001), 'The cultural industries mapping document', London: DCMS.

Devins, D., J. Gold, S. Johnson and R. Holden (2005), 'A conceptual model of management learning in micro businesses: implications for research and policy', *Education and Training*, **47** (8–9), 540–51.

Gibb, A.A. (1996), 'Entrepreneurship and small business management: can we afford to neglect them in the twenty-first century business school', *British Journal of Management*, **7**, 309–21.

Gibb, A.A. (1997), 'Small firms' training and competitiveness: building on the small firm as a learning organization', *International Small Business Journal*, **15** (3), 14–29.

Gibb, A.A. (2001), 'Creating conducive environments for learning and entrepreneurship', address to the First Conference of the Entrepreneurship Forum: Entrepreneurship and Learning, Naples, 21–24 June.

Gibb, A.A. (2002), 'In pursuit of a new "enterprise" and "entrepreneurship" paradigm for learning, creative destruction, new values, new ways of doing things and new combinations of knowledge', *International Journal of Management Reviews*, **4** (3), 233–69.

Gibb, A.A. and J. Ritchie (1982), 'Understanding the process of starting a small business', *European [now International] Small Business Journal*, **1** (1), 26–45.

Good, D. and S. Cooper (2009), 'SPEED and evaluation', presented at SPEED national final event, Crewe Hall, July.

Heartfield, J. (2000), *Great Expectations: The Creative Industries in the New Economy*, London: Design Agenda.

Heinonen, J. and S.A. Poikkijoki (2006), 'An entrepreneurial-directed approach to entrepreneurship education: mission impossible?', *Journal of Management Development*, **25** (1), 80–94.

Henry, C. (ed.) (2007), *Entrepreneurship in the Creative Industries: An International Perspective*, Cheltenham, UK and Northampton, MA, USA: Edward Elgar.

Heron, J. (1996), *Co-operative Inquiry*, London: Sage.

Honey, P. and A. Mumford (1992), *The Manual of Learning Styles*, Maidenhead: Honey Publications.

Institute for Innovation and Enterprise (IIE) (2008), 'SPEED biennial report', University of Wolverhampton, Wolverhampton.

Jones, O. and R. Holt (2008), 'The creation and evolution of new business ventures: an activity theory perspective', *Journal of Small Business and Enterprise Development*, **15** (1), 51–73.

Jones-Evans, D., W. Williams and J. Deacon (2000), 'Developing entrepreneurial graduates: an action-learning approach', *Education and Training*, **42** (4–5), 282–88.

Kolb, D. (1984), *Experiential Learning: Experience as the Source of Learning and Development*, Englewood Cliffs, NJ: Prentice-Hall.

Lave, J. and E. Wenger (1991), *Situated Learning: Legitimate Peripheral Participation*, Cambridge: Cambridge University Press.

Leadbeater, C. and K. Oakley (1999), *The Independents: Britain's New Cultural Entrepreneurs*, London: Demos.

Lewin, K. (1951), *Field Theory in Social Science*, New York: Harper & Row.

McElwee, G. and D. Rae (2008), 'Creative enterprise in the rural economy', paper presented at 31st ISBE conference, Belfast, November.

Marsick, V. and K. Watkins (1990), *Informal and Incidental Learning in the Workplace*, London: Routledge.

Marsick, V. and K. Watkins (1997), 'Lessons from informal and incidental learning', in J. Burgoyne and M. Reynolds (eds), *Management Learning: Integrating Perspectives in Theory and Practice*, London: Sage, pp. 295–.

Matlay, H. (2000), 'Organisational learning in small learning organisations: an empirical overview', *Education and Training*, **42** (4–5), 202–10.

Mumford, A. (1995), 'Effective learners in action learning sets', *Employee Counselling Today*, **8** (6), 5–12.

Munro, J. and R. Cook (2008), 'The small enterprise as the authentic learning environment opportunity (SEALEO)', *Aslib Proceedings: New Information Perspectives*, **60** (6), 686–700.

Murray, L. and B. Lawrence (2000), *Practitioner-based Enquiry: Principles for Postgraduate Research*, London: Falmer Press.

National Council for Graduate Entrepreneurship (NCGE) (2007), *Enterprise and Entrepreneurship in Higher Education*, Birmingham: NCGE.

Pankaj, P. and B. Conklin (2009), 'The balancing act: the role of transnational habitus and social networks in balancing transnational entrepreneurial activities', *Entrepreneurship Theory and Practice*, **33** (5), 1045–78.

Pedlar, M. (1991), *Action Learning in Practice*, 2nd edn, Aldershot: Gower.

Pedler, M., J. Burgoyne and T. Boydell (1997), *The Learning Company*, Maidenhead: McGraw-Hill.

Penaluna, A. and K. Penaluna (2006), 'Cox review of creativity in business: implications for entrepreneurship educators', paper presented at 29th ISBE conference, Cardiff, November.

Potts, J. and S. Cunningham (2008), 'Four models of creative industries', *International Journal of Cultural Policy*, **14** (3), 238–48.

Potts, J., J. Hartley, J. Banks, J. Burgess, R. Cobcroft, S. Cunningham and L. Montgomery (2008), 'Consumer co-creation and situated creativity', *Industry and Innovation*, **15** (5), 459–74.

Rae, D. (2000), 'Understanding entrepreneurial learning: a question of how?', *International Journal of Entrepreneurial Behaviour and Research*, **6** (3), 145–9.

Rae, D. (2003), 'Entrepreneurial identity and capability: the role of learning', PhD thesis, Nottingham Trent University.

Rae, D. (2005), 'Entrepreneurial learning: a narrative-based conceptual model', *Journal of Small Business and Enterprise Development*, **12** (3), 323–35.

Rae, D. (2007a), 'Achieving business focus: promoting the entrepreneurial management capabilities of owner-managers', *Industry and Higher Education*, **21** (6), 415–26.

Rae, D. (2007b), 'Creative industries in the UK: cultural diffusion or discontinuity?' in C. Henry (ed.), *Entrepreneurship in the Creative Industries, an International Perspective*, Cheltenham, UK and Northampton, MA, USA: Edward Elgar, pp. 54–71.

Rae, D. (2009), 'Entrepreneurship: too risky to be let loose in a stormy economic climate?', *International Journal of Entrepreneurship and Innovation*, **10** (2), 137–47.

Rae, D., S. Gee and R. Moon (2009), 'The role of an entrepreneurial learning team in creating an enterprise culture in a university', *Industry and Higher Education*, **23** (3), 183–97.

Revans, R. (1980), *Action Learning: New Techniques for Managers*, London: Blond & Briggs.

Revans, R.W. (1982), *The Origin and Growth of Action Learning*, London: Chartwell Bratt.

Schon, D.A. (1983), *The Reflective Practitioner*, London: Temple Smith.

Shorthose, J. (2000), 'The ecology of the creative community', in R. Aubrey and H. David (eds), *Nottingham's Lace Market, Greater Nottingham in the 21st Century*, Nottingham: Work Institute, Nottingham Trent University, pp. 223–8.

Shorthose, J. (2004), 'A more critical view of the creative industries: production, consumption and resistance', *Capital and Class*, **84** (1–10).

Smith, L. and S. Robinson (2006), *Leading Enterprise and Development Programme Evaluation Report*, Lancaster: Lancaster University Management School.

Taylor, D.W. and R. Thorpe (2004), 'Entrepreneurial learning: a process of co-participation', *Journal of Small Business and Enterprise Development*, **11** (2), 203–11.

Vincett, P. and S. Farlow (2008), '"Start-a-Business": an experiment in education through entrepreneurship', *Journal of Small Business and Enterprise Development*, **15** (2), 274–88.

Watson, T.J. (1994), *In Search of Management: Culture Chaos and Control in Managerial Work*, London: Routledge.

Wenger, E. (1998), *Communities of Practice: Learning, Meaning and Identity*, Cambridge: Cambridge University Press.

Woodier, N. (2008), 'Our SPEED students a year on: a case study approach', paper presented at 31st ISBE conference, Belfast, November.

7. Reconciling economic and creative performance: insights from a creative business service start-up

Brian V. Tjemkes*

INTRODUCTION

Creative industries essentially supply products and services with aesthetic, broadly educational or entertainment purposes rather than any immediate technical function (Throsby, 2001). Compared with other creative industries, including arts, media and publishing, however, creative business services (CBS) possess distinct properties (Moeran, 1996), in that such firms typically produce and sell informational media content on a commercial basis (Stam et al., 2008). To this end CBS are customer-oriented and employ creative professionals with jobs of a clearly creative nature to develop tailor-made services for their corporate clients. Advertising agencies are typical, as these firms design and sell advertising campaigns that their clients use to communicate with their (potential) customers. The primary aim of this type of firm is to achieve differentiation in its services, making its activities and outcomes highly innovative. Taken together, these characteristics suggest that CBS confront a unique challenge: achieving the twofold objective of economic and creative performance.

On this front however, prior research on creative industries only provides partial understanding of this puzzle (Lawrence and Phillips, 2002; Thompson et al., 2007) since it has primarily focused on factors that influence creative performance. For example, studies report that specific individual characteristics (Rae, 2004) and organizational designs foster creative performance (Moultrie and Young, 2009; Townley et al., 2009). However, the insights of this research have limited application within a CBS context: organization designs that enable CBS to obtain high levels of creative performance may not enable them to achieve economic performance and vice versa (Banks et al., 2002). To address this concern, other studies examined high-performing firms and reported that these firms design organizations in which creativity-enhancing conditions receive support from a professional management structure (Lampel et al., 2000; Tschang, 2007) or employ creative persons who align their artistic creativity with business interests (Chaston, 2008; Griffith and Taylor, 1994). Yet due to the static focus of these studies on performance, they provide little understanding on organization development. Despite organization development being a critical management activity, there are still relatively few empirical studies that explicitly explore how a CBS firm's organization design evolves toward one that reconciles economic and creative performance.

I address this gap in the literature by developing an integrative and multilevel process model of a CBS firm start-up. To accomplish this research objective, I conducted a longitudinal case study of the establishment of an advertising agency in the Netherlands. Building on the findings I make two key contributions. First, I validate prior studies on creative industries by showing that the organizational design in which creativity is managed functions as an important driver of a CBS firm's ability to realize the twofold objective of economic and creative performance. Second, I advance prior CBS literature by showing that during the start-up period an organization design progresses through (positive and negative) adaptation cycles toward a design that would enable it to achieve the twofold objective of economic and creative performance. More specifically, by disentangling venture development, I demonstrate how distinct types of creative persons' behaviour positively and negatively influence rationalization of the organization (that is, initiatives to improve the organization design), a relationship mediated by team dynamics. Moreover, the interplay among rationalization, team dynamics and creative persons' behaviour is influenced by venture performance.

The remainder of the chapter is structured as follows. First, I discuss the theoretical background and present the research question. Second, I outline the case study approach. Third, I report the case study results. Fourth, I introduce the proposed multilevel process model and propositions. Fifth, I conclude with a discussion of the results and conclusions.

THEORETICAL BACKGROUND

A common thread in prior literature on creative industries is that creativity is an important aspect and should be encouraged to ensure organizational success (Banks et al., 2002). In addition to factors such as the development of creative capabilities (Napier and Nilsson, 2006) and organizational creativity (Moultrie and Young, 2009), studies investigating creative industries argue that creativity flourishes in specific organization designs

(Townley et al., 2009). Such designs are often characterized by flexibility, creative working climates, decentralization of decision-making, separation of supporting and creative tasks, participative leadership and creative organizational capabilities (Napier and Nilsson, 2006). However, this research forgets that organizational designs enhancing individual creativity and processes, and thus creative performance, may not attend to economic performance.

To address this gap, some studies examine design conditions that enable firms in creative industries to achieve the twofold objective of economic and creative performance (Kennedy, 2000; Lampel et al., 2010). For example, Cohendet and Simon's (2007) analysis of video games illustrates how tight and decentralized control aligned with loose and informal management serve to balance the demands of creativity and mass production. Moeran (2009) examines a Japanese advertising agency and finds that differentiation between account managers and production teams, and installing dual creative–administrative roles of key personnel are pivotal to creative and economic performance. A key contribution of these studies is their demonstration that organizational design solutions for economic performance may enhance creative performance and vice versa.

Other studies postulate that individual creative persons' behaviour also may influence a CBS venture's ability to achieve superior economic and creative performance (de Bruin, 2005). Creative persons may act upon an internal desire to create artistic content irrespective of business objectives (Kerrigan and Ozbilgin, 2004), or they may act in response to business-driven triggers, suggesting that they apply creativity to realize economic objectives. For example, Griffith and Taylor (1994) find that high-performing firms, compared with low-performing ventures, employ creative persons who are able to align business objectives with their creative aspirations. Chaston (2008) reports that creative firms whose owners or managers exhibited a financial–artistic orientation outperformed those whose owners or managers revealed an artistic–creative orientation. These results suggest a continuum of behaviours, ranging from a total focus on creative output to a complete commitment to economic performance.

Despite these advances, only a few studies have provided insights into organization development and rationalization (Mathieu, 2006): the processes by which a CBS venture seeks to develop an organization design to achieve its economic and creative objectives (Tschang, 2007). For example, Banks et al. (2002) examine new media ventures and find that venture performance depends on creativity management and that as these firms mature, creativity becomes less unfettered and increasingly subject to managerial control. Tschang's (2007) results indicate that firms should alternate between more or less innovative strategies to meet the dual objectives of creativity and economic performance in the video gaming industry. These studies have produced a fruitful foundation proffering a systematic understanding of relationships between organization design and development and economic and creative performance. However, their focus is on established firms, so it remains questionable whether these insights generalize to venture start-ups in the creative industry.

Taken together, despite the widespread recognition of the importance of finding the right persons, supported by the right organizational design, to achieve the dual objective of economic and creative performance, the implementation of these attributes requires founder-managers of a new venture to engage in a difficult and complex balancing act. Building on the logic that creativity is essential to a creative firm's competitive advantage, it is unlikely that proposed solutions for fostering economic performance relate to creative performance; conversely, solutions enhancing creative performance may be considered barriers to economic performance. Moreover, in part because of the tension between economic and creative performance, a new firm may not settle into a dominant organization design. Prior research also suggests that distinct types of creative persons' behaviour differently affect economic and creative performance, such that organizational designs can be developed to attend to both performance objectives. Building on this foundation, I attempt to provide a richer understanding of the connections between the rationalization of the organization design and creative persons' behaviour in the context of a new CBS venture. Specifically, I explore the following research question: how do rationalization of the organization design, creative persons' behaviour and venture performance (that is, economic and creative performance) interact during the start-up stage of a creative business service venture?

METHODOLOGY

Research Design

I adopt a case study approach to build a more integrative perspective of CBS venture start-up that explains how rationalization of the organization design, creative persons' behaviour and venture performance are connected. A case study is appropriate for theory building because it enables us to: (1) answer questions about events over which we have little or no control (Yin, 1984); (2) draw on multiple observations of complex processes (Eisenhardt, 1989); and (3) examine the interrelatedness of the different levels of analysis in depth (Hall, 2006). I follow Faems et al.'s (2008) approach and develop a multilevel process model with a case study analysis.

I conducted a longitudinal case study of the start-up of an advertising agency and refer to it as ADDESIGN (a pseudonym, for anonymity). ADDESIGN is appropriate for the purposes of this study for three reasons. First, its core business fits with my definition of CBS. To reconcile the dual objectives of economic and creative performance ADDESIGN relies on six founder-managers (that is, copywriters and art directors) to design and sell advertising campaigns, which requires them to perform significant amounts of creative thinking. Second, during the start-up period, ADDESIGN experienced economic and creative successes and setbacks, which resulted from and were caused by shifts in founder-managers' behaviour and changes in the organization design. Third, the research team had full access to the company.

Data Collection and Analysis

Data on the ADDESIGN case were collected in a participatory and retrospective way. One of the researchers was involved in the firm as member of the Board of Advice (BoA). The main advantage of this unique position was that communication with the founder-managers about organization development was open and transparent. A disadvantage, however, is that participative research may introduce bias in data interpretation. To overcome this concern, two independent researchers joined the research team within two months of the start of data collection. Retrospective data collection offered a deeper understanding of critical events after they occurred, reducing the risk of redundant data. However, respondents have a tendency to filter out events that render their story less coherent. Thus, to improve the validity of reports and prevent respondent bias, the research team first triangulated data using multiple data sources. Second, we asked informants to reflect on concrete events rather than abstract concepts to reduce the risk of cognitive biases and impression management. Third, we attempted to verify individual reports by asking similar questions, organizing interviews with multiple respondents and having the interview reports checked by other interviewees.

The case study data were collected between September 2007 and February 2009. Because a long data collection period creates the danger of data overload and unusable data, we followed suggestions from prior case study research (Faems et al., 2008; Pentland, 1999) that recommend theory-building efforts should move from the surface level to deeper levels of data collection and analysis. Therefore, the research team adopted three data collection strategies: (1) unstructured and semi-structured interviews; (2) observation and internal documents; and (3) case report writing.

First, the research team used both unstructured and semi-structured interviews to obtain an understanding of ADDESIGN's organization development. The unstructured interviews were designed to identify initial key events and obtain detailed information about them. For example, during the first four months the results of these interviews enabled us to understand the rationale behind adaptations made to the organization. The research team used these findings and theoretical considerations to develop a semi-structured interview tool (see Appendix), which allowed it to focus on research efforts. The six founder-managers were interviewed on multiple occasions, both separately and together. Interviews were conducted in their native language (that is, Dutch) to maximize their ability to express their thoughts, feelings and opinions. The interviews offered an in-depth understanding of the sequence of events during the start-up phase. The length of the more than 20 interviews ranged from ten minutes to two hours. The interviewees explicitly requested their interviews not be recorded. To overcome data analysis and interpretation concerns, all interviews were therefore conducted by two researchers, who processed the results (including quotes) immediately after the interviews. These documents were subsequently returned to interviewees as an accuracy check.

Second, the research team used observation and internal documents to collect data. The research team had full access to ADDESIGN and attended multiple management and project meetings. Although the researcher acting as a member of the BoA was actively involved in some of these meetings, the other two researchers always maintained their objective and independent role. In addition, to obtain insights into the inner workings of the firm, the research team observed the founder-managers at work in their office. Although these observations provided valuable insights, they were subject to interpretation biases. Therefore, the research team also obtained access and studied relevant documents. The research team performed document analyses of internal reports, such as minutes of meetings, client reports and proposals for organizational change, and it had permanent access to the project management system. In the comparison of the results of these observations and document analyses, any inconsistencies were resolved through discussion.

Third, building on the available data, the research team wrote an extensive case report that encompassed the company's background, chronological development, key events, external environment, internal organization and progress. In this report the research team also made extensive use of its observations, interview data and documents to ensure internal consistency. Two interviewees checked this case report for accuracy. Thus, data triangulation was accomplished with multiple respondents at different times in multiple settings, as well as different sources of data (that is, interviews, observation and documentation; Eisenhardt, 1989).

After the data collection, the research team examined the data and moved to the theory-building stage (Faems et al., 2008). First, building on the data each member individually identified critical events tied to shifts in individual behaviour, team dynamics and organization development. Analysis also resulted in visual maps of organizational development across levels of analysis. Comparing the results, some discrepancies existed, but they were resolved through returning to the data, contacting interviewees and discussion. Second, the research team moved to a more theoretical level to arrive at an explanatory model. It focused on identifying links between its initial core concepts, but also allowed for additional concepts to enter the analysis. For example, as data analysis progressed, it became clear that the research team needed to add 'commercial' and 'institutional' pressures to rationalize, 'constructive' and 'destructive' team dynamics and founder-managers' 'resistance to' and 'compliance with' rationalization to its model. This multistage process of continuous interaction between research team members resulted in a multilevel process model. As data analysis progressed, the findings were also contrasted with prior literature, further validating the research team's unique insights.

THE START OF AN ADVERTISING AGENCY

In this section, I describe chronologically the start-up of ADDESIGN from the initial foundation meeting in September 2007 to a major organizational restructuring in February 2009. Building on the data, the research team decided to distinguish six periods; each period demarcates a critical venture development stage. Period 1 describes the establishment of ADDESIGN; Period 2 describes initial attempts to professionalize the organization; Period 3 describes the emergence of conflicts between founder-managers; Period 4 describes a second attempt to reorganize; Period 5 describes economic and creative successes; and Period 6 describes the introduction of a new organization design. The research team decided to discontinue data collection upon the occurrence of a critical event, namely, the successful implementation of a matrix structure. This chronological description provides the background for the multilevel process model, presented in the next section.

Period 1: Establishing ADDESIGN (September 2007–March 2008)

In September 2007, six freelance professionals founded a new advertising agency, ADDESIGN. Building on their expertise in various disciplines, they together formed a multidisciplinary team, including an art director, creative director, account manager and interaction designer. Each founder-manager was primarily responsible for their individual specialization, but they all possessed equal decision-making rights with respect to management decisions. Confronted with a competitive environment, ADDESIGN positioned itself as a niche player that could offer multidisciplinary, highly creative and innovative products and services (for example Internet design and advertising campaigns). It focused on tailor-made products, thereby avoiding head-to-head or price competition with established competitors. The founder-managers' combined expertise and the small size of the venture enabled them to respond quickly to customer demands. As one interviewee stated: 'We are small, flexible and we are able to align different specializations. The campaigns we design, will really add value to our clients.'

During this initial start-up period the organization was functionally organized around specializations, decision-making was decentralized and conflicts and unexpected problems were resolved through informal communication and mutual adjustment. The founder-managers worked in close quarters in a small office, creating a climate in which ideas and knowledge could easily be exchanged. They were highly motivated to deliver state-of-art services that capitalized on their individual areas of expertise. Every day they produced numerous new ideas and creative concepts, though only some of these had economic viability. Creative processes and individual creative expressions dominated ADDESIGN's internal workings.

Immediately after the start-up ADDESIGN attracted a major client, which commissioned the development of an online advertising campaign. Creatively the project was a huge success, as the website's innovative design and functionality increased hit rates substantially. However, due to a continuous quest for creativity at the expense of budget control, and ad hoc collaboration between concept designers, art directors and the account manager, many additional hours were required to meet the client's specifications. Although *ex post* calculations were not made, the founder-managers felt that financially the project underperformed. After completing this first project, ADDESIGN sent its first invoice at the end of March 2008 and one of the founder-managers expressed satisfaction: 'I really feel that I can express my creativity in an interesting project. I have an idea and immediately I can share it with five others, who understand where I come from.'

Despite some minor efforts to professionalize the internal organization, management activities remained disorganized. For example, supplier invoices were paid, but it was unclear how much money ADDESIGN had in the bank; potential clients were approached, but the status of

these efforts was unclear to the wider organization; a project management system was set up, but it contained numerous disconnected entries.
Creatively however the founders accelerated their efforts and invested
substantial hours in creative concepts and projects, which were commissioned by new clients.

Period 2: Minor Organizational Changes (April 2008–June 2008)

To improve its service delivery system, ADDESIGN decided to restruc-
ture its internal organization. Several meetings were organized to discuss
the problems and challenges ahead, and it was decided that ADDESIGN
needed to operate in a more professional manner. Terms and conditions
had to be written, and an account management system, project management system and financial system had to be put in use. New clients forced
ADDESIGN to professionalize its organization further. For example,
clients requested that ADDESIGN register with the chamber of commerce,
become officially registered as a company and comply with Dutch tax
regulations (for example VAT). During this period, ADDESIGN officially
became a cooperative and thereby obtained legal status, which enabled
the company to hire an accountant. Due to the founder-managers' lack
of knowledge about running a business, they also decided to establish a
BoA that consisted of three persons with different forms of expertise. One
was an assistant professor in business, another was the general counsel for
an oil and gas company, and the third provided personal coaching to top
management team managers.

The founder-managers also worried that organizational and functional
responsibilities were being mixed, and after extensive meetings they
created task descriptions. During these meetings the founder-managers
collectively sought solutions to professionalize the organization; the meetings were characterized by dialogue and transparency. Two key decisions
resulted. First, each founder-manager was assigned one management
and one functional task. For example, the account manager was made
responsible for office management, whereas the interactive web designer
became responsible for bookkeeping. The founder-managers supported
these decisions:

> Luckily our clients provide us with feedback. We have no idea where to start with
> this management and their feedback is important. They make us understand
> what everyone has to do, not only creatively, but also about how we should com-
> municate. One result is that I also have been assigned management tasks.

During this period ADDESIGN continued to have economic and
creative successes. The founder-managers were able to fulfil their creative

aspirations with ADDESIGN projects; they willingly participated in organizational development; the internal organization slowly professionalized; and money was coming into the bank.

Period 3: Emerging Conflicts (July 2008–August 2008)

After these initial successes and improvements to the internal organization, ADDESIGN experienced some serious setbacks. For various reasons – failing to capitalize on their personal networks, refraining from cold calls and slow communication with potential clients – the founder-managers were not able to obtain commitments from potential clients, resulting in a drop in revenues.

This failure to attract new projects had several negative consequences. First, the founder-managers expressed aspirations to be more creative and searched for creative challenges in arenas other than ADDESIGN projects. The need for personal income also pushed them into external freelance activities. For example, two founder-managers frequently worked part-time for other advertising agencies and one founder worked almost full-time on non-related projects. Second, the founder-managers became less concerned about fulfilling their management tasks. Client status and financial reports were no longer regularly updated or communicated, resulting in a backlog. The combination of poor financial performance, lack of creative inspiration and task evasion increasingly contributed to conflicts. The founder-managers accused and blamed one another for this decrease in performance. Emergency meetings were organized, but conflicts surged and tensions rose, as one interviewee stated:

> It seems that we only talk to one another about difficult issues. Every discussion seems to end in a conflict, upset people, who basically walk away if they disagree. Also, no one is taking the blame and it is always someone else's fault. I am getting fed up with my colleagues.

To resolve these conflicts, the founder-managers decided to organize meetings specifically to discuss and deal with ADDESIGN's management problems. These meetings temporarily shifted their focus from external projects toward organizational development, yet they were not particularly effective and characterized by hostility. For example during one meeting, one of the founders threatened to leave ADDESIGN, which was resolved after some tense discussions. The increasing frequency and nature of the meetings reduced founder-managers' commitment to professionalizing the organization. They also started to develop diverging views on clients' projects, the service delivery system and the internal organization, which triggered them to avoid participating in ongoing organizational development. Moreover, they became increasingly detached from ADDESIGN, engaged in free-riding behaviour and evaded their responsibilities to pursue their creative aspirations. This non-compliant behaviour resulted in a shift toward more external activities, which damaged the founder-managers' collective identity and sense-making.

Period 4: Organizational Adaptation (September 2008–October 2008)

In the period between September 2008 and October 2008 matters became worse and the downward spiral continued. Conflicts increased and founder-managers became increasingly detached. They became worried about ADDESIGN's future and asked the BoA, by then reduced to one member due to financial problems, to intervene. Under the guidance of the BoA, the founder-managers jointly decided to develop new task descriptions. All received individual-specific tasks that outlined their responsibilities for both their creative and their management tasks. The main improvement was the degree of formalization and the level of detail in the task descriptions, which allowed founder-managers to keep track of one another's task fulfilment. Creative and management tasks were differentiated, decision-making was distributed across tasks, and task descriptions required client status reports to be updated weekly and published on the project management system, followed by joint discussions of the reports during monthly meetings.

The BoA supervised meetings were characterized by focus and dialogue, rather than hostility and secrecy. Moreover, the BoA encouraged founder-managers to direct their creativity toward ADDESIGN projects, which resulted in constructive interactions and greater individual awareness of the need to combine creative aspirations with business interests. Although these interventions contributed to collective efforts and improved team dynamics temporarily, a full implementation of the proposed revision to the organizational design was delayed. Tensions remained relatively high, as the founder-managers remained primarily concerned with their individual creative projects and continued to evade their management tasks. Their frustration was clear: 'How do these changes make ADDESIGN work again? I am willing to discuss solutions, but it is not clear to me how they will help us. I rather focus on my creative projects.'

Period 5: Regained Venture Success (November 2008–December 2008)

During the period November 2008–December 2008 ADDESIGN regained its creative success. The renewed focus on internal creative projects led to some unexpected success. During the preceding months, two founder-managers had worked on an ADDESIGN project designed to create consumer awareness about how to live a luxury lifestyle without spending too much money. The project functioned as a creative catalyst and all founder-managers became involved in planning and executing it. By mid-December, ADDESIGN launched the project with great success, attracting substantial attention from several media, including television and the Internet. As one interviewee emphasized: 'This project was really brilliant. It was great to work together and make it into a great success. Everyone was involved and felt responsible. We were able to be really innovative, while considering our commercial objectives.'

The success of the project triggered several changes within ADDESIGN. First, the project involved substantial financial investments in web design and marketing events, which required immediate transparency in financial administration. Second, to realize this project, constructive team meetings were required about the management of the project and the creative concepts underpinning the project. The founder-managers started to communicate about various topics including creative ideas (for example concept design, marketing events, potential sponsors) and organizational design (for example account management, project administration). Third, each founder-manager shifted their creative aspirations back to ADDESIGN projects. In addition, they started to fulfil their management tasks. Their increased commitment to and compliance with ongoing professionalization contributed to a productive working climate, characterized by positive informal and formal communication.

Period 6: Major Organizational Change (January 2009–February 2009)

Driven by this project's success, the founder-managers agreed to engage in a new attempt to professionalize the organization. Prior experiences and performance setbacks made it clear that ADDESIGN's functional, decentralized, informal organizational design was not equipped to handle large, complex projects. Despite the improved task descriptions, tasks and responsibilities had not been defined clearly enough, so some tasks were not executed, while others were performed by multiple founder-managers. In addition, communication processes needed improvement, such as during meetings when founders discussed management issues and client projects. Guided by the BoA, the founder-managers decided to implement a business-functional matrix design.

The founder-managers formed the board of ADDESIGN, supported by the BoA. The board comprised five functional specializations (sales and account management; traffic and production; concept strategy; concept design; and concept execution) as well as three business units (customer-driven projects, ADDESIGN-driven project and non-commercial projects). In addition: (1) distinct founder-managers became responsible for the functional areas; (2) distinct founder-managers became responsible for management tasks; and (3) two founder-managers became responsible for business activities. Meetings were organized around client projects or management topics, meaning that founder-managers only attended if topics in their interest were on the agenda. The compliance of founders-managers reinforced their collective identity, thereby establishing a path to their future economic and creative performance, which even they saw clearly:

> I really think this will work. This new matrix design accommodates all my wishes. With it we can work on creative projects and make a profit. More importantly, I understand why it is important: to be competitive and viable!

MULTILEVEL PROCESS MODEL

Drawing on the chronological description, I develop a multilevel process model that separates the organizational, team, and individual levels of analysis. At the organizational level I distinguish between pressures to rationalize, forms of rationalization and venture performance. At the team level I focus on team dynamics and at the individual level I focus on creative persons' behaviour (see Figure 7.1).

Commercial and Institutional Pressures

Building on the data, I consider two organization-level forces that have driven ADDESIGN's founder-managers to improve the organization design to achieve their economic and creative objectives (that is, rationalization): commercial and institutional. Consistent with prior work on CBS venture development (Tschang, 2007; Powell, 2008), the findings indicate that commercial pressure, originating with (potential) client feedback, functions as a trigger to rationalize the organizational design. A key characteristic of a CBS venture is clients' involvement in the service delivery process, and to ensure a timely and cost-effective completion of commissioned projects they demand an efficient and effective organization. For example, during Periods 1 and 2 clients enforced rationalization. First, clients offered feedback during formal meetings and informal conversations, not only about advertising campaigns but also about the service delivery process. They demanded, among other things, designated account managers to improve communication and timely invoices. Second, clients

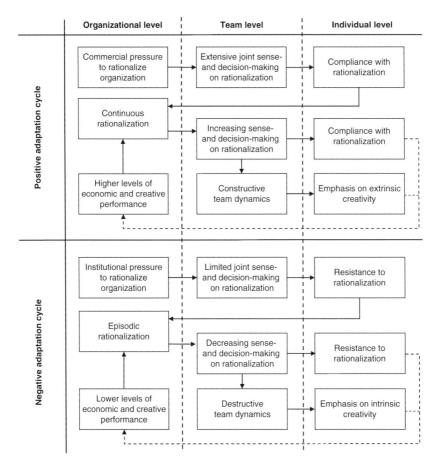

*Figure 7.1   A multilevel process model of organizational development in a
CBS venture*

demanded tax registration, chamber of commerce registration and an
account management system. As such, clients coerced ADDESIGN to
engage in acts of organizational development.

Institutional pressures pertain to regulative forces that coerce a firm to
develop and implement professionalization initiatives. Prior work on CBS
has recognized that pressures originating internally, such as advice boards,
or externally, such as chambers of commerce, push a CBS to professionalize (Tschang, 2007). The data support these insights, as ADDESIGN was
subject to institutional pressure to modify its organization design. For
example during Period 1, ADDESIGN experienced institutional pressure

to make a definitive choice of its legal form and submit necessary documentation from external government entities. This pressure however was replaced by commercial pressures after the first client commission. During Periods 3–4 institutional pressure reached a peak, as the BoA pressured ADDESIGN to improve its organization design.

The Impact of Commercial and Institutional Pressures on Team Dynamics

A unique property of this agency was that it was established by six founders who formed a management team. Consistent with prior work (Moeran, 1996, 2009), the results suggest that team dynamics are affected by commercial and institutional pressures to rationalize. Team dynamics refer to joint sense-making processes and collective decision-making about the degree, timing and content of rationalization. The results suggest a distinction between constructive and destructive team dynamics though.

Constructive team dynamics refers to creative persons' open and transparent discussions (formal and informal) about the need to rationalize the organization. A collective interest and concern exists about how to improve the organizational design. For example during Periods 1 and 5, management meetings were transparent, constructive and focused, and the founder-managers interacted through dialogue. They listened carefully to one another, put forward proposals to improve the service delivery system and found compromises easily. Constructive team dynamics thus suggest that founder-managers' interactions were characterized by a joint understanding about the need, ability and ways to rationalize: 'These management meetings are really working. We have a clear agenda, everyone is prepared and discussions are friendly. I sense that everybody is willing to make professionalization efforts work [in Period 5].'

In contrast, destructive team dynamics suggest that creative persons have conflicts, disagreements and misunderstandings about the degree, timing, and content of rationalization. They are subject to tunnel vision and become secretive about their motivations and activities. Proposals to professionalize the organization are met with hostility and likely to be rejected without proper analysis or discussion. The data indicate that destructive team dynamics entail a working climate in which joint sense- and decision-making are virtually absent. For example in Period 3, management meetings were often ad hoc and characterized by conflicts and fights about tasks and responsibilities. Occasionally, several founder-managers made 'threats to leave the organization' and as one interviewee stated: 'I start to dislike these meetings. They are long, unproductive and I feel that my co-founders are hiding information about their activities. It seems that we have developed diverging views on how to proceed.'

Commercial and institutional pressures differently influence team dynamics. Commercial pressure prompts creative persons' collective awareness of the need to professionalize and, thus, nurtures the quality of joint sense-making and decision-making. In Period 2 when clients demanded transparency in financial, marketing and production activities, founder-managers jointly considered their professional backgrounds and started to think about how they could contribute to the rationalization of the organization. During meetings they discussed possibilities to distinguish between management and creative tasks and identified distinct roles, including gatekeepers (for example account manager), facilitators (for example office manager) and production (for example art director). They collectively understood the need for organizational development. As one interviewee stated: 'We like working for clients. They enable us to work on highly innovative projects. But, they also force us to reconsider our service delivery system. We discussed this constructive feedback extensively during meetings.'

In contrast, institutional pressure inhibits joint sense-making and collective decision-making. Initially in Periods 1 and 2 institutional pressure, as manifested by repeated demands to comply with laws and regulations, resulted in destructive team dynamics. In Period 4 the BoA participated in management team meetings to enforce adaptations to the organizational design. When the BoA demanded an organization redesign destructive team dynamics emerged; the founder-managers, with two exceptions, did not recognize the need for financial, budgetary or project controls. As a team, the founder-managers acted evasively, conflicts arose and more meetings were required to enforce organizational development. However, this enforced process invoked more dysfunctional conflicts and hampered sense-making and decision-making processes. As one interviewee expressed it: 'We share ADDESIGN's core values, but it looks like that we have diverging views on what is good. Forcing us to adopt solutions frustrates joint decision-making.' Taken together, these results indicate that whereas commercial pressure prompts intrateam understanding, institutional pressure stimulates dysfunctional conflicts and team disintegration.

The Impact of Team Dynamics on Creative Persons' Disposition towards Rationalization

The data indicate that creative persons have a natural inclination to dislike management tasks. This tendency also translates into a negative disposition toward rationalization, manifested by a propensity to contest and resist it. However, the results also indicate that a creative person's disposition may be positive and they may actively participate in organizational development. More specifically, team dynamics influence creative persons' disposition toward rationalization, in the form of resistance or compliance.

Destructive team dynamics positively influence creative persons' resistance to rationalization. Team frictions reduce creative persons' proactive participation in professionalization trajectories. Without a collective understanding, creative persons feel no need to fulfil their management tasks, and engage in evasive behaviour, expecting others to take care of management activities. For example in Period 3, the surge in dysfunctional conflicts prompted founder-managers to engage in unrelated projects, which meant that they disengaged from the organization. As their aspirations to be creative were thwarted by frequent team meetings, conflicts and enforced professionalization, the founder-managers reacted opportunistically and developed resistance. As one interviewee stated: 'Talking for hours about topics I don't care about: let other people solve those management issues. I just want to work on my creative projects, if not for ADDESIGN then for other organizations [in Period 4].'

In contrast, constructive team dynamics positively influence creative persons' compliance and proactive engagement in organizational development. For example in Period 2, founder-managers reached consensus about the need to professionalize, which resulted in widespread compliance with ongoing organizational adaptation. They actively participated in activities, such as implementing financial and marketing reporting systems, formalizing operating procedures and quickly providing management reports. Thus constructive team dynamics boosted individual compliance, as expressed by one interviewee: 'The meetings are constructive and they make me understand that it is important to professionalize ADDESIGN. Moreover, I am actively involved in making our company better [in Period 6].' In summary, I identify connections between the pressures to rationalize the organization (commercial and institutional), team dynamics (constructive and destructive) and creative persons' disposition in terms of resistance and compliance to rationalization. Thus, I propose that:

Proposition 1: Commercial (institutional) pressure to rationalize the organization triggers constructive (destructive) team dynamics, which prompt a creative person's compliance with (resistance to) rationalization of the organization.

The Impact of Creative Persons' Dispositions on Rationalization

Within the context of CBS, rationalization pertains to organizational adaptation processes, which aim to develop an organization design suited to realize the dual objective of economic and creative performance. In line with prior work on organizational development (Weick and Quinn, 1999), and building on the data, I identify two types of rationalization: continuous and episodic. Continuous rationalization entails incremental, timely and flexible changes to the organization design, and creative persons are actively involved through self-organizing. Organizational change is a pattern of endless modifications and is driven by reactions to internal and external contingencies. Furthermore, changes are internally coherent, suggesting that adaptations in the organization reinforce one another and build on prior modifications. For example, the matrix structure implemented at the end of Period 6 incrementally built on prior adaptations to the organization design, it was proposed and implemented at an appropriate point in venture development and it depicted a coherent design in such a way that changes in the degree of differentiation (high), centralization (high for supporting tasks and low for functional tasks) and formalization (high for supporting tasks and low for functional tasks) strengthened one another.

Episodic rationalization suggests that the processes surrounding organization development exist, yet they are detached from historical decisions (that is, discontinuous), are not the result of participatory processes (that is, infrequent) and are essentially externally developed and imposed (Weick and Quinn, 1999). It sustains an inadequate organization design, and changes are often delayed or postponed. A CBS venture is not likely to realize its long-term objectives of economic and creative performance with episodic change, due to the enforced nature of adaptations. For example, in Period 4, attempts to improve the organization design began, including the following: the founders were assigned management and specialist roles; the hierarchical structure was developed by appointing project leaders and project teams; the production and supporting tasks were externalized; and the management information system came under greater formalization. However, these efforts failed to achieve their purposes, because they made little sense to the founder-managers, as they were imposed upon them. As one interviewee asked:

> Why would I contribute to further professionalizing my company? I do not see the short or long-term benefits of the proposed solutions. Implementing them for the sake of implementation does not make sense to me. I would rather spent my time on other, more fun, projects [in Period 4].

Creative persons' compliance with rationalization fosters continuous rationalization. Compliant creative persons are more likely to see the short-term benefits obtained through incremental adaptations and are, therefore, more likely to accept changes. For example, in Period 2 all founder-managers participated in the development and implementation of new task descriptions, installing a project management system and a management information system. These changes were successful, even though they directly affected how the founder-managers worked, because each founder-manager was actively involved in developing them. Similarly in Period 6, they were all involved in organization changes related to the matrix structure, with a clear distinction of business units, functional specializations and supporting departments. The matrix structure entailed significant implications, including changes in the service delivery system, the establishment of a hierarchy and formal communication lines, yet each founder-manager supported the new design.

> The new organization structure felt good. I obtained a clear idea what my contribution was to ADDESIGN and, moreover, I didn't have to communicate with everyone about everything. Past changes gave me confidence that we could pull it off and I liked being actively involved [in Period 6].

In contrast, creative persons' resistance to rationalization triggers episodic rationalization. When creative persons contest organizational adaptations and their behaviour becomes evasive, they are more likely to fail to execute their management tasks; thus contributing to organizational inertia (Weick and Quinn, 1999). During Periods 3 and 4, characterized by increasing levels of free-riding behaviour, the implementation of new design elements, such as task descriptions and standard operating procedures, was delayed. Individual resistance to professionalization hampered the enhancement of the organization, as design decisions were not fully supported. Taken together, I propose that:

Proposition 2: Individual compliance with (resistance to) rationalization increases the probability of continuous (episodic) rationalization.

Positive and Negative Adaptation Cycles

Taking the individual level of analysis, the results suggest that in addition to creative persons' dispositions toward rationalization, creative persons may possess different orientations toward expressing creativity. In line with prior research (Kerrigan and Ozbilgin, 2004; Paige and Littrel, 2002), I find that creative persons employed in a CBS, on the one hand, can be highly and intrinsically motivated to act upon their artistic creativity. That is, if a person is driven by intrinsic creativity, their behaviour is primarily directed toward the fabrication of artistic content, neglecting the economic objectives of creative expressions in a CBS. On the other hand, if a person is driven by extrinsic creativity, they put creative abilities to use to realize economic objectives. This distinction between intrinsic and extrinsic creativity enables us to theorize about the relationships between rationalization at the organization level of analysis (continuous and episodic), team dynamics (constructive and destructive) and creative person's individual behaviour (that is, disposition toward rationalization and creative orientation) that I refer to as an adaptation cycle.

A positive adaptation cycle suggests that continuous rationalization fosters constructive team dynamics, which increase individual compliance with rationalization. In addition, a creative person's compliance encourages extrinsic creativity. Flexible and incremental adaptation processes induced through self-organizing, thus, nurture and facilitate collective sense-making, which positively reinforces creative people's dispositions toward rationalization and prompts them to use their creative ability to achieve economic objectives. Periods 1 and 2 are illustrative of a positive adaptation cycle. At the end of Period 2, the six founder-managers engaged in a process of continuous rationalization, manifested in incremental changes to task descriptions, formalization of work procedures and the separation of functional and supporting tasks. These changes were instigated by extensive sense-making and decision-making during team meetings, which motivated founders/managers to work on ADDESIGN projects. In turn, they developed a positive and urgent disposition toward the need to rationalize, which they aligned with their creative orientation (that is, extrinsic). The implementation of the matrix structure at the end of Period 6 was preceded by a similar pattern of individual behaviours and team dynamics.

In contrast, a negative adaptation cycle suggests that episodic rationalization fosters destructive team dynamics, which increase creative persons' resistance to rationalization. In addition, individual resistance encourages intrinsic creativity, that is, creativity for the sake of creativity. Due to its interruptive nature, episodic rationalization contributed to dysfunctional conflicts between creative persons about the need and urgency to reorganize ADDESIGN. These distorted interactions within the management team shifted their attention away from management tasks and increased individual resistance and intrinsic creativity. Periods 3 and 4 represent negative adaptation cycles. At the end of Period 4, organizational adaptations, such as detailed task descriptions and detailed management information systems, were met with great resistance by founders-managers who perceived the proposed changes as constraints on their artistic freedom. Team discussions marked by tunnel vision and withholding of relevant information about individual projects and activities preceded this process of episodic rationalization. Furthermore, the founder-managers increased their freelance activities to escape organizational constraints on their creativity, which reinforced their already negative disposition toward rationalization. I therefore propose:

Proposition 3: During the start of a new creative business service venture, founder-managers engage in a balancing act between positive and negative adaptation cycles. A positive adaptation cycle suggests that continuous rationalization triggers constructive team dynamics, which prompts individual compliance with rationalization and thus extrinsic creativity. A negative adaptation cycle suggests that episodic rationalization triggers destructive team dynamics, which prompts individual resistance to rationalization and thus intrinsic creativity.

Impact of Venture Performance on Adaptation Cycles

Consistent with prior work on CBS performance (Paige and Littrell, 2002; Tschang, 2007), the results indicate that the founder-managers assessed venture performance in terms of economic and creative performance. Economic performance refers to overall profitability, but project cost calculations, investments and revenues per account were also indicators. Creative performance refers to the unique and differentiating qualities of services. For example, the degree to which an advertising campaign satisfies customer preferences and tastes, as well as media exposure and individual gratification, were important indicators. The results suggest that whereas Periods 1, 2, 5 and 6 were characterized by economic and creative success, during Periods 3 and 4 ADDESIGN experienced serious performance setbacks.

I suggest that high venture performance interacts with a positive adaptation cycle, whereas low venture performance interacts with a negative adaptation cycle. High levels of venture performance reinforce positive adaptation cycles and accelerate continuous rationalization in three ways. First, satisfactory venture performance triggers individual commitment. For example, successfully completing the first commissioned project resulted in commitments by all founder-managers to participate in ADDESIGN's growth ambitions. Second, good venture performance fostered collective sense-making. The success of the first project was extensively discussed during meetings, resulting in insights into how the next projects could be handled better, more creatively and more economically. Third, success attracts success, so ADDESIGN acquired new clients after this first project through positive referrals, which meant that commercial pressure increased.

In contrast, underperformance during the start-up period of a CBS reinforces a negative adaptation cycle, as it triggers episodic rationalization in three ways. First, low venture performance created individual detachment; the founder-managers disliked being associated with or made responsible for the lack of success. For example, in Periods 3 and 4, none of the founder-managers took responsibility for the drop in revenue and all pointed toward one another. Second, poor venture performance resulted in highly frustrating team dynamics. During meetings in Periods 3 and 4, conflicts surged as some founder-managers attempted to avoid discussing the performance problem. Third, low venture performance induces institutional pressure, because stakeholders may sense a need to become more actively involved. For example, in Period 4 the BoA intervened, and though these initiatives were welcomed, their suggestions were rarely implemented. Thus, building on the notion that venture performance functions as an important catalyst of rationalization, I propose that:

Proposition 4: During the start of a new creative business service, high (low) venture performance (economic and creative) reinforces positive (negative) adaptation cycles.

DISCUSSION AND CONCLUSION

The start-up of a CBS requires founder-managers immediately to create and sustain a competitive advantage in a highly competitive industry. The key challenge that founder-managers therefore need to address is developing an organization design that can achieve the dual, potentially conflicting objectives of becoming profitable and being recognized as creative. By conducting a longitudinal case study of a new CBS venture, I have developed an integrative perspective on organization development. More specifically, the findings suggest that a CBS venture's organization design during the start-up period progresses through adaptation cycles. That is, ventures may evolve through positive adaptation cycles, in which continuous rationalization fosters constructive team dynamics, which prompts compliance with rationalization and extrinsic creativity. However, ventures may also evolve through negative adaptation cycles, in which episodic rationalization fosters destructive team dynamics, which prompts resistance to rationalization and intrinsic creativity. Venture performance appears to function as an important catalyst of adaptation cycles.

Building on these results, I make two contributions to literature on CBS. First, CBS studies acknowledge that distinct organizational contexts nurture the achievement of the conflicting objectives of economic and creative performance. The results validate prior research by revealing that organization designs can be structured to accommodate both types of performance objectives. For example, the matrix design – characterized by the separation of support and creative tasks, centralized managerial decision-making for support tasks and decentralized decision-making for creative tasks, and high formalization of support tasks and low formalization of creative tasks – enabled ADDESIGN to realize the twofold objective of economic and creative performance.

Second, by disentangling venture development I also advance CBS research by showing that to develop and sustain their competitive advantage, founder-managers need to engage in a complex balancing act between different forces operating at different levels: organization, team and individual. The longitudinal perspective shows that a CBS venture may progress through a series of positive and negative adaptation cycles. Commercial pressure to rationalize an organization induces a positive adaptation cycle, in which continuous rationalization, constructive team dynamics and creative persons' compliance to rationalization and extrinsic creativity reinforce one another. Furthermore, commercial pressure gets reinforced by higher levels of venture performance, and business growth in turn triggers continuous rationalization. In contrast, institutional pressure induces a negative adaption cycle, in which episodic rationalization, destructive team dynamics and creative persons' resistance to rationalization and intrinsic creativity reinforce one another: organization development comes to a halt. Institutional pressure accelerates if venture performance decreases, because the likelihood of venture failure activates stakeholders to intervene, triggering ineffective enforcement by stakeholders. Taken together, a CBS venture start-up is likely to improve its organization design through trial and error.

Although not incorporated in the multilevel process model, the data also suggest that through interventions, shifts from a negative to a positive adaptation cycle are possible. For example, as ADDESIGN progressed, the initially homogeneous team transformed into multiple heterogeneous teams (that is, through increasing task differentiation and external sourcing) fostering constructive team dynamics. Interventions may also target an individual creative person's behaviour. Creative professionals lean toward creativity at the expense of business objectives, and training and creating awareness may shift their disposition. Future research may examine the viability of these and other interventions.

An important theoretical implication is that the tension between economics and creativity across levels makes a CBS venture unlikely to achieve a single dominant organization design. Active management of rationalization and creativity is critical to organizational development.

Creativity is an important aspect of a CBS venture's competitive advantage and should be encouraged to ensure business growth (Banks et al., 2002). However, in light of the uncertainty of CBS venture survival, organization designs that solely nurture creative outcomes may have unintended consequences, because they likely forget the realization of economic outcomes. A primary focus on creativity may therefore have adverse impacts on start-up success. Yet a dominant focus on economic outcomes may also jeopardize start-up success, because efficiency-based organization designs can constrain creative employees' creativity. Thus CBS ventures are more likely to develop and sustain competitive advantages if their organization design grows continuously (Weick and Quinn, 1999). Decision-makers need to learn about and exploit prior experiences and avoid enforcing their predetermined conceptions of appropriate organization designs. Further research should explore the underlying learning processes.

I also note a key limitation of the study. My findings are based on an in-depth, exploratory study of a new venture in the creative industry. The use of a single case enabled me to capitalize on the richness of the data, though these highly contextualized findings hamper generalizability (Eisenhardt, 1989). For example, the specific founding conditions for ADDESIGN included a small size, lack of external investors and a founding team of six creative persons. Further research should investigate other new ventures to explore potential contingencies. In addition, research could empirically test (parts of) the proposed multilevel process framework across contexts to validate our findings.

To obtain and sustain a competitive edge new entrants in the creative business service industry must be both creatively recognized and economically profitable. Drawing on prior literature on creative industries and a longitudinal case study, I develop a more integrative multilevel process model that reveals how founder-managers reconcile the tension between economic and creative performance during the start-up process. Building on the findings and in contrast to the common wisdom that organizational problems can be fixed with instant solutions, I conclude that economic and creative performance objectives can be reconciled over time, through incremental steps as a new venture becomes established.

NOTE

* I would like to express gratitude to Renée Scheerman and Yuri Narayen for their research assistance. Furthermore, I would like to thank Colette Henry, Anne de Bruin, Olivier Furrer, an anonymous reviewer and participants of the Institute for Small Business and Entrepreneurship (ISBE) 2009 conference for their constructive and insightful comments on prior versions of this chapter.

REFERENCES

Banks, M., D. Calvey, J. Owen and D. Russel (2002), 'Where the art is: defining and managing creativity in new media SMEs', *Creativity and Innovation Management*, **11** (4), 255–64.

de Bruin, A. (2005), 'Multi-level entrepreneurship in the creative industries: New Zealand's screen production industry', *International Journal of Entrepreneurship and Innovation*, **6** (3), 143–50.

Chaston, I. (2008), 'Small creative industry firms: a development dilemma?', *Management Decision*, **46** (6), 819–31.

Cohendet, P. and L. Simon (2007), 'Playing across the playground: paradoxes of knowledge creation in the videogame firm', *Journal of Organizational Behaviour*, **28** (5), 587–605.

Eisenhardt, K.M. (1989), 'Building theories from case-study research', *Academy of Management Review*, **14** (4), 532–50.

Faems, D., M. Janssens, A. Madhok and B. van Looy (2008), 'Toward an integrative perspective on alliance governance: connecting contract design, trust dynamics, and contract application', *Academy of Management Journal*, **51** (6), 1053–78.

Griffith, M.W. and B. Taylor (1994), 'Entrepreneurs in entertainment: putting on the top hat', *Long Range Planning*, **27** (6), 96–107.

Hall, P.A. (2006), 'Systematic process analysis: when and how to use it', *European Management Review*, **3** (1), 24–31.

Kennedy, H. (2010), 'Net work: the professionalization of web design', *Media, Culture and Society*, **32** (2), 187–203.

Kerrigan, F. and M. Ozbilgin (2004), 'Film marketing in Europe', *Non-profit and Voluntary Sector Marketing*, **9** (3), 229–38.

Lampel, J., T. Lant and J. Shamsie (2000), 'Balancing act: learning from organizing practices in cultural industries', *Organisation Science*, **11** (3), 263–9.

Lawrence, T.B. and N. Phillips (2002), 'Understanding cultural industries', *Journal of Management Inquiry*, **11** (4), 430–41.

Mathieu, C. (2006), 'Transforming the Danish film field via "professionalization", penetration and integration', *Creativity and Innovation Management*, **15** (3), 242–9.

Moeran, B. (1996), *A Japanese Advertising Agency: An Anthropology of Media and Markets*, London: Curzon.

Moeran, B. (2009), 'The organization of creativity in Japanese advertising production', *Human Relations*, **62** (7), 963–85.

Moultrie, J. and A.R.R. Young (2009), 'Exploratory study of organizational creativity in creative organizations', *Creativity and Innovation Management*, **18** (4), 299–314.

Napier, N.K. and M. Nilsson (2006), 'The development of creative capabilities in and out of creative organizations: three case studies', *Creativity and Innovation Management*, **15** (3), 268–78.

Paige, R.C. and M.A. Littrel (2002), 'Craft retailers' criteria for success and associated business strategies', *Journal of Small Business Management*, **40** (4), 41–51.

Pentland, B.T. (1999), 'Building process theory with narrative: from description to explanation', *Academy of Management Review*, **24** (4), 711–24.

Powell, S. (2008), 'The management and consumption of organisational creativity', *Journal of Consumer Marketing*, **25** (3), 158–66.

Rae, D. (2004), 'Entrepreneurial learning: a practical model from the creative industries', *Education and Training*, **46** (8–9), 492–500.

Stam, E., J. De Jong and G. Marlet (2008), 'Creative industries in the Netherlands: structure, development, innovativeness and effects on urban growth', *Geografiska Annaler: Series B Human Geography*, **90** (2), 119–32.

Thompson, P., M. Jones and C. Warhurst (2007), 'From conception to consumption: creativity and the missing managerial link', *Journal of Organisational Behavior*, **28** (5), 625–40.

Throsby, D. (2001), *Economics and Culture, Melbourne*, Cambridge: Cambridge University Press.

Townley, B., N. Beech and A. McKinlay (2009), 'Managing in the creative industries: managing the motley crew', *Human Relations*, **62** (SI), 939–62.

Tschang, F.T. (2007), 'Balancing the tension between rationalization and creativity in the video games industry', *Organizational Science*, **18** (6), 989–1005.

Weick, K.E. and R.E. Quinn (1999), 'Organizational change and development', *Annual Review of Pscyhology*, **50**, 361–86.

Yin, R.K. (1984), *Case Study Research: Designs and Methods*, London: Sage.

APPENDIX: SEMI-STRUCTURED INTERVIEW INSTRUMENT

The semi-structured interview instrument is built on theoretical considerations and initial observations and unstructured interviews. The instrument depicts an overview of questions, which the research team used to guide interviews. If applicable, new insights were further explored during the interviews. The research team also asked questions about the connectedness between the concepts.

Questions on organizational development:

- Provide a list of initiatives to professionalize the organization, in light of the dual objective of economic and creative performance
- Consider issues such as differentiation (for example division of tasks), centralization (for example establishing hierarchy) and formalization (for example reporting structure)
- Provide a brief description of the initiative (that is, key events):
  - antecedents;
  - consequences;
  - people involved.
- Additional topics: financial system (invoices, legal, reports), account systems (pitches, reports), personnel and organization (task descriptions), service delivery system (concept design and production); board of directors, advisors, and so on.

Questions on team dynamics:

- Provide a list of key events during founders'/managers' meetings and provide a description
- Consider issues such as decision making, mutual understanding, nature of communications, frequency of meetings and agenda of meetings.
- Explain the antecedents, consequences and people involved for each key event
- Additional topics: quality of communication, distinction between management and creative meetings, and so on.

Questions on creative persons' behaviour:

- Provide a list of behaviours you observed. Which types of behaviour do you recognize? What are typical characteristics?
- Provide a description of typical behaviour (for example compliance, resistance, etc)

- Explain the antecedents and consequences for each type of behaviour

Questions on venture performance:

- What dimensions/indicators of venture performance do you consider?
  – Consider economic and creative performance.
- How does venture performance affect organizational development?
- How does venture performance affect team dynamics?
- How does venture performance affect individual behaviour?

8. The emergence of the serious game industry: to play or not to play

Patricia G. Greene*

INTRODUCTION

> How incredible would it be for a professor to say 'Pull out your laptops, load up '*Investhor: Lord of Wall Street*', and begin your midterm?' (Greene, 2009)

The study of emerging industries from a socio-economic platform has been conducted through an analysis of a variety of innovations in spaces such as cochlear implants (Van de Ven and Garud, 1989, 1993), American film (Mezias and Kuperman, 2001), windsurfing, skateboarding and snowboarding (Shah, 2000), and recycling in the United States (Lounsbury et al., 2003). These types of studies explore questions on topics such as the emergence of innovations, where and how individual businesses start and grow, how the markets are defined and developed, and what are the growth trajectories of the industries themselves. As a framework, this approach has the potential to help us better understand the phenomena of serious games, providing an industrial perspective to explore questions of definition, stakeholders, boundaries and markets.

Advancing our understanding of serious games as an industry also contributes to building the body of knowledge around creative economies. Serious games can be technically classified as interactive media, and the creative industry is built on: 'activities which have their origin in individual creativity, skill, and talent and which have the potential for wealth and job creation through the generation and exploitation of intellectual property' (DCMS, 2001, p. 5). Much of our interest in creative economies is driven by our need to better understand economic development, in particular postmodern economies built on the generation of knowledge. Games fit quite neatly into this approach as evidenced by the fact that activity in the serious games industry has increased to the point where numerous geographic areas are promoting these types of ventures in a systematic manner as an economic development strategy, with prime examples including the Research Triangle area, North Carolina, USA

(DFC Intelligence, 2009); Valenciennes, France (e.2009, 2008); and the West Midlands, UK (Future Making Serious Games Blog, 2007).

This chapter is grounded in an institutional approach to develop an emerging research agenda while investigating the overarching preliminary research question: what does the serious game industry actually look like? The chapter goes further to suggest practical lessons to be learned and shared with entrepreneurs who are interested in working in this area. To answer these questions I use a triangulation of methodologies, including secondary research through industry reports, academic articles and trade publications, observation at the 2009 Serious Games Summit of the annual Game Developers Conference and the 2010 Games Beyond Entertainment conference, and a set of expert interviews with various types of stakeholders. The chapter concludes with suggestions for a future research agenda.

WHAT IS A SERIOUS GAME?

The simple definition of a serious game must be expanded beyond that of a game used for education or training. On the one hand that definition is overly wide, while on the other it still does not capture the range of the opportunity. Even limiting the game technology to a digital base, the definition remains ambiguous. Sawyer and Smith (2008) recognized that a shared, consistent terminology would help the development of the field and compiled an extensive inventory of defining terms, including educational games, simulation, virtual reality, alternative purpose games, edutainment, digital game-based learning, immersive learning simulations, social impact games, persuasive games, games for change, games for good, and synthetic learning environments and Game based 'X'. About the same time, a report by Forrester Research drew upon an eLearning Guild categorization and applied the term 'immersive learning simulations' as an umbrella term to include interactive learning tools that are representative of a real-life situation, combine simulations, learning and competition, and use 'Serious Games' to engage employees (Schooley et al., 2008). This report went even further to suggest four types of simulations: software, role-playing, spreadsheet and immersive. These categories, while loosely bounded, give a sense of evolution to the industry. However, it is another Forrester definition that may be the most helpful, describing serious games as: 'the use of games or gaming dynamics not simply to entertain the player, but rather to inspire a particular action, effect some type of attitudinal change, or instill a particular lesson in the service of an organizational goal' (Keitt, 2009, p. 3). While one might question the explicitly organizational goal, given individual interest in and options for learning, it does put the focus on the outcomes. This is often considered to be a defining criterion for a serious game.

Another critical characteristic is the concept of game play, as that 'governed by rules that are both artificially constraining on participants yet at the same time productive of the pleasure of play' (Lastowka, 2009, p. 380). The dimensions of 'rules' and 'play' are two of the primary distinctions between simulations and serious games. Lastowka (2009) provides an insightful discussion of the definition and importance of 'game' and 'play', including the definition by the Dutch historian Huizinga:

> [A] free activity standing quite consciously outside 'ordinary' life as being 'not serious', but at the same time absorbing the player intensely and utterly. It is an activity connected with no material interest, and no profit can be gained by it. It proceeds within its own proper boundaries of time and space according to fixed rules and in an orderly manner. (Huizinga, 1938 as cited in Lastowka, 2009, p. 383)

While Huizinga's definition might be considered as the archetype of play, the explicit and significant message is that play is the opposite of productive work. This approach, even though questioned as to motivation and extent, has largely stayed with most discussions of play since Huizinga.

For games, however, even discussions of the earliest games recognize their dual role of entertaining and teaching – often actually teaching children survival skills (Shubik, 2009). However, the modern consideration of games for didactic purposes is generally mapped as growing from the war games of the Second World War (Verzat et al., 2009; Shubik, 2009; Cohen and Rhenman, 1961). Serious games can be further considered as those offered through the use of commercially available games, and those that are custom created for a unique learning need. The range of styles and scope is vast, but again the focus is upon the goal:

> Serious games when they started out were conceived as this [sic] completely non-commercial things . . . Today, serious games can be seen as a reconception of the old edutainment chestnut. Even commercial off-the-shelf games like *Half-Life* or *Civilization* can be repurposed for education, if creatively applied the basic concept of a serious game . . . must be the use of game hardware and software as applications for life, rather than merely as diversions in and of themselves. Within that scope lies limitless practical potential to use video games for the betterment of the individual, yet much depends on the creativity and motivation of the end user, to make that crucial MacGuyveresque shift of perspective. Not everything can be listed on the box, and a tool can only do so much on its own. (Waugh, 2008)

THEORETICAL FRAMEWORK: EMERGING INDUSTRIES

The social sciences offer a selection of theoretical foundations from which to explore organizational questions at a variety of levels, including individual businesses and industries (Swedberg, 2001–02). Swedberg's useage of Emile Durkheim's 'collective effervescence' in his description of innovation as 'when the intensity of social interaction reaches such a pitch that it practically boils over' seems particularly apt for a consideration of serious games (Durkheim, 1912 in Swedberg, 2001–02, p. 28).

Much of the traditional discussion on industries is anchored by the industrial economic definition of industry as: 'the group of firms producing products that are close substitutes for each other' (Porter, 1980, p. 5). This definition works well for more mature industry sectors, but is less helpful when investigating the innovations for which the markets and producers of products are still emerging and the 'close substitutions' are less obvious. Therefore, in this chapter I use the expansion of the concept of industry as introduced by Van de Ven and Garud (1989). Under this approach, the new industry sector is recognized as an emerging system: 'consisting of the key firms and actors that govern, integrate and perform all of the functions required to transform a technological innovation into a commercially viable line of products or services delivered to customers' (Van de Ven and Garud, 1989, p. 206). This use of this approach is further supported by the work of Mezias and Kuperman (2001) when they describe 'one way of conceptualizing the community of relevance might be in terms of populations of organizations that constitute the value chain' (p. 209). This approach is particularly relevant to the consideration of a creative industry in recognizing what aspects are needed for launch, growth and eventual sustainability of the industry. In order to provide a foundation for investigating these aspects, this chapter focuses upon understanding the answers to four basic questions:

1. Where do serious game innovations come from?
2. Where do the businesses come from?
3. Who is in the market for serious games?
4. What is the growth trajectory of the industry?

METHODOLOGY

Methodology is the means of thinking, studying and learning about organizational realities (Strauss and Corbin, 1998), and methodological choices are driven by the form and focus of the study (Van Maanen, 1979). This chapter is focused upon learning more about the existing nature of the serious game industry in order to better design and contribute to the emerging research agenda. As such, the specific methods used are qualitative techniques, in the Van Maanen tradition of 'an array of interpretative techniques which seek to describe, decode, translate and otherwise come to terms with the meaning, not the frequency' (Van Maanen, 1983). The approach further builds on Daft's suggestion that: 'The research craft is enhanced by respect for error and surprise, storytelling, research poetry, emotion, common sense, firsthand learning, and research colleagues' (Daft, 1983, p. 544). While the chapter may not be 'research poetry', collecting the data was filled with surprise, and some error, firsthand learning, and benefited from the generosity of research colleagues. The intended result is one of commonsense storytelling. To be precise, this chapter is built upon data collection through a variety of means, including content analysis of industry and media materials, observations at industry events, and a series of semi-structured interviews over the space of 18 months.

Given that the industry is still emerging, the source of industry data is rather limited, with sources in this category mostly consisting of reports that were actually developed outside the industry; but for the industry, including those by Forrester Research, websites of organizations such as the Entertainment Software Association and the Serious Games Institute, conference proceedings such as the Interservice/Industry Training, Simulation, and Education Conference, and magazines on a variety of topics, such as *Training Magazine, Defense Horizons* and *Simulation and Gaming.*

I attended and observed at two industry conferences. First, the Serious Games Summit of the annual Game Developers Conference (GDC). This conference was held on 23–24 March 2009 in San Francisco, California. This event is considered the primary annual gathering for all types of game professionals, including designers, programmers and publishers. The Serious Games Summit is the segment of the GDC devoted to the educational and training markets. The second conference was the Games Beyond Entertainment conference held in Boston, Massachusetts on 24–27 May 2010. This conference is a new expansion of the former Games for Health conference and is also a gathering for a wide range of game professionals. In this conference all discussion is connected to some type of serious games. These conferences were particularly useful not only for the content presented, but also as a source of expert interviews.

A series of semi-structured interviews with stakeholders in the field was designed to expand upon the product, practice and process of serious gaming in order to better delineate a research agenda. These interviews began in a separate research project focused upon virtual and augmented realities, and subsequently led me to the topic of serious games. The interviewees were first identified through a convenience sample and this ultimately became a snowball approach as each person suggested who else might be helpful. (Please see the Appendix for a list of interviewees.) Given the early stage of the research agenda, the qualitative data from the interviews were combined with the information from the other sources and used to inform the description of the industry and to support suggestions of practical tips for entrepreneurs as well as to guide future research.

FINDINGS AND DISCUSSION: WHAT HAVE WE LEARNED TO DATE?

Overview: What is the Serious Game Industry?

Industry data present striking numbers as far as the size and the growth of activity are concerned. The Entertainment Software Association (ESA) (www.theesa.com/gamesindailylife/education/asp) provides a useful place to start:

- US computer and video game software sales grew 22.9 per cent in 2008 to $11.7 billion.
- 68 per cent of American households play computer or video games.
- The average game player is 35 years old and has been playing games for 12 years.
- 40 per cent of all game players are women.

Building on the ESA data, a number of other sources help further flesh out the picture of the game industry. From Gamer Generation (http://www.sharenator.com/Gamer_Generation/) we learn that if you combine the software and hardware, consumers spend $258 billion per year on computer games and game systems and that 800 million people worldwide are regular players. In their book, *Total Engagement* (2009), Reeves and Read provide the somewhat unexpected statistic that 26 per cent of game players are older than 50. This is particularly relevant in helping us to think beyond the stereotype of gamers as teenagers, or at the most young adults. Reeves and Read (2009) further provide the growth statistic that the game software industry has posted an annual growth rate of 17 per cent with 5 per cent annual employment since 2003.

However, the numbers above are for the full computer game industry. The interest for this chapter is in the subset of the serious game industry, and that portion is tricky to parse out of the overall statistics. What is available, however, provides a compelling reason to dig deeper:

- In 2007 the serious game market was estimated at $400 million (Masie, 2007).
- One estimate was that in 2007 there were 70 serious game companies in the US (www.wired.com/gamelife/2007).
- The US government has evaluated more than 16 educational technology-based products.
- The Apply Group estimates that approximately 20 per cent of Global Fortune 500 companies will have adopted gaming for learning purposes by 2012.
- Four million people played the United Nations World Food Programme game, *Food Force*, in the game's first year.
- The US Army created its own video group unit with the intent of investing up to $50 million for game training systems (www.theesa. com/gamesindailylife/education/asp).

Accepting that there is a significant amount of size, scale, and activity in the area of serious games, I now turn to the four research questions driving the remainder of the chapter.

Where do the Innovations Come From?

The first question explored in this preliminary study considers the emergence of innovations that ground the industry. We can track sources of innovations from the starting point of the triggers for the increased growth of the serious game industry. Sawyer and Smith (2008) attribute it to changes in the audience, the technology, Web 2.0, and increased interest from academics regarding theories of learning and cognition. In a quite parallel manner, Smith (2008) summarizes the forces as personal, technology, social and financial. For the purposes of this chapter, I build on the themes from the existing data and the interviews conducted, and suggest that the categories can be summarized into three sources of innovation: educational, technological and business models. These categories are not linear or hierarchical; indeed there is more of a chicken-and-egg relationship, especially between the educational and the technological categories.

Educational innovations

Much has been written in the last few years on the changing nature of how generations learn and, equally importantly, how they want to work (Tapscott, 1998, 2009; Palfrey and Gasser, 2008; Gee, 2007; Beck and

Wade, 2004; Pink, 2005; Edery and Mollick, 2009; Reeves and Read, 2009). There is certainly increased attention paid throughout academia to theories of learning and cognition. As we conceptualize more about how we best learn particular types of content and skills, we are more confident in adopting a greater variety of pedagogies. (While the term 'pedagogy' has historically referred to the education of children, increasingly the more common usage includes the educational approach to almost any audience.) Overall, the approach is that we understand our brains better and therefore need new ways to teach and learn.

The research changing the way we think of our brains informs part of the innovations in this area. However, the other innovation entering the classrooms is not new in its relation to learning, but is certainly newer in its acceptance into those classrooms. This involves the idea of combining instructional design use with game mechanics for higher retention of learning. As John Geiger describes it, 'The play, the interaction, the rules, the value system in the games' combines with the other needed parts of the trajectory, 'the pedagogy, the instruction, and making sure the learning outcome is met' (Geiger, 2010). Not all are in favour of this approach. The debate about the effect of computer games on children continues and has a great impact on the consideration of games for educational purposes. The positive side includes the ability of the games to intrinsically motivate learners while the negative side generally focuses upon the perceived link between violent video games and aggressive behaviour (Foster and Mishra, 2009). However, from a post-secondary perspective, students arrive in university classes having already grown up using digital media for entertainment, learning, communicating and shopping (Tapscott, 1998). The challenge is to think about education in a manner that engages students immersed in that digital lifestyle (Tapscott, 2009; Palfrey and Gasser, 2008).

People of all types and ages can be students, and in a world in which people increasingly rely on training and development for professional advancement, this becomes another prompt for innovation. The training and development market in the US was $134.39 billion in 2007 with one-third of the programmes based on e-learning and a notable increase in using gaming approaches (ASTD, 2008). As gamers reach the classrooms of higher education and the workplaces beyond, their learning approaches are different than previous generations. 'Simulations are growing in importance because they address the radically different needs of next-generation employees' (Schooley et al., 2008). The projection is that the trend toward gaming as educational and business tools will continue to grow as people who grew up as gamers become the decision-makers regarding approaches toward education and learning, as well as the resource allocation to support those approaches.

Technological innovations

From the technological approach, advances in computing and visualization techniques, gaming platforms and newer 'middleware' (Jarvis, 2010)
engines, as well as the rise of mobile functions, all contribute to opening up
markets for this industry. These types of technological innovations lower
the cost of producing the games while also raising the attractiveness and
appeal of the games, resulting in the potential for existing markets to grow
and new markets to open. At the same time, changes in and limitations of
the technologies also drive related changes in other aspects of the industry:

> Opportunities are huge because the demand is there. We have to look at such
> things as how the iPad is going to change interaction, in general and in the
> classroom. There are finally budgets for building tools. Plus, all the mechanics
> of social networking will play a huge part. These games have broken all the
> gender and age barriers. Before it was only because of the gamers, now it has
> opened the doors for games all over the place with mobile and location aware
> experiences. (Geiger, 2010)

Changes in technology also support a serious game environment.
Decreased cost and increased availability of the technologies support the
development of increasingly sophisticated gaming experiences. There is
an accompanying rise in the understanding of how to use and adapt commercially available games for teaching and training purposes. Examples
of this include using the *The Sims Open for Business* to teach the creation
of entrepreneurial culture (Greene and Brush, 2009) and *SimCity* for civil
engineering and government (Van Eck, 2006). Others include *Civilization*,
CSI, and *RollerCoaster Tycoon* for teaching history, forensics and physics,
respectively. Once considered 'slightly eccentric' or the domain of 'specialist companies', serious games are now becoming much more mainstream,
a trend attributed back to that 'increasingly sophisticated and affordable
technology' (Damon, 2009).

Another consideration of the game is the delivery system, which then
feeds into the distribution channel. While some games are played online,
others are played through gaming systems such as the Xbox, PlayStation3,
Wii, and so on. The role of mobile applications is another consideration
with iPhone applications leading the charge, but other types of opportunities are emerging (Tori, 2008; Greene, 2009), including those related to
virtual worlds:

> *Second Life* is one such virtual environment development platform. Its immer-
> sion, ease of use, wide availability and low barrier to entry are essential quali-
> ties that make it an excellent choice for use in education. Many educators have
> already made impressive contributions by using *Second Life* in their courses
> and projects. (Simteach, 2006, in Mason and Moutahir, 2009, p. 2)

However there are variations within each, as well. A person or organization wanting to use a game for learning purposes can buy an existing commercial game off the shelf (COTS), either using it as designed, or modifying when necessary and possible. An organization may also create its own, working in-house or working with a custom developer (Schooley et al., 2008). For instance, a commercial game may be used, but rather than playing the actual game, the commercial video game may be used as the development platform. For instance, Rizwan-uddin (2009) discusses using *Unreal Tournament* for the 'developer platform'. He sees that a 'synergistic fit between the needs of the nuclear industry and built-in features in computer games make them specifically suitable to educate and train personnel destined for work at nuclear power plants' (Xi et al., 2009, p. 1). Some game editor software companies encourage such use, others do not. In the case of nuclear engineering, when a virtual model of the lab was needed, the cost was $60 for the game and 20 hours of graduate assistant time (priceless) (Rizwan-uddin, 2009). This approach can be very beneficial given that every computer game requires a game engine; however, few serious game companies have their own actual game engine. Indeed, most still survive on using Flash, an easy-to-program web application made by Adobe. Flash is the most commonly used application of serious games, although serious games are not even a fraction of its usage (Greene, 2009).

The rise of social networking and an emphasis on Web 2.0 and collaboration also contribute to advancing the serious game industry in almost a fractal manner, with the social networking experience grounding the experience inside the game and inside the industry: 'The web of relationships between players – competitive, cooperative, and collegial – sustains the computer game industry, no less than the latest 3D engine, facial animation algorithm, or high-speed graphics card' (Herz and Macedonia, 2002 in Smith, 2008, p. 14). Social games are not only attracting new markets of players, they are also gathering up most of the venture capital in the overall gaming area (Sheffield, 2010). The increased importance of social connections draws our attention to other gaming dimensions as well. Smith (2008) emphasizes the global nature of these communities, with time as the limiting factor, not geography. While some of the innovations supporting these changes are the technological approaches allowing the social interaction, others might be considered as based upon business models as well.

Business model innovations
The evolution of business models is one of the more fascinating areas of discussion, both at the industry conferences and from the interviews.

Lewis (2010) describes the present business model of the commercial gaming industry as:

> more focused on making a game and then selling millions of copies if it does well, and that's obviously a better business model than ours which is just like painters. Someone calls to have us paint their house, and once it's done there's nothing we can do with that but point it out to others and say, hey we did a nice job and hope they want us to paint their houses as well.

Lewis describes it as a 'relentless business structure'. Lewis further commented that: 'We make custom stuff all the time – no shelf products. The business model is based on getting enough work in the door to support us in what we do. We're kind of like sharks – we've just got to keep swimming' (Lewis, 2010).

However, there have been various changes in the business model in the past few years. This is affirmed by Koster when he describes predicting the rise of the Indie game community on the web in 2006 and recognizing the drastic changes this would make in the industry. At that time Koster predicted that the giant budget game on a disc was going to be a casualty. Part of this evolution of the business model may also be seen as a result of changes in the industry markets. The funding of serious games is also changing. Koster (2010) posits that corporate players have to be in the market in order for serious games to get funding, suggesting that: 'Large media is finally starting to move into social games, corporations will follow.'

Several corporations tested the gaming area through large-scale alternative-reality games (ARG) which blended activities in the physical and digital worlds. Early examples such as World Without Oil (http://www.worldwithoutoil.org/) and Evoke (http://www.gamesetwatch. com/2010/02/evoke_arg_looks_to_change_the.php) were designed to address global-scale challenges, and sponsored by corporations through community outreach. While Jarvis (2010) recognizes the involvement of 'cause' or 'charity' games by describing a whole category of 'influencers', Koster reports that there is a serious debate as to whether or not these even constitute a serious game. These games include things like tying coral reef preservation to a game about saving coral reefs. Others are perceived as using the approach as a marketing hook, with micro-transactions as a revenue model, and some portion of the proceeds subsequently donated to 'the cause'. Koster (2010) states that: 'Games and advocacy and propaganda have been around for a long time.'

Grant funding is increasingly a part of the business model, particularly for games designed to influence (Koster, 2010; Greene, 2009). The John D. and Katherine T. MacArthur Foundation funded an immersive game, *Participatory Chinatown*, in order to advance the planning process for Boston's Chinatown. The project collaborators included the Massachusetts serious game company, Muzzy Lane, the Metropolitan Area Planning Council, the Asian Community Development Corporation and Emerson College (http://www.participatorychinatown.org; Jarvis, 2010). Another example can be seen in the US NIH (National Institute for Health) providing US$3.4 million for a dental health game (http://www.healthgamers.com/2009/research-theory/nih-funds-34m-dental-health-game/). Grant funding also is becoming more prevalent in the training field. Also, while militaries around the world have been early adopters, other approaches include *Triage Trainer*, a game created by TruSim to train about the prioritization of medical care during crises. The game is based on an earlier project funded by the UK's Ministry of Defence (http://gamefwd.org/index.php?option=com_content&view=article&id=85:triage-trainer-game-developed-for-emergency-responders&catid=51:serious-games&Itemid=51). Each of these examples represent a particular game. The Robert Wood Johnson Foundation went even further to establish its Pioneer Portfolio as a means of investing in games for health (www.rwjf.org.pioneer), and is a primary supporter of the annual conference Games for Health.

While in general the business models are still primarily based on business-to-business (B2B) transactions (Sawyer, 2010), companies are increasingly experimenting with other models. Startup.com's revenue model for *8D World*, an English language training game for children, is targeted to the consumer market. This company follows the casual game practice of providing 60 days free usage, followed by the choice between continuing on at a minimal level for free, or upgrading to a premium user for a monthly fee. Micro-transaction activities are also available throughout the game (Goodman, 2010).

Finally, at the emerging extreme end of the business model is the suggested application of serious games actually to perform the work of the organization (Reeves and Read, 2010). This would represent the extreme of usage: not just games to learn, but games to accomplish specific work tasks such as scheduling or inventory control. In these cases the business model would be based upon internal productivity advances versus specific revenue increases. This approach is a work in progress.

Where do the Businesses Come From?

Where are the companies within the industry coming from? Businesses are entering the industry from a variety of places. New small businesses are sometimes started as extensions of businesses in related fields; for example John Geiger founded Tracer Media as a producer of multimedia and interactive projects, largely focusing on converting textbooks into interactive experiences. Tracer grew into the serious game segment as an outcome of where it saw the demand for its type of work. Similarly, Richard Lewis of Chedd-Angier-Lewis describes his company as dedicated to increasing the interactivity of the museum exhibit, with the gaming aspect one tool it uses to increase user engagement. Differently, Raph Koster entered from more of a technology space, founding Metaplace to launch a tool suite that would allow anyone to create a virtual world.

Given that innovations are coming from a variety of sources, and due to a variety of innovations, it is not surprising that there is a corresponding variety of types of businesses participating in the industry. After all, games become serious in a variety of ways. Keitt (2009) categorizes the producers as: (1) traditional video game companies; (2) serious game vendors; (3) large software producers such as IBM and Microsoft; and (4) multimedia companies who do serious games as a part of their business.

The training industry has also been a source of some of the serious games, most often developing games for large clients. For instance, Games2Train.com, founded by Marc Prensky, includes among its clients American Express, Bank of America, Charles Schwab & Co., Estée Lauder Companies, Inc., IBM, JP Morgan Chase & Co., Nokia Corporation, and Pfizer Inc. (ESA, 2009). The ESA projected that by 2010 20 per cent of Global Fortune 500 companies would be using serious games for training and development (ESA, 2009). Other companies have largely focused upon military applications.

Some serious games are coming from university centres such as *Environmental Detectives* by the Education Arcade; *Hazmat* by the Entertainment Technology Center at Carnegie Mellon University; *River City* by Professor Chris Dede, the Harvard Graduate School of Education and George Mason University (Van Eck, 2006). These games might be considered as emerging from technology transfer or commercialization approaches in that they are based upon the research of the professors and then moved into the commercial market.

Finally, we should recognize that for-profit serious game companies (or divisions of larger companies) are not the only organizations that have emerged as part of this industry. The Serious Game Institute (SGI) is part of an economic development effort in the West Midlands of the UK. Games for Health is part of the Robert Wood Johnson approach. Organizations are also emerging through public–private partnerships to develop serious games, such as 'Entertainment Arts (EA) one of the largest game-development companies partnering with the National Endowment for Science, Technology and the Arts (NESTA)' in the UK (Van Eck, 2006, p. 7).

Who is in the Market for Serious Games?

The question of market for serious games is one of primary concern to those in the industry, with descriptions ranging from 'anyone who wants to learn anything' (Greene, 2009), to tightly focused industry targets. In other words, the markets for serious games can best be defined as emerging, and doing so in a broad manner. A variety of lists and taxonomies have already been suggested to summarize market demand, or potential demand (Table 8.1) (Sawyer and Smith, 2008; Smith, 2008; Keitt and Jackson, 2008). These lists vary to some degree, largely around the broadness of the categories; however, they are unanimous in reporting the military and defence, education and healthcare as prime markets for these games. While these lists can be reclassified in a number of ways in order to answer different sets of questions, it is striking that they are all positioned at the organizational level, rather than targeting the consumer directly. In fact, even more notably, most of the market-makers inside these categories are governmental and, indeed, represent governments in a number of countries around the world.

Another way to consider the markets is less about the industrial sector of the user and more focused upon the usage of the serious games. Jarvis (2010) describes the primary use categories as: (1) academic, for use in schools at all levels; (2) influencers, used to promote causes or practices; and (3) training, those used within organizations for types of professional development and job training. However, for these categories as well, the lines become blurred. As seen above, the examples of the use of serious games for learning, education, and training are wide-ranging. Loyalist College in Canada uses the virtual world *Second Life* as a site for simulating border officer training (www.discussions@nasaga.org). Hilton Garden Inns uses a PlayStation game to train staff in customer service (Kervella, 2009). The Federation of American Scientists developed a 'first-person shooter' genre game to teach cellular biology (Amarelo, 2009). And in one of the largest examples (for budget and usage), the US Army developed *America's Army* to be accessible on a number of platforms to inform, teach and ultimately recruit (www.America's Army.com).

What is the Growth Trajectory of the Industry?

The impetus of the innovations and the size and scope of the markets each suggest an upward curve for the industry. Koster (2010) provided an extremely helpful overview of his perception of the growth trajectory of the industry. As mentioned previously, he believes there is a hierarchical participation model needed to foster industry growth. He suggests that

Table 8.1   Summary of market demand and sites of game usage

Smith (2008)	Sawyer and Smith (2008)	Keitt and Jackson (2008)
Military	Defence	Military
Education	Education	Education
Emergency Management	See Government & NGO below	Emergency Services & Healthcare
Architecture		
Civil & Civil Planning		
Corporate Training		
Health Care	Healthcare (also included in Government & NGO below)	See above
Politics		
Religion		
Movies & Television		
Scientific Visualization & Analysis		
Sports		
Exploration		
Law		
	Government & NGO (defined as Public Health Education & Mass Casualty Response Marketing & Communication (largely advertising and opinion research)	
	Corporate Industry	Business

corporate players have to be in the market in order for serious games to get funding (Koster, 2010), and offers several examples of this happening around the world:

- the purchase of Playfish (developer of social games, founded in 2007) by Electronic Arts in 2009;
- Deutsche Telecom launching games through a contract with a game developer (http://www.deutschetelekom.com/dtag/cms/content/dt/en/744592); and

- two UK television channels (Channel 4 and the BBC) deploying games from the web (http://www.bbc.co.uk/schools/games).

Koster (2010) notes that when the serious game and the entertainment industry 'marry', one outcome is increased attention and resources dedicated to production value. This is when the serious money comes into play. Examples of these are the Bayer glucose meter Nintendo game and the Pokemon pedometer. These types of partnerships also helped lead to the next step, the involvement of grant money and pressure from game industry. 'Things like *Guitar Hero*, Wii, and Brain Training. *Guitar Hero* demonstrated that you could do a serious game about music education in a way that the music educators had never managed to do. We started seeing an interesting meld of gameplay and educational or serious components, including *Darfur is Dying* and the *Peacemaker Project'* (Koster, 2010). Koster stills sees the mainstream industry as lagging behind the military and the healthcare industry, recognizing earlier games such as *Full Spectrum Warrior*, *America's Army* and medical simulation groups, driven largely by the pediatric area, with a prime example being Steven Spielberg's Starlight Starbright Foundation. Geiger convincingly sums up the future:

> Growing up and getting serious about what we are doing is a challenge. There is going to be pretty explosive growth because everyone is diving into it but there is no infrastructure. There are tech people making educational games but they have no business background and vice versa for the educators. The big challenge is surviving the growth without coming out in an embarrassing state. There is no solid research and no solid metrics on success. We are striving for rubrics for evaluation but we have no standardization on technology or instruction. A year back there was no threat for being disorganized because there wasn't that much demand. Now there is. (Geiger, 2010)

PRACTICAL IMPLICATIONS AND CHALLENGES FOR ENTREPRENEURS

The serious game industry as part of the creative industries movement is one of great potential. The rise of these businesses has been tied to major global demographic, technological, economic and social trends. However, if broken up into entrepreneurial opportunities and resources, challenges can be delineated for emerging businesses as well as the industry:

1. Opportunities span multiple markets, including (but not necessarily limited to) primary and secondary school systems, universities,

military forces, governments at various levels, and large and small businesses. However, often the buyer is not sure of what they need or want or how they will benefit (Keitt and Jackson, 2008). Creating a market is always more difficult and more expensive than meeting a market. Entrepreneurs need to understand a consultative sales model, and be prepared for a long sales cycle (Greene, 2009).

2. Several of those interviewed talked of the difficulty in selling to a school district. Challenges included not only the procurement process and timetable, but also the challenge of fitting into a prescribed curriculum. Keitt (2009) quotes Impact Games co-founder Asi Burak: 'the K through 12 market is slow moving, hard to penetrate, and poorly funded, with all material needing to be tied to state curriculum'.

3. 'Probably the biggest thing holding back serious games is we don't have a marketplace where different players can connect, Bates says.' (www.gamasutra.com. SGS: Inside the Army Game. Jill Duffy, Oct 31, 2006).

4. The entrepreneurial team needs to include someone who understands the educational content and process, or be able to identify alternative ways of reaching the market.

5. Margins are generally thin on custom projects (Kaitt, 2009) and often do not include large enough budgets for marketing (Greene, 2009).

FUTURE RESEARCH

A research agenda is needed to understand better the size, scope and structure of the serious game industry in order to inform theory, practice and policy at both the micro and macro levels. This chapter begins to lay the groundwork through an institutional analysis focusing on innovations, businesses and markets. The proposed research agenda has three related prongs: (1) conduct an inventory of serious game companies and related organizations in order best to understand who is in the industry; (2) complete the theoretical analysis using the institutional framework, particularly moving into the questions of institutional legitimacy; and (3) continue the translation of findings into tools useful for entrepreneurs and entrepreneurship educators. The completion of each of these should advance our understanding of the serious game industry and how it fits into a creative industry economic strategy.

The agenda described above is necessary for knowing the industry and advancing our understanding of creative economies and their potential for economic development. However, there is an even larger potential contribution to be made through the study of the serious game industry as part of a creative economy, and this approach would consider more deeply what it means actually to live in a knowledge economy. How deep might the use of serious games go in our lives? Can games (and an emphasis on fun) have an actual impact on the way individuals and organizations work internally as well as together? What is the impact of the digital divide on the advancement of such games (and therefore a knowledge economy)? Future research should not only focus on the 'what is', but also most certainly push to propose new innovations and experiments in this area.

NOTE

* With special thanks to Babson College, MA, USA graduate student, Teague Hopkins, for his help in conducting a set of stakeholder interviews.

REFERENCES

Amarelo, M. (2009), 'Immune attack sheds light on the molecular world: teen video gamers acquire immunity', Federation of American Scientists, News, accessed at www.fas.org/press/news/2009/dec_immuneattack.html.

American Society for Training and Development (ASTD) (2008), 'State of the industry report', accessed at www.astd.org/ASTD/aboutus/trainingIndustry-FAQ.htm.

Beck, J.C. and Mitchell Wade (2004), *Got Game*, Boston, MA: Harvard Business School Press.

Cohen, K. and E. Rhenman (1961), 'The role of management games in education and research', *Management Science*, **7** (2), 131–66.

Daft, R.L. (1983), 'Learning the craft of organizational research', *Academy of Management Review*, **8** (4), 539–46.

Damon, N. (2009), 'Serious training games: let the games begin', *Personnel Today*, accessed at www.personneltoday.com/articles/2009/02/09/49335/serious-training-games-let-the-games-begin.html.

Department for Culture, Media and Sport (DCMS) (2001), 'Creative industries mapping document', London: DCMS.

DFC Intelligence (2009), 'DFC Industry Report: Game development at Research Triangle Park', accessed at www.trianglegameconference.com/news/view/91153-DFC-Industry-Report-Game-Development-at-Research-Triangle-Park.

Durkheim, E. (1965 [1912]), *Elementary Forms of Religious Life*, New York: Free Press.

e.2009 (2008), 'e-creators', November, accessed at www.e-virtuoses.net/uk/index.php.

Edery, David and Ethan Mollick (2009), *Changing the Game: How Video Games are Transforming the Future of Business*, Upper Saddle River, NJ: FT Press.

Entertainment Software Association (ESA) (2009), 'Video games and the workplace', accessed at www.theesa.com/gamesindailylife/workplace.asp.

Foster, Aroutis and Punya Mishra (2009), 'Games, claims, genres and learning', in Richard D. Ferdig (ed.), *Handbook of Research on Effective Electronic Gaming in Education*, New York: Information Science Reference, pp. 33–50.

Future Making Serious Games Blog (2007), blog assessed at http://futuremaking-seriousgames.blogspot.com/2007/02/west-midlands-uk-serious-about-games.html.

Gee, James Paul (2007), *What Video Games Have to Teach Us About Learning and Literacy*, New York: Palgrave Macmillan.

Geiger, J. (2010), personal interview.

Goodman (2010), conference presentation, Games Beyond Entertainment, Boston, MA.

Greene, P.G. and C.G. Brush (2009), 'Entrepreneurial influence on culture in emerging organizations', presentation to USE conference, Denmark.

Greene, S.G. (2009), personal interview.

Herz, J. and M. Macedonia (2002), 'Computer games and the military: two views, *Defense Horizons*, **11**, accessed at www.neu.edu/inss/DefHor/DH11/DH11.htm.

Huizinga, J. (1938), *Homo Ludens: A Study of the Play Element in Culture*, Boston, MA: Beacon.

Jarvis, R. (2010), conference presentation, Games beyond Entertainment, Boston, MA.

Keitt, T.J. (2009), 'Demand insights: serious games break through', 11 March, Forrester Research Inc.

Keitt, T.J. and P. Jackson (2008), 'It's time to take games seriously', 19 August, Forrester Research Inc.

Kervella, D. (2009), 'Hilton ultimate team play for the PSP', presentation at Game Developers Conference, Serious Games Summit, 23 March, San Francisco, CA.

Koster, R. (2010), personal interview.

Lastowka, G. (2009), 'Rules of play', *Games and Culture: A Journal of Interactive Media*, **4** (4), 379–95.

Lewis, R. (2010), personal interview.

Lounsbury, M., M. Ventresca and P.M. Hirsch (2003), 'Social movements, field frames and industry emergence: a cultural-political perspective on US recycling', *Socio-Economic Review*, **1**, 71–104.

Masie, J. (2007), 'Business and games', accessed at www.businessandgames.com/blog/2007.

Mason, H. and M. Moutahir (2009), 'Multidisciplinary experiential education in *Second Life*: a global approach', Johnson and Wales University working paper.

Mezias, S.J. and J.C. Kuperman (2001), 'The community dynamics of entrepreneurship: the birth of the American film industry, 1895–1929', *Journal of Business Venturing*, **16** (3), 209–33.

Palfrey, John and Urs Gasser (2008), *Born Digital: Understanding the First Generation of Digital Natives*, New York: Basic Books.

Pink, Daniel H. (2005), *A Whole New Mind*, New York: Penguin Group.

Porter, M. (1980), *Competitive Strategy: Techniques for Analyzing Industries and Competitors*, New York: Free Press.

Reeves, Byron and Leighton Read (2009), *Total Engagement: Using Games and Virtual Worlds to Change the Way People Work and Businesses Compete*, Boston, MA: Harvard Business School Publishing.

Rizwan-uddin (2009), personal interview, University of Illinois at Urbana-Champaign, USA.

Sawyer, B. (2010), 'The state of serious games and where it goes next . . .' presentation at Serious Games Day Conference, 24 May, Boston, MA.

Sawyer, B. and P. Smith (2008), 'Serious game taxonomy', conference presentation, Game Developers Conference, Serious Games Summit, 19 February, San Francisco, CA.

Schooley, C., C. Moore, T. Schadler and S. Catino (2008), 'For stickier learning, try a dose of serious gaming', 19 September, Forrester Research Inc.

Shah, S.K. (2000), 'Sources and patterns of innovation in consumer products field: innovations in sporting equipment', MIT Sloan School of Management working paper 4105, Cambridge, MA.

Shaw, S.K. (2000), 'Sources and patterns of innovation in consumer products filed: innovations in sporting equipment', MIT Sloan School of Management working paper 4105, Cambridge, MA.

Sheffield, B. (2010), 'Players vs users', *Game Developer*, June/July, 2.

Shubik, M. (2009), 'It is not just a game!' *Simulation and Gaming*, **40** (5), 587–601.

Simteach (2006), 'Simteach Second Life Education Wiki', accessed August 2006 at http://simteach.com/wiki/index.php?title=Second_Life_Education_Wike.

Smith, R. (2008), 'Game impact theory: the five forces that are driving the adoption of game technologies within multiple established industries', proceedings of the 2008 Interservice/Industry Training, Simulation, and Education Conference, Orlando, FL.

Strauss, A. and Juliet Corbin (1998), *Basics of Qualitative Research Techniques and Procedures for Developing Grounded Theory* 2nd edn, London: Sage Publications.

Swedberg, R. (2011–02), 'The social science view of entrepreneurship: introduction and practical applications', ESBRI; reprinted from Richard Swedberd (ed.), *Entrepreneurship: The Social Science View*, Oxford: Oxford University Press, pp. 7–44.

Tapscott, Don (1998), *Growing Up Digital*, New York: McGraw Hill.

Tapscott, Don (2009), *Grown Up Digital*, New York: McGraw Hill.

Tori, Romero (2008), personal interview, Centro Universitario Senac, Sao Paulo, Brazil.

Van de Ven, A.H. and R. Garud (1989), 'A framework for understanding the emergence of new industries', *Research on Technological Innovation, Management and Policy*, **4**, 195–225.

Van de Ven, A.H. and R. Garud (1993), 'Innovation and industry development: the case of cochlear implants', *Research on Technological Innovation, Management and Policy*, **5**, 1–46.

Van Eck, R. (2006), 'Digital game-based learning: it's not just the digital natives who are restless . . .', *EDUCAUSE Review*, **41** (2), 16–30.

Van Maanen, J. (1979), 'Reclaiming qualitative methods for organizational research: a preface', *Administrative Science Quarterly*, **24** (4), 520–26.

Van Maanen, John (ed.) (1983), *Qualitative Methodology*, Beverly Hills, CA: Sage Publications.

Verzat, C., J. Byrne and A. Fayolle (2009), 'Tangling with spaghetti: pedagogical lessons from games', *Academy of Management Learning and Education*, **8** (3), 356–69.

Waugh, E. (2008), 'Sawyer, Smith on serious gaming for life', 18 February, Serious Game Summit.

Xi, C., M. Khasawney, Rizwan-uddin (2009), 'Innovative training tools for improved human performance', presentation to the ANS/ENS CONTE – the Conference on Nuclear Training and Education, Florida.

APPENDIX: INTERVIEWEES

Individual respondent	Organization
John Geiger	Tracer Media
Greene, Shaun	Muzzy Lane
Koster, Raph	Metaplace
Lewis, Richard	Chedd-Angier-Lewis
Rizwan-uddin	University of Illinois – Champaign/Urban

9. Coping with the cutting edge: enterprise orientations and the creative challenges of start-up in the fashion design sector in New Zealand

Colleen Mills

INTRODUCTION

Creative industries are an important economic focus in many countries, but particularly in New Zealand where the last ten years have seen several creative sectors move from the fringes to become viable economic forces. This is particularly true for the film and the fashion industries. Both recently burst into the international limelight and their subsequent successes have contributed significantly to a broadening of New Zealand's economic profile. The prominence of these sectors has both led to and been facilitated by, at least in part, the fifth Labour government's recognition of the potential of the creative sector to be a significant contributor 'to the future economic growth and global positioning of the country' (de Bruin, 2005, p. 143). The recent and rapid rise to prominence of such creative industries is not mirrored in the literature on creative industries. Scant attention has been paid to exploring the experience of creative start-up, particularly in the vibrant and fiercely competitive New Zealand designer fashion industry (DFI). Successful enterprises in this industry sector represent the tip of a growing iceberg of enterprises that operate on a 'knife edge of risk' (Gregg, 2003, p. 13), yet they are already making a significant contribution to the country's gross domestic product (GDP). We need to know more about the genesis and process of business consolidation of these enterprises if we are to develop supportive policy and training opportunities to maximize their chances of survival and fully realize their potential to contribute to the nation's economy.

This chapter presents findings from a study that it is responding to the paucity of studies on creative business start-up in New Zealand by examining new fashion designers' stories of how they have managed to navigate this knife-edge. After briefly reviewing the scant DFI literature and relevant literature on start-up, entrepreneurs' self-identity and social capital, the study's narrative approach is discussed. The chapter then presents an original conceptual framework that explains how nascent designers approach the tension between creative processes and business practice. It is argued that, when considered alongside the findings on designers' business development trajectories and social capital, this framework has considerable practical and theoretical value. In particular it has the potential to help policy and training agencies in a demanding but vibrant and rapidly growing sector to target their industry support and development activities more effectively.

NEW ZEALAND'S DESIGNER FASHION INDUSTRY

New Zealand is a country of small and medium-sized enterprises (Ministry of Economic Development, 2010, p. 11) with 97.2 per cent of all businesses employing 19 or less people. Given the predominance of small businesses, it is surprising that we still know relatively little about the experience of establishing and operating such businesses, particularly those in non-traditional and emerging industries such as the creative industries. Relatively few studies have been conducted on creative businesses generally, or those in the DFI in particular.

The paucity of empirical studies examining the New Zealand DFI can be attributed in part to the fact that, despite the rapid expansion and international acknowledgement the industry has experienced since four trailblazers, i.e. World, Zambesi, Nom.D and Karen Walker, took their labels – to the 1999 London Fashion Week, the New Zealand designer fashion industry is 'just a baby by international standards' (Gregg, 2003, pp. 7–8). It is little more than a decade since the industry began emerging from a handful of designers, boutiques and discerning consumers into what Lewis et al. (2008, p. 43) term 'subjects for the new economy'. Despite this recent rise to prominence, designer fashion, according to Lewis et al. (2008, p. 48), now produces approximately 50 per cent of New Zealand's footwear and apparel exports.

Much of the literature on the New Zealand fashion industry has appeared in popular press publications (for example Bailey and Stretton, 2007; Gregg, 2003), popular or industry magazines (for example *Her Magazine, Lucire, New Zealand Business Magazine*) or as parts of reports commissioned by government agencies and local authorities on the creative industries, (for example on the textile and clothing industry (Burleigh

Evatt and New Zealand Institute of Economic Research, 2001) or the fashion industry (for example Blomfield, 2002). Exceptions include an industry-level analysis of a fashion cluster in Dunedin (Thompson-Fawcett, 2007), the writings of the New Zealand Designer Fashion Project centred at the University of Auckland and the recently released *New Zealand Fashion Design* (Lassig, 2010), which provides in-depth profiles of 25 established designers and sits in a space of its own between the academic and popular press.

Most of these sources characterize the New Zealand DFI similarly, as tough, competitive, high-end focused, dynamic and based upon small companies (Thompson-Fawcett, 2007). In 2002 Blomfield reported that 69 per cent of the businesses in the sector employed ten or less full-time people and 72 per cent had turnovers of less than $2 million in the year prior to his report being published. Six years on in 2008, designer-led businesses employing over 70 people and with cash flows in excess of 5 million dollars (Lewis et al., 2008) constituted the tip of this growing industry sector's iceberg.

The DFI sector in New Zealand has a wide range of stakeholders, including training providers, business incubators, local and regional authorities, business associations, research agencies, government departments and agencies, industry agencies, suppliers, wholesalers, promoters, media representatives, sponsors, retailers, the fashion-conscious New Zealand consumer and, last but not least, fashion designers. Thus, not only is there scant literature on the industry, but there are also many perspectives that need to taken into account if we are to develop a comprehensive understanding of the FDI experience in New Zealand.

ORIENTATIONS TO THE BUSINESS START-UP EXPERIENCE

Business start-up is arguably the major theme in the entrepreneurship literature. It has been studied from a wide variety of angles, including the antecedents of new venture formation (for example Davidson and Honig, 2003), business founders' personal attributes (for example, Locke and Baum, 2004) including their need for achievement (for example McClelland, 1961) and orientation to risk (for example Forlani and Mullins, 2000; McCarthy, 2000; Petrakis, 2005; Pinfold, 2001), and financial and economic decision processes (for example Amit et al., 2001). Overall, quests for definitive patterns of entrepreneurial behaviour, distinguishing orientations (for example Cartland et al., 1984; Kropp et al., 2008) and a general profile of the entrepreneur have dominated this literature.

The construct, 'entrepreneurial orientation' (EO) has been proposed as a way to conceptualize entrepreneurs' processes, practices and decision-making activities (Covin and Slevin, 1986, 1989, 1991; Lumpkin and Dess, 1996, 2001; Miller, 1983; Runyan et al., 2008; Zahra, 1991). The dimensions that are used to measure EO are typically proactiveness, risk-taking and innovativeness (Covin and Slevin, 1986, 1989, 1991) and, as such, these essentially provide a psychological assessment (Krauss et al., 2005). Proactiveness refers to the forward-looking and opportunity-seeking mindset that focuses on producing new products or processes in the expectation that these will generate demand (Lumpkin and Dess, 2001). Risk-taking refers to boldness and moving forward in the face of limited knowledge and where outcomes are uncertain (Kropp et al., 2008, p. 104). Innovativeness refers to being creative and experimental or supporting creativity and experimentation in the quest for new products. These dimensions, which according to Kropp et al. (2008, p. 104), are the most used dimensions in entrepreneurship enquiry, have been employed to differentiate other types of small business owners from entrepreneurs and to propose a contrasting construct, the 'small business orientation' (SBO) (Stewart and Roth, 2001). This refers to the orientation of those small business owners who score poorly on the three dimensions of EO. Both orientations address general operating styles, which differ according to both short- and long-term goals (Cartland et al., 1984). Runyan et al. (2008) consider that the pursuit of growth distinguishes the two orientations, with the pursuit of growth being much more aligned with the EO than the SBO.

Other dimensions have also been explored in relation to EO and SBO, including beliefs (for example Kolvereid and Isaken, 2006), motivation (for example Segal et al. 2005) and intentionality (for example Krueger and Carsrud, 1993). There has also been a wide range of studies that have explored the relationship between EO and firm performance, although analysis of these reveals ambiguous results and recurring methodological weaknesses (Andersén, 2010). As a result, EO and SBO have featured in a range of entrepreneurship studies and have gained a general explanatory appeal that has encouraged a generalized trans-sector view of entrepreneurship and business start-up. Ironically, this has occurred in the face of mounting contradictions in the literature, increasing acceptance of the complexity (Cohen and Musson, 2000, p. 32) and variability of enterprise development, and recognition that business start-up does not occur in a vacuum (Hindle, 2004, p. 584) but is situated in the local economic, social, cultural and industry circumstances. In responding to these developments and calls for more situated and process-based approaches in the study of entrepreneurship (for example Steyaert, 1997) a gradual refocusing of research activity has occurred, which is encouraging researchers to pursue an understand of the idiosyncrasies of start-up in specific industries rather than common entrepreneurial patterns.

SELF-IDENTITY AND ENTREPRENEURSHIP

Identity is a complex and ambiguous concept (Kohonen, 2005, p. 23). Attempts to define it are complicated by the fact that a person can have multiple identities, which draw on psychological, social and cultural resources and are the result of the dynamic interplays between physicality, psyche and social processes. Entrepreneurship scholars have invested considerable effort in their quest to define the entrepreneurial identity and those with an aptitude to assume this identity (for example Brockhaus, 1980; Locke and Baum, 2004; McClelland, 1961; Schaper and Volery, 2004; Stewart and Roth, 2001), as well as how such an identity is achieved and maintained. Much attention has been paid to the extent to which individuals can shape their entrepreneurial identity (Down and Warren, 2008, p. 6). Some scholars feel this identity is a stereotypic script or label that is created and sustained by public representations (for example Somers, 1994) and generally accepted definitions (for example Blumer, 1969), and is acquired retrospectively (for example Cohen and Musson, 2000; Ritchie, 1991). Others question whether the identity is strongly preordained by the cultural context in which the entrepreneur operates. They see entrepreneurs as having the agency to purposefully manipulate entrepreneurial identity, to varying degrees, through their enterprising activities (for example Down and Warren, 2008; Down and Reveley, 2004; Downing, 2005; Lounsbury and Glynn, 2001; Warren and Anderson, 2005). Lounsbury and Glynn (2001), for instance, argue that one of the key challenges of the entrepreneur is to engage with institutionalized notions of the entrepreneur in a way that allows them to create a unique yet socially legitimate sense of their entrepreneurial self (Lounsbury and Glynn, 2001, p. 554), or in other words, their self-identity.

Self-identity is a concept used to denote 'the character that the individual takes themselves to be' (Watson, 2009, p. 255), and is understood reflectively within the context of their constantly evolving biography (Giddens, 1991, p. 53). Discursive processes seem to play important roles in the creation and maintenance of this identity (Cohen and Musson, 2000; Down and Warren, 2008; Mallon and Cohen, 2001; Mills and Pawson, 2006a; Warren, 2004) as these processes sustain the range of externally determined social identities that shape this internal view that the individual holds of himself or herself. Watson (2009, p. 256) goes so far as to say that an individual's self-identity and social identities are intimately and inevitably linked 'in a "looking glass" way' even though the individual does not passively accept the external social realities as their self-identity. Instead, to varying degrees, individuals purposefully act in ways designed to influence how others see them, and in so doing engage in what is commonly termed 'identity work'.

SOCIAL CAPITAL

Social capital captures the fundamental proposition that positive outcomes are associated with sociability (Portes, 1998, p. 2) and that mutual goodwill results from shared social relations. Adler and Kwon (2002, p. 17) suggest social capital is: 'understood roughly as the goodwill that is engendered by the social fabric of social relations and that can be mobilized to facilitate action'. It is intimately related to considerations of reciprocity, trust, social networks and mutual benefit.

The concept is used in many disciplines. In entrepreneurship studies its utility as a concept is increasingly being acknowledged (Lee and Jones, 2008, p. 550). For instance, Ikeba (2008, p. 181), in a discussion of the meaning of social capital in the context of market processes, brings the notions of reciprocity, trust, social networks and mutual benefit together by suggesting that social capital: 'consists of norms of generalized reciprocity and networks of trust that emerge unplanned over time, that operate in public space among members of an open-ended community, and that help to promote entrepreneurial discovery'.

Unfortunately, the concept's widespread application has both elaborated and brought 'an unhelpful vagueness' to its meaning (Ikeba, 2008, p. 167). Adler and Kwon (2002, p. 19) consider that part of this vagueness is due to the fact that the concept has been defined variously in terms of its substance, sources or effects. For example Bourdieu (1986, p. 243), in defining social capital as 'made up of social obligations ("connections"), which are convertible, in certain conditions, into economic capital and may be institutionalised in terms of a title of nobility', focuses on substance. In contrast, Nahapiet and Ghoshal's (1998) definition focuses on sources. They propose that social capital is: 'the sum of the actual and potential resources embedded within, available through and derived from the network of relationships possessed by an individual or social units' (p. 243). Putnam (2000), on the other hand, focuses on effects when distinguishing between 'bridging' and 'bonding' social capital, characterizing bridging social capital as that which promotes openness in a community by allowing strangers to be admitted and form relationships within it.

Bonding social capital, in contrast, creates a sense of solidarity between community members which works to exclude non-members and make the community boundaries somewhat rigid.

Adler and Kwon (2002) address all three definitional dimensions when they propose the following working definition for social capital: 'Social capital is the goodwill available to individuals or groups. Its source lies in the structure and content of the actor's social relations. Its effects flow from the information, influence, and solidarity it makes available to the actor' (p. 23).

In order to understand these effects it is helpful to distinguish between three dimensions of social capital: structural, relational and cognitive (Naphapiet and Ghoshal, 1998). The structural dimension refers to how frequently members of a network are in contact and the level of connectivity they share. Both bridging and bonding social capital, mentioned above, are forms of structural social capital. The relational dimension refers to the normative codes that guide network interactions and encourage trust, reciprocity, obligation and expectations (Adler and Kwon, 2002), while the cognitive dimension addresses the 'shared representations, interpretations, and systems of meaning between parties' (Nahapiet and Ghoshal, 1998, p. 244) that are revealed in language-based resources. According to Lee and Jones (2008, p. 562), structural and relational social capital have been found to reduce transaction costs in business but there is little research that explains the effects of cognitive social capital. What we do know is that the development of common understandings is facilitated when entrepreneurs use similar narratives, codes and languages (Hatzakis et al., 2005). Such common understandings are likely to contribute to an entrepreneur's credibility by ensuring that they make sense to those whose support they seek to enlist (for example investors and customers). Little wonder then that there is a widespread acceptance that relational (that is, social) competence and social capital influence business success (for example Holt and Macpherson, 2010; Johansson, 2004; Lounsbury and Glynn, 2001; O'Connor, 2002). What is also of significance for the study reported here is that relational competence and social capital generally shape the social identities which are intimately related to self-identity (Watson, 2009, p. 256).

Taking a Narrative Approach to Examine Entrepreneurial Experience

According to Fisher (1987, p. 24), life is experienced and interpreted 'as a series of ongoing narratives, as conflicts, characters, beginnings, middles, and ends'. We tell stories to understand our past and these stories in turn shape the unfolding story in which we live (Johansson, 2004, p. 274) as the central character. Stories provide us with a means to organize and understand the past and present and shape our expectations of the future (Gergen, 1994, p. 208). This means that when we ask people to tell their stories, we tap into their current sense of reality, who they are in that reality, and their notions of purposeful activity (O'Connor, 2002, p. 36). Each story is rich with people, places, actions, reactions, beliefs, judgements and reasons. Thus, an entrepreneur's start-up story not only provides the researcher with a chronology of actions and events, but also puts these into the social, personal and industry context in which these actions and events occurred and reveals the meaning the story has to the narrator. Furthermore, such stories, by providing a means to capture the business founder's enterprise development experience from their point of view (for example Mills and Pawson, 2006a, 2006b), allow their sense-making to be explored.

Despite well-developed narrative traditions in other disciplines (for example social linguistic and literary studies) (Riessman, 2008, p. vii), it is only recently that researchers have recognized the value of using narrative approaches to study entrepreneurship (Johansson, 2004). The number of narrative studies is now rising steadily, with narrative approaches being used both as the primary research method and in mixed-method studies (for example de Bruin and Flint-Hartle, 2006) to investigate such dimensions as the transition to self-employment (Mallon and Cohen, 2001), international entrepreneurship (Fletcher, 2002 referred to in Johansson, 2004), intergenerational succession in family businesses (Hamilton, 2006), entrepreneurial learning (Rae, 2005), the influence of gender and family on entrepreneurial activity in New Zealand (Kirkwood, 2004, 2007), sense-making of new-start entrepreneurs in the information technology (IT) industry (Mills and Pawson, 2006b) and the way narrative sense-making provides the connection between business formation and legitimacy (Holt and Macpherson, 2010).

It is important to recognize, however, that 'Narrative scholars are a diverse bunch' (Riessman, 2008, p. 13) and that narrative research approaches vary considerably in their epistemological assumptions (Johansson, 2004, p. 286). If we focus on the purpose that narratives can serve, we can identify approaches that have a content orientation which focuses on what Fletcher (2007) calls the 'realist text', where the narrative primarily is used to provide rich and contextualized data about specific dimensions of entrepreneurship. Then there are approaches with a more processural orientation that focus on the social performance of narrative and how this produces entrepreneurial understanding and meanings (for example Jones et al., 2008; Rae, 2005). Intersecting with both are those approaches with a sense-making orientation which use narrative as a means to solicit both narrative content and the narrators' sense of this (for example Mallon and Cohen, 2001; Mills and Pawson, 2006a).

THE NARRATIVE APPROACH EMPLOYED

The study described in this chapter had a sense-making orientation. It sought to understand the sense designers made of their start-up experiences; in other words, the meaning ascribed to this experience. A narrative approach therefore fitted the research objective perfectly, given that 'narrative is a form of "meaning making"' (Polkinghorne, 1988, p. 36). Because interviews inevitably produce collaboratively created texts that 'can be considered stories, that is, interpretations of some aspect of the world occurring in time and shaped by history, culture, and character' (Fisher, 1995, p. 170), they were employed to collect participants' start-up narratives.

Each interview commenced with an invitation for the designer to tell their business start-up story. They chose where their story started and what events, actions and decisions it contained. Because the research objective was to understand how each designer made sense of their experience, the researcher's primary inputs were related to asking for clarification, prompting elaboration and soliciting explanations of actions, events or decisions when these were not volunteered. Open-ended prompts such as 'Why do you say that?' or 'What was your reasoning there?' or 'How did you account for that decision?' were used. In this way, the narrative's structure was, in the first instance, provided by what the designer chose to volunteer rather than by a set of preconceived themes or concepts or questions determined by the researcher.

This approach, which was taken to give the designer's experience and the sense they made of this experience pre-eminence in the narrative created, does not deny the inevitable contribution that a researcher makes to any text gathered in an interview situation (Johansson, 2004, p. 286). After all, as Riessman (2008, p. 50) observes: 'By our interviewing and transcription practices we play a major part in constructing the narrative data that we then analyse.' The researcher was aware of this inevitability and so took care to enhance the possibility that each narrative had one principal narrator. Not only were the interviews relatively unstructured and the researcher's inputs limited, but also any significant themes and patterns that emerged from the analysis of previous interviews were not explored in a subsequent interview until the end of the interview. This strategy facilitated the comparative analysis by allowing emergent themes and patterns to be considered in the light of new data without allowing questions about these to shape the interviewee's narrative.

Each narrative was subjected to a preliminary analysis prior to conducting the next interview or transcription, that involved reflecting on the notes taken in the interview and comparing these with earlier interviews. It was this preliminary analysis that provided any themes that were explored at the end of the subsequent interview.

The main analysis occurred once the interview was transcribed. This entailed reading and rereading each transcribed interview in order to identify the overall flavour, persistent themes, key concepts, arguments and structural features (for example plot, characters, positioning of the primary narrator) of the narrative, and any evidence suggesting that the designer had a consistent way of presenting his or her ideas. Once an overall 'feel' for the narrative was achieved, then a finer analysis occurred whereby sections relating to or illustrating these features were coded and clustered. The codes used were suggested by the data rather than by any extant conceptual framework. Findings from these analyses were subsequently considered in relation to broader contextual issues (for example local economic conditions, designers' access to resources such as technical information and business advice) and demographic information. Comparative analyses were then made across all narratives to identify broad patterns and disjunctions that allowed the data to be conceptualized as a whole. Only after this stage did the researcher consider the findings in relation to the extant literature. This chapter reports on the section of the data analysis that relates to the ways designers reported approaching the tension between the creative process and business activities – the creativity–business tension. The concepts of self-identity and social capital resonated closely with the findings that emerged from this analysis and so are used here to frame their presentation. Using the extant literature in this way is consistent with conducting research from an interpretive research perspective.

A narrative approach is not without limitations. It introduces the possibility of 'hindsight bias'. This refers to: 'the tendency for individuals to see past events as being more predictable, or to believe after an event, their prediction of the outcome was more accurate than it really was' (Cassar and Craig, 2009, p. 6). Narrative approaches also raise questions about the degree to which *post facto* rationalizations generate a coherence that is not an accurate representation of the 'real' nature of experience, due to the fact that a narrator creates linkages between decisions and events in order to create their story that may have been rather random and disconnected even though they were sequenced chronologically (Kohonen, 2005; Gergen and Gergen, 1983; Linde, 1993). The study here, however, was not founded on a desire to tap into the 'factualities' of experience. Instead, it took an essentially sense-making approach, seeking to understand and conceptualize the sense designers made of their start-up experiences in the

DFI. Thus, it was concerned with stories judged plausible by the partici-pants rather than any objective truths – a key feature of a sense-making approach (Weick, 1995).

THE DESIGNERS

The designers were selected because they met the working definition of an entrepreneur: 'a business person in the development phase of a new enterprise, which they own and manage' in the designer fashion sector. The development phase was defined as being within seven years of label launch, as start-up is often a gradual process with many designers main-taining part-time employment in other people's businesses for some years to fund the early phases of their own enterprise development process.

The total population of new designers in the DFI was not readily iden-tifiable, so representative sampling was not possible. Instead local tertiary education, business development agency and word-of-mouth referrals were used to identify potential participants. Those chosen represented the identifiable population that met the working definition and were able to be accessed within the time constraints of the study.

Forty-four designers' start-up narratives were examined. Of these six were from male and 38 from female designers.[1] This ratio approximates the strongly female-dominated industry in New Zealand. Culturally the designers were predominantly Pakeha (that is, New Zealanders with European ancestry) but included four Maori (Indigenous New Zealanders), one Tongan and one Chinese designer. The designers were aged from their early 20s to over 60, and had businesses based in Auckland, Hamilton, Wanganui, Palmerston North, Wellington, Nelson, Christchurch or Dunedin or the region immediately surrounding one of these cities.[2] These cities represent New Zealand's four main fashion design centres (Auckland, Wellington, Christchurch and Dunedin), a large city that is emerging as a fashion design centre (Hamilton), and two pro-vincial centres known for their design activities (Wanganui and Nelson). One Palmerston North designer, with strong associations with Wanganui, also participated in the study. The designers' training backgrounds ranged from those with no formal design, industry or business training to others who had engaged in all three types of training.

The designers typically preferred to contract out aspects of production or employ casual staff during the labour-intensive phases of the produc-tion cycle, rather than have permanent employees. None employed more than ten permanent staff. Fifteen designers were in partnerships with other designers with whom they shared premises and, in some cases, retail outlets. Fourteen designers operated retail outlets, while the remainder chose to sell their designs online or to wholesale to retailers in New Zealand and in some cases overseas (for example Australia and the USA). Overall, the labels spanned high-end fashion through to smart street wear, fashionable sportswear and fashion jewellery, shoes and hosiery.

FINDINGS

Self-Identity and Enterprise Development

The way designers approached the creativity–business tension was found to relate strongly to the self-ascribed sense of self that the designers discursively created in the process of narrating their enterprise development story. The designers presented these self-identities in various ways, but most recognizably through self-labelling. Some designers labelled themselves as 'designers' while others preferred the labels 'artist', 'tailor', 'entrepreneur', 'business person', 'creative business person' or simply 'creative person'. The analysis of this labelling gave rise to a self-identity spectrum that ranged from identities that made no reference to business to ones that positioned business as a central self-identity dimension. Below are examples of how three designers (D1, D2 and D3) labelled themselves in their narratives (note that R designates the researcher):

D1: I guess a businesswoman and an entrepreneur. I just love being able to create things in terms of creating a business. Creating systems and creating . . . just building this business so that's business woman, but it's starting from scratch so it's entrepreneur as well.

D2: No, I'd say I'm more of an entrepreneur. I'm more interested in the business side of things . . . I struggle to say that I'm actually a designer in a huge sense of the word at the moment because . . . There isn't really a label to speak of . . .

D3: . . . when I was back at university I knew that I was doing fashion design and I knew that I wanted to do fashion design for my career but I always felt uncomfortable when people asked me what I did, to say 'I'm a fashion designer' cos [sic] I wasn't quite there. Um, and I never really have had that feeling for a while, which was like, yeah, and I hadn't thought about it until you asked me.

R: So how do you account for the fact that you're now comfortable?

D3: Um I think just, I've actually got my own label and selling it throughout the country, got my own shop, um, whereas back when I did, made designs and I didn't really sell them to anyone, made them for friends and family and for myself and for my university project, um, but I wasn't really out there in the market.

Often self-identification 'work' was done in the interview when discussing the values underscoring the designer's business practices, their motivation for starting a business or their aspirations for their business. For instance, designers reported endeavouring to develop their businesses in ways that allowed their actions to be consistent with their values and their sense of self. Many, but certainly not all, reported making deliberate choices to achieve this alignment. Running through the data was a strong theme of being challenged in pursuit of this alignment by the demands of establishing and sustaining a business in the fashion sector. At the same time the narratives included expressions of satisfaction when satisfactory degrees of alignment were achieved. Below are narrative excerpts from two designers (D4 and D5) that reveal this issue of alignment. D4 talks about having to do ranges, something that doesn't fit with being an artist, in order to sell garments at realistic prices. In comparison, D5 considers such compromises a 'trap' to be avoided. She reports being uncompromisingly in her pursuit a good fit between values and business decisions:

D4: . . . every artist wants to create something new every time and while in the reality of fashion that's not always possible because every piece would be so expensive it would be unsaleable and that's why we do ranges . . .

D5: I mean I know now we have to satisfy the market a little bit but [business partner] and I try very hard not to fall into that trap. Um.

R: You call it a trap . . .

D5: Well because it sort of goes against what we really are, so we decided right from the beginning it was going, it wasn't ever, we never wanted it to be hard. We wanted it to suit our lifestyles, we wanted it to fit in with what we love and and [sic] we, we've remained quite strict on that, so if we're not enjoying it and it's not happening or working for one reason or another, um, it doesn't, and it doesn't feel right, then it's not right [laughs]

The Creativity–Business Tension

Designers grappled in many ways and to varying degrees with what is being called here and elsewhere (Mills, forthcoming) the creativity–business tension. This tension is captured in the following narrative excerpt:

Business comes first, before creative considerations. The creative side is important but must be put in its place.

It was the 'putting creativity in its place' that created the tension. For some designers, this tension was experienced simply as time pressure. Business activities required time that they would rather use to complete their design-related tasks. Others experienced the tension as a pressure to modify their sense of self to include the notion of being a 'business person'. Some reported making this adjustment, while others reported seeking (and in many cases securing) ways to retain their sense of being a 'creative person' (for example by going into partnership with someone who would do the business management side of their business). Such experiences suggested that at the heart of the tension was a mismatch between the participant's sense of self (that is self-identity), their expectations about how this sense should be enacted and the identities the business models they worked within demanded of them. The narrative excerpt below illustrates how one designer (and reportedly her business partner) responded to this mismatch between her sense of herself as a creative person capable of creating competition-level designs, and the activities demanded of her by being a business woman:

> . . . but of course, the business um, is set up for us to earn an income, you know, um, and that's the idea of it, which is fair enough, and we all, for example, I know that eventually I'll have the opportunity to be more creative and design something of my ideas. I'm really really keen to, to do that. It's what I really wanna [sic] do but of course we've got to set things up to pay the bills first before we can go off and do what we want to do, but eventually I see myself doing that and entering competitions.

This designer's response to the disjunction between self and the roles required to be in business was to assume that eventually the situation would change and allow her to enact her uniquely creative self, which currently was not being adequately expressed. Other designers suggested that they would limit or shape their business activities so they could stay true to their sense of self. The following narrative excerpt illustrates this:

> You know, I think I've got a little bit of a negative connotation of fashion. I'm not into the whole catwalk side of things. I couldn't bear to do that, and I think that's, um, I wouldn't want to make my business big enough that it would go that [sic], to that side of things. I don't, to me, it sounds awful, but I find it quite bitchy sort of, too competitive, um, yeah, it's not me.

Enterprise Development Orientations

While each designer's story was unique, in terms of both what it contained and how it was told, several discernible integrating themes emerged in the comparative narrative analysis. The most obvious related to how designers positioned themselves in their stories. This orientation was revealed when the data on how the designers approached the tension between their creative processes and the business practices that sustained their participation in the designer fashion industry were compared with how they talked about themselves and why they went into business. This orientation was labelled their 'enterprise orientation'. The word 'enterprise' captures the fact the orientation is in relation to enterprise development, and the word 'orientation' captures the positioning dimension (that is, how the designers positioned themselves in relation to creativity, business and the fashion industry).

Three interrelated dimensions – self-identity, start-up motivation and aspirations – were found to determine the designer's position in relation to their enterprise development, and thus distinguished one enterprise orientation from another. The three general enterprise orientations identified (see Table 9.1) delineated a triangular conceptual space (see Figure 9.1). Designers' orientations can be mapped onto this space according to how strongly their self-identity, start-up motivation and aspirations match the three defining orientations. In this study some mapped exactly onto one of the three orientations, while others mapped across orientations.

Table 9.1 Enterprise orientations

Orientation	Creative enterprise CEO	Creative business CBO	Fashion industry FIO
Motivation	To realize his/her creative potential	To work for oneself	To participate in the fashion industry
Aspirations	To become known as a designer	To make a living by building a successful label	To be successful in the industry
Self-identity	Creative person	Creative business person	Creative and/ or style-focused business person

Source: Mills (2011, forthcoming).

The first enterprise orientation is the 'creative enterprise orientation' (CEO). Start-up was seen by those with this orientation as a way of realizing their creative potential. They were primarily motivated by a quest for self-expression and recognition rather than by a desire to be in business or to make money. Those classified as expressing a CEO presented themselves primarily as creative individuals, seeking an outlet for their creativity rather than a means to achieve self-employment, make a good living or create a particular sort of lifestyle. The following excerpts capture the centrality of creativity to the orientation of designers with this orientation:

I'm a creative person. I need to create things and feel good about it.

Design is who I am.

> Wanting to design is more my drive [compared to having a retail business].

Designers who had a clear CEO often found dealing with the tension between creativity and business rather tough. As one noted:

> Learning to create a business doesn't come naturally to a creative person.

For those who fitted perfectly into the CEO category, business tasks and the demands of staying in business provided a brake on creativity and self-expression. The following two excerpts capture this 'brake' effect:

> I am losing the ability to get scared about things any more. I am more accustomed to the nature of the industry . . . You spend two weeks twice a year designing and then you spend the rest of the year picking up the pieces of those decisions.

> [I] really like design but sometimes push it too far. [Partner] puts the brakes on. She knows what sells.

For designers who clearly exhibited the second enterprise orientation, the 'creative business orientation' (CBO), start-up was primarily a way to become self-employed and make a living. They reported having business aspirations and positioned themselves in their narratives as essentially creative business people taking advantage of business opportunities. Those who reported taking advantage of an unexpected business opportunity all fell into this orientation category. The more mature designers tended to fall between this and the CEO category, suggesting that life's experiences had produced an appreciation of the need for creating a viable venture and a recognition of the value of appropriate prior business experience. The following excerpts capture the essence of the CBO category:

> It's not enough for me to do something that I am interested in because I don't like being broke.

> Business comes first, before creative considerations. The creative side is important but must be put in its place.

> What we are doing with the business is commercial, and is about making money, and . . . it means there are restrictions on my creativity. You know, I can't make the most way-out things all the time because they won't sell.

> . . . we both come from business backgrounds and so the business part of the business was always as much a part of starting as the fashion. In fact probably more . . . than the fashion.

The 'fashion industry orientation' (FIO) is the third orientation category. Designers who clearly fitted in to this category did not primarily account for business start-up in terms of meeting a need to express their creativity, or achieving self-employment or business goals. Rather, they were primarily motivated by a desire to participate in the fashion industry. The following quotes from two different designers illustrate ways in which a FIO was presented in the narratives:

> I see myself as being the Michael Hill jeweller [successful New Zealand-based retail jewellery chain] of the fashion world.

> Why did I choose the garment industry? I think a lot of it comes back to both [partner] and my belief that at the end of the day people should live well and be happy and feel confident and I guess the garment sector gave us the vehicle in which to really celebrate those values . . . From the walls [of the retail outlet] to where we go next with the . . . what part of the industry we go into next harks back to those values.

This orientation, while it was industry-focused, included motivations that could overlap with those exhibiting more of a CBO. One participant stood out in this respect. She was clearly motivated by a desire to have her own business and sell fashionable garments to her niche market of the larger woman, and was designing a range that did this, but she did not see herself (or her business partner) as a designer. This was despite being recognized by the industry as a fashion designer. Her self-identity was expressed in her narrative in opposition to her notion of a designer. Her narrative suggested that she saw herself as a business woman who retailed her own label in the fashion industry. Her orientation is captured in the excerpts below:

> . . . I said to [partner] that that was it, I was, getting out [of her paid employment], and I was going to get a temporary job until, you know, I could sort out what we wanted to do and she said 'look', she said. 'We've always been talking about opening the shop. Why don't we do it now?' . . . what we wanted to do was, we wanted, um, clothes that suited the average woman and at a reasonable price and we wanted to extend the size range and there was absolutely nothing that they could buy, um, in New Zealand basically . . . [partner] and I are not fashion designers by anything but we do do, we do do the drawings of what we want, yeah . . . and we design the clothes but we're not, we're not a [sic] fashion designer at all. We get ideas and say 'this would be really cool to wear' . . . our dream was for always good quality you know, wearable clothing.

Figure 9.1 depicts the relationship of the orientations to each other and to the creativity-business tension and shows how the three orientations define a conceptual space onto which designers' enterprise orientation can be mapped. These are represented by the faces.

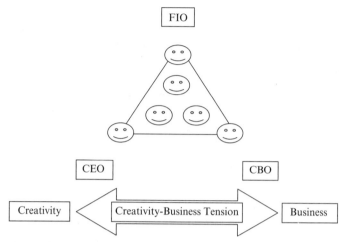

Figure 9.1   The enterprise orientation space

Overall, the narratives suggest that fashion start-up in the FDI is most challenging for those with a strong CEO, many of whom were very young designers who had used tertiary design courses as their entry into the world of fashion design. Often their work experience during these design courses was their only pre-start-up industry or business experience. Designers with more industry experience and/or business training seemed were more likely to tell enterprise development narratives consistent with possessing a CBO. However, even designers with a CBO were typically strongly experiential in their approach to business development, learning how to respond to the creativity-business tension as they went along, so it is possible that their early enterprise development narratives may have revealed a more CEO. For this reason, the concept of enterprise development orientation needs to be understood as a space within which individual designers move as they establish their business, rather than as a typology of fixed orientations.

Social Capital and Enterprise Development

An experiential rather than strategic approach to enterprise development was evident across the entire dataset. As an approach it runs counter to the anticipatory and systematic strategic models of business development. For many designers, but especially those with a CEO, design revolves around a type of 'being' (that is, being creative) whereas business models focus on 'becoming' something different (that is, getting bigger, richer and gaining greater market share). Creating a fashion design business requires working with both these aspects and marrying the creative self to the business activities required in order to pursue business growth. The challenge of doing this prompted participants either to make conceptual shifts or to develop strategies that allowed both aspects to coexist (for example hiring a business manager to release them from business administration tasks), or a combination of both. The following narrative excerpt captures how one designer was experiencing this challenge of marrying the creative self and business activities:

> Because in business you cannot do everything and at this point in time I'm, um, facing a bit of a dilemma. I am the designer for the company. I also manage production and I do the PR. [public relations] . . . so I think I've got too much on my plate and I have considered offloading some of those activities to other people and I have indeed tried some other people with that [business responsibilities] but they haven't brought, even though they have followed our, um, framework, guidelines and so on, they haven't brought the results that I can bring when I do that, these things myself so there is a bit of a worry. I'm not sure how to manage that, uh, in terms of, uh, offloading the design to somebody else, I have tried that too but then the, the items lose the unique flavour that they got. People seem to know that, I will not tell them, this person actually designed this part of the range but those things are not bought [laughs]. They want what I do, and that is a bit of a curse sometimes. That kind of limits my time. So what I will have to do is perhaps as I grow and become a little bit larger financially [is] involve another interested party, [to] focus on the business side of things, cos [sic] I thought, you know, at the end of the day, nobody can replace a designer really because the identity of the label would be lost. And it's a catch twenty-two situation. If the identity is lost then what [label] is made of will disappear, [label] will collapse.

The narratives contained many examples of social strategies that allowed designers to develop and realize the social capital associated with their social networks, and balance design and business tasks. Generally, designers reported turning in the first instance to members of their personal social networks for advice, assistance and finance. Those with limited personal networks were forced to be relatively more self-reliant and were often among those who reported encountering major challenges in the business side of start-up. This is consistent with the findings from Taylor and Thorpe's (2004) study of an entrepreneur's social relations, which found that social networks significantly influence the business development process. Like the study reported here, their findings highlighted the value of social capital for enterprise development. What was suggested by the narratives in the study reported in this chapter, however, was that the lack of social capital often meant designers did more in their businesses, and this then limited the time available to network and rectify the situation. Below is an example of how one designer narrated her experiences of the support from professional and friendship networks in relation to business promotion:

> I think I wouldn't have been able to get as far without being able to speak to [a particular promotions consultant] who was the man behind [another fashion business]. [Associate], she's been a huge part as well. It's not really a professional relationship I have with her, it's more of a personal friendship base. She's given me great insight. I mean I've only been hunting [for promotional ideas] a couple of times and don't actually . . . haven't really roughed it, so she's on TV, she's been on the magazine, so she's sort of like a spokesperson who will be able to help me get out there as well. Having a quote from her would be more than some other type of advertisement. Definitely contacts have been great. She's been able to get me onto other people.

The degree to which each designer's enterprise orientation generated a disjunction between their self-identity and those identities supported by the prevailing business model was linked to the designer's available social capital and their ability to mobilize this to create supportive synergistic networks around their business. The findings reveal that those designers who reported facing a tension between their creative practice and business yet successfully navigated this tension accessed different levels and types of social capital to those who reported being trapped and limited by this tension.

The narrative analysis also revealed that the significance and nature of social capital was indexed to, and at the same time shaped, the plot of a designer's enterprise development narrative. While each enterprise development narrative had its own unique plot, there was a meta-plot or general pattern to the form these plots took. This meta-plot consisted of four overlapping stages, each with its related decisions, learning and development points. These stages were termed '*do it yourself*' (DIY), '*collaborative action*', '*streamlining*', and '*diversification or downsizing*' (see Figure 9.2). This proved to be a useful framework for exploring the relationship between social capital and enterprise development.

DIY → COLLABORATIVE ACTION → STREAMLINING → DIVERSIFICATION or DOWNSIZING

Figure 9.2   New enterprise development trajectory

In the DIY stage designers reported endeavouring to do as much as they could themselves. This produced different challenges depending on the skills and experience of the designer. Some reported having to learn a wide variety of skills, including how to do accounts, file tax returns, keep records, make patterns and 'go out on the road' promoting their range of designs. Other designers who had previous business or industry experience were faced with less steep learning curves. The fact that some reported very steep learning curves highlighted the naive optimism of many new-start designers. Networks at this stage were particularly important for providing encouragement, money and practical assistance such as helping to attach labels, collect fabrics from suppliers and child-minding.

In the *collaborative action stage* time and production pressures often required designers to engage help. In many cases this help was sought from within family and friendship networks, but in other instances it involved contracting out functions or enlarging operations by hiring staff. Designers reported making decisions that forced them to consider extending their social contacts and engaging with others outside their personal networks. Some, for example, sought out training providers who operated internship programmes so that they could host student interns. Others reported enlisting the professional assistance of professional contractors such as a promotional agency. What was interesting was that existing networks were generally used to guide such decisions.

In the *streamlining stage* designers reported engaging in activities designed to refine their business operations, such as selling online, moving to more functional premises, ceasing to make made-to-measure garments or substantially increasing the price of these garments and thinking more deeply about their brand. These activities and the decision-making processes that led to them involved discussions and advice from both existing networks and newly identified industry sources. It was at this stage in the business trajectory that business and industry networks became particularly important because of the nature of the information and advice they could offer. A comparison of the narratives suggested that differences existed between geographic regions with regard to the availability of face-to-face industry networks and support agencies. Relational social capital mattered, and this was harder to acquire in the smaller cities. Auckland designers had significant advantages with regard to developing and sustaining relational social capital because of the concentration of industry-related businesses and development support agencies in that city.

The final stage identified in the start-up narratives was the *diversification or downsizing stage*. Those designers who had reached this stage reported facing some of their most challenging decisions. These decisions typically centred on the question of 'Where to from here?' and were related primarily to production levels. For some, the challenges associated with meeting large orders forced them to confront the question of whether they should diversify or downsize their other operations to cope while, for other designers, falling margins or reduced sales raised this question. Associated with this stage were decisions about such matters as whether to approach banks for development capital, the level of debt that could be serviced, the desirability of developing supplementary ranges or starting additional labels, the wisdom of producing garments for a different demographic or opening a retail outlet or, alternatively, the long-term consequences of reducing production to one collection in a year or producing only existing designs for a year.

These sorts of decisions taxed those relying on friendship and extended family networks more than those who could access industry-based networks for advice and information. This finding highlights how highly strategic decisions in a challenging competitive industry, such as the DFI, require quality information and innovative ideas. Little wonder, then, that those who were confident that their personal and social capital could be employed to gain such inputs felt more relaxed. These tended to be the designers who expressed creative business and fashion industry orientations (CBO and FIO). In contrast, those expressing a more creative enterprise orientation (CEO) often had restricted networks and limited access to appropriate resources. Their networks were often more personal and contained fewer individuals with industry experience. They often reported relying on family or individual contacts rather than interacting more widely and developing industry networks. In this regard, accountants had significant influence as they were often the most trusted and readily available source of business information despite having little or no industry knowledge.

Overall, the social capital acquired through industry networks influenced how quickly designers moved through the stages of the business development trajectory. Below is an excerpt from the narrative of a designer with a CEO at the DIY stage in her business development. It illustrates how limited designers' industry networks can be:

R: Tell me about the significant people in this story? Who's been an important part of your development to this point?
D: Um, my husband, and my children. And I'm not sure who else really.
R: Have you at any stage gone to get funding from a bank or had a mentor?
D: No.
R: Right. So how would you describe your contact with the industry?
D: Um, very lacking [laughs]. Yup, very lacking. I haven't had a lot to do with, oh, even the other designers, or um, retail or yep, no I haven't.

Then later this designer observes:

I think I would have liked to have gone and worked under someone first in the fashion industry and learnt a lot more about it than trying to work it out myself. I feel quite lost at times, yeah.

The consequences for this designer of such isolation were a lack of all three dimensions of industry-specific social capital and a business that was stalled at the DIY stage in the DFI enterprise development trajectory suggested by this study

At all stages in the business development trajectory, the tertiary educators and local enterprise support agencies could be particularly important for designers as they provided a doorway to information and support that others with high levels of relational and structural social capital found elsewhere. Without such doorways the likelihood of the businesses of the designers with strong CEOs stalling was relatively high.

The analysis suggested that the development trajectory captured by the meta-plot was defined more by business decisions than by creative design decisions. Thus, for those who began their engagement in the industry as a result of their motivation to express their creativity by becoming a fashion designer, their continued participation in the industry propelled them in a direction that made a shift towards a creative business orientation more likely as they grappled with a succession of business decisions. The successive stages of this business trajectory facilitated a broadening of the networks that designers accessed, and encouraged them to engage more with industry support agencies and industry-related networks. This broadening of networks and engagement was often accompanied by a heightened recognition of the value of feedback, from retailers and customers, the industry at large and the media. These developments reflected a shift in focus from self-expression to industry engagement and required, among other things, heightened networking and social skills in order to develop or realize sufficient social capital to remain operational. Thus, designers reported spending more time communicating as their business progressed, in order to understand and manage the wider context in which they were operating.

Overall, the trajectory for all those interviewed was experienced as an incremental and increasingly 'peopled' process. There were no overnight success stories among the narratives. What the narratives did reveal, however, were designers who spent differing periods at each stage in the development trajectory and accounted for their unique journey through these stages in quite different ways. Common to all narratives was the importance the designers placed on the information, influence and solidarity they achieved as a result of being part of family, friendship and industry networks.

Designers' comments about the assistance gained from industry networks suggested that clear norms of engagement existed that served to support the image of the industry as a tough, constrained and pressured industry. For instance, there was an expectation that everyone 'did the hard yards'. Such norms were important in terms of realizing the benefits of industry-specific social capital. For designers who were seen to be working hard at their businesses, information and assistance from others in the industry were more forthcoming than if they were not seen to be, 'putting in the hard yards'.

DISCUSSION

This chapter has presented a section of the findings from a study that set out to extend the scant literature on creative start-up in New Zealand. It did this by exploring the start-up experiences of 44 fashion designers using a narrative approach. The particular approach employed allowed the researcher not only to tap into the rich fabric of each designer's start-up experience in a holistic fashion, but also to appreciate the sense the designer made of this experience.

The analysis of the narratives that were created in this process suggested that in order to understand a designer's start-up experience it was necessary to appreciate their enterprise orientation and where this was located within a conceptual space delineated by three enterprise orientations: the creative enterprise orientation (CEO), the creative business orientation (CBO) and the fashion industry orientation (FIO). The value of this conceptual framework lies in the way that it captures how designers describe their approach to enterprise as they navigate the tension between creative processes and business practice that is a fundamental and defining aspect of their chosen industry sector.

Enterprise orientation is defined in terms of the designers' self-ascribed identities and reported start-up motivations and aspirations. These dimensions distinguish this new concept from the familiar concept of entrepreneurial orientation (EO) (Covin and Slevin, 1986, 1989, 1991; Lumpkin and Dess, 1996, 2001; Miller, 1983; Runyan et al., 2008; Zahra, 1991), which is defined and measured in terms of three dimensions; proactiveness, risk-taking and innovativeness (Covin and Slevin, 1986, 1989, 1991). These dimensions are taken-for-granted requirements for participation in New Zealand's dynamic and highly competitive DFI. Just to survive at a marginally profitable level in this industry requires levels of proactiveness, risk-taking and innovativeness that might be considered exceptional in other industries. This is a result of many factors, including the small size of the domestic market; the limited availability of reasonably priced local options for manufacturing; and the industry's commitment to short seasonal cycles of innovative design, production and retailing. This industry reality reduces the utility of the EO concept and the EO–SBO framework as a means for distinguishing one designer from another, and predicting their likelihood of success. If we accept the findings from the narrative analysis reported here, this lack of fit is not just because the industry is fundamentally risky and requires an ability to be both innovative and proactive. It is also because there are other dimensions that need to be taken into account if we are to understand nascent designers' start-up experiences and how they make sense of them. These dimensions include the designer's self-identity, motivation and aspirations and how they develop and use social capital to effectively align these dimensions (that is, their enterprise orientations) with the demands of the creativity-business tension as it is manifested in each stage of their business development trajectory.

It is the interface that creative industries like the DFI provide between artistic endeavour and entrepreneurial activity that generates this tension and makes new conceptual frameworks like the enterprise orientation necessary if we are to fully appreciate the challenges that business founders face. De Bruin (2005, p. 144) defines the artist as: 'a person who draws on his or her inspiration and inherent artistic bent to fabricate an initial creative piece or an embodiment of his or her ideas'. In contrast, the entrepreneur is typically portrayed as a person who sees the commercial opportunity and makes it happen (Schumpeter, 1991, p. 413). Creative start-up requires grafting artistic and entrepreneurial enterprise together. The EO-SBO framework does not help us to understand how this is done, as it neglects the qualities associated with effective artistic expression (for example a sense of having an aesthetic and being a creative person). In contrast, the conceptual space being proposed here is defined by three orientations that to varying degrees incorporate a creative sense of self and motivations and aspirations that are specific to the DFI. It accommodates the possibility that people are in business in order to be creative rather than being creative in order to be in business.

The second contribution of this study, the general enterprise development trajectory, and designers' strategies for developing and using social capital, complete the framework this chapter is proposing for appreciating how this process of grafting artistic and entrepreneurial enterprises together occurs. The narratives revealed that designers with different orientations move along the enterprise development trajectory at different rates and in different ways, often tied to their available social capital and how they employ this. By identifying a designer's orientation, then person-specific support can be provided.

Those designers whose enterprise orientations align most strongly with a CBO or FIO experience less disjunction between their self-identity and the identities required to run a successful design business than those whose narratives suggest a strong CEO. The analysis suggests that this is because those with creative business and fashion industry orientations were more likely to develop and/or mobilize the relational and structural social capital needed to gain appropriate resources to make critical business decisions. In contrast, the CEO was linked more closely to relational social capital based on friendship and extended family networks, which was less likely to provide access to industry-specific information and resources. This suggests that designers with a CEO are less able than those with a CBO or FIO to gain the industry-specific information and inspiration needed to make the harder strategic decisions required for business development.

Finally, the study also contributes to our understanding of the lived-in experience of start-up in the DFI by revealing ironies that have implications for both policy and designer education. For example, the desire to be creative and gain an outlet for this creativity is reported as a prime start-up motivation by designers with a CEO, yet increasingly their creativity is compromised by, or redirected towards, their business management activities. Their intention to realize a particular self-identity or 'state of being' (that is, to be a fashion designer) increasingly gets supplanted by a pressured 'state of doing' (that is, engaging in business management activities required to keep pace with the cyclic demands of the FDI). This was often resented, yet at the same time being in business was often the only option these designers had considered as a means to realize their creative intent. This raises the question of whether policy-makers and educators should be doing more to promote alternatives to business start-up for those with creative flair and a strong CEO. The narratives of those with CEO suggest that more effort needs to go into highlighting the fact that success (in business terms) in the DFI often means that designers end up engaging in less design work than when they first entered the industry. This is explained by the finding that the general trajectory of business development in the FDI requires increasing levels of business activity that necessitate quite high levels of collaboration (for example with suppliers, retailers and contractors) in order for the designer to develop and maintain the social capital necessary for their business to thrive. This highlights a second irony: that designing is widely viewed, particularly among intending and new-start fashion designers, as something individuals do, but successful participation in the DFI demands the sort of social capital that can only be achieved and accessed by those with high levels of collaborative competence.

These findings have significant implications for many stakeholders in the sector, but particularly for those whose role it is to encourage and support successful new fashion design ventures. They provide valuable insights into the way social capital and self-identity, motivation and aspirations shape the start-up process. If taken into account when designing business training or developing enterprise support policy, they could facilitate education and support that is targeted to individual designers' needs at each stage in their business development trajectory. They also provide a basis for further research which examines the link between long-term business success and designers' enterprise orientations.

CONCLUSION

This chapter makes several contributions. Firstly, it contributes a new conceptual framework to the entrepreneurship literature that is grounded in the experiences of nascent entrepreneurs in a creative industry and takes into account the creativity-business tension that is created when artistic and entrepreneurial enterprise activity must coexist. Secondly, it adds to the scant literature on creative start-up in New Zealand. Thirdly, it illustrates the way a narrative approach can lead to the development of conceptual frameworks that are sensitive to the complexities of both the subjects and the local industry. Finally, it has contributed a framework that has the potential to assist policy-makers and training providers to more precisely target their industry support and development activities to the start-up needs of individual designers in an industry where everyone is operating on a knife-edge of risk (Gregg, 2003), and the nascent designer is often only one bad collection away from business failure.

NOTES

1. Earlier papers were based on the analysis of narratives from designers in just the four main fashion centres. For the analysis reported here, this sample was extended to include designers operating from three provincial centres.
2. New Zealand is a country of just over 4 million people distributed across two main islands, the North and South Islands, and a series of sparsely populated minor islands. Auckland, the largest city in the country, has a population in excess of 1.4 million people and is located towards the north of the North Island. Hamilton, a smaller but still significant city, is located 126 kilometres (78 miles) further south. Palmerston North and Wanganui are in the lower third of the island while Wellington, the political capital, is located at the southern tip of the North Island. The largest city in the South Island is Christchurch. This is situated slightly less than half-way down the east coast of this island while the second-largest city in this island, Dunedin, is located on the same coast but approximately 362 kilometres (225 miles) further south. Nelson is located at the northern tip of the South Island.

REFERENCES

Adler, P.S. and S.-W. Kwon (2002), 'Social capital: prospects for a new concept', *Academy of Management Review*, **27** (1), 17–40.

Amit, R., K.R. MacCrimmon, C. Zietsma and J.M. Oesch (2001), 'Does money matter? Wealth attainment as the motive for initiating growth-oriented ventures', *Journal of Business Venturing*, **16** (2), 119–43.

Andersén, J. (2010), 'A critical examination of the EO-performance relationship', *International Journal of Entrepreneurial Behaviour and Research*, **16** (4), 309–28.

Bailey, Jo and Annah Stretton (2007), *From Rag Trade to Mag Trade: The Business of Annah Stretton*, Morrinsville, NZ: Stretton Publishing Company.

Blomfield, Paul (2002), *The Designer Fashion Industry*, Wellington: Industry New Zealand.

Blumer, Herbert (1969), *Symbolic Interactionism: Perspective and Method*, Berkely, CA: University of California Press.

Bourdieu, Pierre (1986), 'The forms of capital', in J.G. Richardson (ed.), *Handbook of Theory and Research for the Sociology of Education*, New York: Greenwood, pp. 241–58.

Brockhaus, R.H. (1980), 'Risk taking propensity of entrepreneurs', *Academy of Management Journal*, **23** (3), 509–20.

de Bruin, A. (2005), 'Multi-level entrepreneurship in the creative industries: New Zealand's screen production industry', *Entrepreneurship and Innovation*, **16** (3), 143–50.

de Bruin, A. and Susan Flint-Hartle (2006), 'Women entrepreneurs in New Zealand: private capital perspectives', in Candida G. Brush, Nancy M. Carter, Elizabeth J. Gatewood, Patricia G. Greene and Myra M. Hart (eds), *Growth-Oriented Women Entrepreneurs and Their Businesses: A Global Research Perspective*, Cheltenham, UK and Northampton, MA, USA: Edward Elgar, pp. 284–307.

Burleigh Evatt and New Zealand Institute of Economic Research (NZIER) (2001), 'Textile and clothing scoping study', July, report to Industry New Zealand.

Cartland, J.W., F. Hoy, W.R. Boulton and J.C. Cartland (1984), 'Differentiating entrepreneurs from small business owners: a conceptualization', *Academy of Management Review*, **9** (2), 354–9.

Cassar, G. and J. Craig (2009), 'An investigation of hindsight bias in nascent venture activity', *Journal of Business Venturing*, **24** (2), 149–64.

Cohen, L. and G. Musson (2000), 'Entrepreneurial identities: reflections from two case studies', *Organization*, **7** (1), 31–48.

Covin, J.G. and D.P. Slevin (1986), 'The development and testing of an organizational-level entrepreneurship scale', in R. Ronstadt, J.A. Hornaday, R. Peterson and K.H. Vesper (eds), *Frontiers of Entrepreneurship Research*, Wellesley, MA: Babson College, pp. 628–39

Covin, J.G. and D.P. Slevin (1989), 'Strategic management of small firms in hostile and benign environments', *Strategic Management Journal*, **10** (1), 75–87.

Covin, J.G. and D.P. Slevin (1991), 'A conceptual model of entrepreneurship as firm behaviour', *Entrepreneurship Theory and Practice*, **16** (1), 7–25.

Davidson, P. and B. Honig (2003), 'The role of social and human capital among nascent entrepreneurs', *Journal of Business Venturing*, **18** (3), 301–30.

Down, S. and L. Warren (2008), 'Constructing narratives of enterprise: clichés and entrepreneurial self-identity', *International Journal of Entrepreneurial Behaviour and Research*, **14** (1), 4–23.

Down, S. and J. Reveley (2004), 'Generational encounters and the social formation of entrepreneurial identity – 'young guns' 'and' 'old farts', *Organization*, **11** (2), 233–50.

Downing, S. (2005), 'The social construction of entrepreneurship: narrative and dramatic processes in the coproduction of organizations and identities', *Entrepreneurship Theory and Practice*, **29** (2), 185–204.

Fisher, Walter R. (1987), *Human Communication as Narration: Towards a Philosophy of Reason, Value and Action*, Columbia, SC: University of South Carolina Press.

Fisher, Walter. R. (1995), 'Narration, knowledge and the possibility of wisdom', in Robert F. Goodman and Walter R. Fisher (eds), *Rethinking Knowledge*, Albany, NY: SUNY Press, pp. 169–92.

Fletcher, Denise (2002), 'Small business narratives of international entrepreneurship', paper presented at the 25th ISBA National Small Firms Policy and Research Conference, Brighton, UK.

Fletcher, Denise (2007), '"Toy Story": the narrative world of entrepreneurship and the creation of interpretive communities', *Journal of Business Venturing*, **22**, 649–72.

Forlani, D. and J. Mullins (2000), 'Perceived risks and choices in entrepreneurs' new venture decisions', *Journal of Business Venturing*, **1**, 305–22.

Gergen, Kenneth J. (1994), *Realities and Relationships: Soundings in Social Construction*, Cambridge, MA: Harvard University Press.

Gergen, Kenneth J. and Mary M. Gergen (1983), 'Narratives of the self', in Theodore R. Sarbin and Karl E. Scheibe (eds), *Studies of Social Identity*, New York: Praege, pp. 254–73.

Giddens, Anthony (1991), *Modernity and Self-identity: Self and Society in the Late Modern Age*, Cambridge: Polity Press.

Gregg, Stacy (2003), *Undressed: New Zealand Fashion Designers Tell Their Stories*, Auckland, NZ: Penguin.

Hamilton, E. (2006), 'Whose story is it anyway? Narrative accounts of the role of women in founding and establishing family businesses', *International Small Business Journal*, **24** (3), 253–71.

Hatzakis, T., M. Lycett, R.D. Macredie and V.A. Martin (2005), 'Towards the development of a social capital approach to evaluating change management', *European Journal of Information Systems*, **14**, 60–74.

Hindle, K. (2004), 'Choosing qualitative methods for entrepreneurial cognitive research: a canonical development approach', *Entrepreneurship Theory and Practice*, **28** (6), 575–607.

Holt, R. and A. Macpherson (2010), 'Sensemaking, rhetoric and the socially competent entrepreneur', *International Small Business Journal*, **28** (1), 20–42.

Ikeba, S. (2008), 'The meaning of "social capital" as it relates to the market process', *Review of Austrian Economics*, **21**, 167–82.

Johansson, A.W. (2004), 'Narrating the entrepreneur', *International Small Business Journal*, **22** (3), 273–93.

Jones, R., J. Latham and M. Betta (2008), 'Narrative construction of the social entrepreneurial identity', *International Journal of Entrepreneurial Behaviour and Research*, **14** (5), 330–45.

Kirkwood, J. (2004), 'One size doesn't fit all: gender differences in motivations for becoming an entrepreneur', unpublished PHD thesis, University of Otago, Dunedin, NZ.

Kirkwood, J. (2007), 'Igniting the entrepreneurial spirit: is the role of parents gendered?', *International Journal of Entrepreneurial Behaviour and Research*, **13** (1), 39–59.

Kohonen, E. (2005), 'Developing global leaders through international assignment', *Personnel Review*, **34** (1), 22–36.

Kolvereid, L. and E. Isaken (2006), 'New business start-up and subsequent entry into self-employment', *Journal of Business Venturing*, **21** (6), 866–85.

Krauss, S.I., M. Frese, C. Friedrich and J.M. Unger (2005), 'Entrepreneurial orientation: a psychological model of success among southern African small business owners', *European Journal of Work and Organizational Psychology*, **14** (3), 315–44.

Kropp, F., N.J. Lindsay and A. Shoham (2008), 'Entrepreneurial orientation and international entrepreneurial business venture start-up', *International Journal of Entrepreneurial Behaviour and Research*, **14** (2), 102–17.

Krueger, N.F. Jr. and A.L. Carsrud (1993), 'Entrepreneurial intensions: applying the theory of planned behavior', *Entrepreneurial Theory and Practice*, **5** (3), 315–30.

Lassig, Angela (2010), *New Zealand Fashion Design*, Wellington: Te Papa Press.

Lee, Robert and Oswald Jones (2008), 'Networks, communication and learning during business start-up: the creation of cognitive social capital', *International Small Business Journal*, **26** (5), 559–94.

Lewis, N., W. Larner and R. Le Heron (2008), 'The New Zealand designer fashion industry: making industries and co-constituting political projects', *Transactions of the Institute of British Geographers*, **33**, 42–59.

Linde, Charlotte (1993), *Life Stories: The Creation of Coherence*, New York: Oxford University Press.

Locke, E. and R. Baum (2004), 'The relationship of entrepreneurial traits, skill and motivation to subsequent venture growth', *Journal of Applied Psychology*, **89** (4), 587–98.

Lounsbury, M. and M.A. Glynn (2001), 'Cultural entrepreneurship: stories, legitimacy and the acquisition of resources', *Strategic Management Journal*, **22**, 545–64.

Lumpkin, G.T. and G.G. Dess (1996), 'Clarifying the entrepreneurial construct and linking it to performance', *Academy of Management Review*, **21** (1), 135–72.

Lumpkin, G.T. and G.G. Dess (2001), 'Linking two dimensions of entrepreneurial orientation to firm performance: the moderating role of environment and industry life cycle', *Journal of Business Venturing*, **16** (5), 429–51.

Mallon, M. and L. Cohen (2001), 'Time for a change? Women's accounts of the move from organisational employment to self-employment', *British Journal of Management*, **12** (3), 217–30.

McCarthy, B. (2000), 'Researching the dynamics of risk-taking and social learning: an exploratory study of Irish entrepreneurs', *Irish Marketing Review*, **13** (1), 46–60.

McClelland, David C. (1961), *The Achieving Society*, Princeton, NJ: Van Nostrand.

Miller, D. (1983), 'The correlates of entrepreneurship in three types of firms', *Management Science*, **29** (7), 770–91.

Mills, C.E. (2008), 'Telling tales: confronting creative tensions in fashion sector start-up', proceedings of the 31st Annual Conference of the Institute for Small Business and Entrepreneurship, Belfast, Northern Ireland.

Mills, C.E. (2011), 'Enterprise orientations: a framework for making sense of fashion sector start-up', *International Journal of Entrepreneurial Behaviour and Research*, **17** (3).

Mills, C.E. and K. Pawson (2006a), 'Enterprising talk: a case of self construction', *Journal of Entrepreneurial Behaviour and Research*, **12** (6), 328–44.

Mills, C.E. and K. Pawson (2006b), 'Gendered risk and start-up behaviour?' proceedings of 29th Institute for Small Business and Entrepreneurship Conference, Cardiff, UK.

Ministry of Economic Development (2010), *SMEs in New Zealand: Structure and Dynamics 2010*, July, Wellington: Ministry of Economic Development.

Nahapiet, J. and S. Ghoshal (1998), 'Social capital, intellectual capital and the organizational advantage', *Academy of Management Review*, **23** (2), 242–66.

O'Connor, E. (2002), 'Storied business: typology, intertextuality and traffic in entrepreneurial narrative', *Journal of Business Communication*, **39** (1), 36–55.

Petrakis, P. (2005), 'Risk perception, risk propensity and entrepreneurial behaviour: the Greek case', *Journal of American Academy of Business*, **7** (1), 233–42.

Pinfold, J.F. (2001), 'The expectations of new business founders: the New Zealand case', *Journal of Small Business Management*, **39** (3), 279–85.

Polkinghorne, Donald E. (1988), *Narrative Knowing and the Human Sciences*, Albany, NY: State University of New York Press.

Portes, Alejandro (1998), 'Social capital: its origins and applications in modern sociology', in E.L. Lesser (ed.), *Knowledge and Social Capital: Foundations and Applications*, Boston, MA: Butterworth-Heinemann, pp. 43–67.

Putnam, Robert D. (2000), *Bowling Alone: The Collapse and Revival of American Community*, New York: Touchstone.

Rae, D. (2005), 'Entrepreneurial learning: a narrative-based conceptual model', *Journal of Small Business and Enterprise Development*, **12** (3), 323–35.

Riessman, Catherine (2008), *Narrative Methods for the Human Sciences*, Thousand Oaks, CA: Sage.

Ritchie, John (1991), 'Enterprise cultures: a frame analysis', in Roger Burrows (ed.), *Deciphering the Enterprise Culture*, London: Routledge, pp. 17–34.

Runyan, R., C. Droge and J. Swinney (2008), 'Entrepreneurial orientation versus small business orientation: what are their relationships to firm performance', *Journal of Small Business Management*, **46** (4), 567–88.

Schaper, Michael and Thierry Volery (2004), *Entrepreneurship and Small Business: A Pacific Rim Perspective*, Milton, QLD: John Wiley & Sons Australia.

Schumpeter, Joseph (1991), 'Comments on a plan for a study of entrepreneurship', in Richard Swedberg (ed.), *Joseph A. Schumpeter: The Economics and Sociology of Capitalism*, Princeton, NJ: Princeton University Press, pp. 406–28.

Segal, G., D. Borgia and J. Schoenfeld (2005), 'The motivation to become an entrepreneur', *International Journal of Entrepreneurial Behaviour and Research*, **11** (1), 42–57.

Somers, M.R. (1994), 'The narrative constitution of identity: a relational and network approach', *Theory and Society*, **23**, 605–49.

Stewart, W. and P. Roth (2001), 'Risk propensity differences between entrepreneurs and managers: a meta-analytic review', *Journal of Applied Psychology*, **86** (1), 145–53.

Steyaert, C. (1997), 'A qualitative methodology for process studies of entrepreneurship', *International Studies of Management and Organization*, **27** (3), 13–33.

Taylor, D.W. and R. Thorpe (2004), 'Entrepreneurial learning: a process of co-participation', *Journal of Small Business and Enterprise Development*, **11** (2), 203–11.

Thompson-Fawcett, Michelle (2007), 'Creative spin? The fashion dividend in Dunedin', in Kerr Inkson, Victoria Browning and Jodyanne Kirkwood (eds),

Working on the Edge: A Portrait of Business in Dunedin, Dunedin, NZ: Otago University Press, pp. 114–24.

Warren, L. (2004), 'Negotiating entrepreneurial identity: communities of practice and changing discourses', *International Journal of Entrepreneurship and Innovation*, **5** (2), 25–37.

Warren, Lorraine and Alistair R. Anderson (2005), 'Michael O'Leary: entrepreneurial fire scorching the landscape', in Chris Steyaert and Daniel Hjorth (eds), *The Politics and Aesthetics of Entrepreneurship*, Cheltenham, UK and Northampton, MA, USA: Edward Elgar, pp. 148–61.

Watson, T.J. (2009), 'Entrepreneurial action, identity work and the use of multiple discursive resources: the case of a rapidly changing family business', *International Small Business Journal*, **27** (3), 251–74.

Weick, Karl (1995), *Sensemaking in Organizations*, Thousand Oaks, CA: Sage.

Zahra, S.A. (1991), 'Predictors and financial outcomes of corporate entrepreneurship: an exploratory study', *Journal of Business Venturing*, **6** (4), 213–32.

10. Music to our ears: new market creation and creative influences in the popular music industry

Erik Noyes, Salvatore Parise and Elaine Allen

INTRODUCTION

The broader transition from industrial economies to knowledge and service economies has increased the need to understand the production and distribution of creative goods in the global economy, including factors that shape the growth and structure of creative industries. This chapter contributes to advancing understanding of the creative industries by seeking answers to the question: in a creative industry, what pattern of creative influences increases the likelihood that an artist will pioneer a new market? We analyse all major artists in the popular music industry between 1950 and 2008 and their unique creative influences to examine if certain structural positions in the complete network of influences make one more or less likely to be a first mover in new markets. Creative influences are the set of recognized social predecessors in a creative industry ('forefathers' or 'foremothers') who are credited for prior achievements in a creative industry; artists commonly recognize, celebrate and give credit to their creative influences. Applying resource dependency theory, we examine each artist's structural pattern of creative influences as an idiosyncratic resource base from which to fashion industry-shaping musical innovations. Our aim is to help disentangle the importance of an artist's individual abilities versus the effect of his or her creative influences in pioneering a new market. Broadly, our analysis examines whether artists who pioneer new markets are tortured individualists who work in isolation (for example those who have few or only peripheral creative influences) or, conversely, highly socialized actors who fashion industry-shaping innovation from cultural touchstones.

Since 1950, the popular music industry has grown into a $4 billion a year industry with wealth creation arising from the creation of 193 separate new markets. We apply network analysis to the social structure of the popular music industry to see whether artists who pioneer new markets occupy and exploit distinct structural positions in the influences network. Our historical data from www.allmusic.com (1950–2008) provide a rich and complex set of artist and industry variables to examine the phenomena.

First, the chapter provides a brief literature review of new market creation as a form of innovation in an industry. Next, there is discussion about the importance of networks in creative industries, including the music, software and gaming industries. Thereafter, we explore theoretical motivations from network research to suggest why an artist's structural position in the creative influences network should impact upon their ability to lead the creation of a new market. Lastly, we present and test network hypotheses, exploiting rich artist and industry longitudinal data from 1950 to 2008 to show that highly socialized, and particularly centrally influenced artists, are most likely to pioneer new markets.

NEW MARKET CREATION

We examine one particular type of innovation in creative industries: new market creation. New market creation is the servicing of newly emergent and newly identified customer needs resulting in a change in an industry's market structure (White, 1981; Bala and Goyal, 1994; Kirzner, 1997; Malerba et al., 1999; Geroski, 2003; Sarasvathy and Dew, 2005). Importantly, new market creation often requires an entrepreneur to invent or exploit different methods of production and distribution. In the automotive industry, for example, the birth of the sport utility vehicle (SUV) market created new consumption patterns in the industry and placed new demands on automotive companies in terms of research and development (R&D), product development, marketing and strategy. Analogously, the emergence of the online subscription-based movie rental market, as led by Netflix, required new investments in technology and operations to satisfy a broad collection of previously unmet needs in the movie rental industry. The fragmentation of an industry into new specialized markets is an important innovation phenomenon because the emergence of a new market can create competitive advantages for industry players, particularly those best positioned in the new market. Also, an entrepreneur's ability to be a first mover in a new market – and potentially shape the creation of that market – can impact upon their future influence and wealth creation in the industry.

New market creation, by definition, shapes an industry's market structure. New market creation has been examined as a process involving a new network of stakeholders (Sarasvathy and Dew, 2005). At a high level, new market creation is arguably an important subprocess of creative destruction, including industry creation and industry evolution (Schumpeter, 1934; Van de Ven and Garud, 1989). Theories of entrepreneurial opportunity discovery emphasizing opportunity recognition, opportunity search and opportunity creation all highlight close relationships between entrepreneurs' successful actions and the formation and formalization of new markets (Hayek, 1945; Kirzner, 1973, 1997; Shane and Venakataram, 2000; Alvarez and Barney, 2007). The creation of new markets is also tightly linked to the diffusion of innovations (Rogers, 1995). According to Bala and Goyal (1994), new markets constantly open up due to technological, political or regulatory changes. One key observation about new markets is that they are regularly emerging.

Knowledge about new markets and knowledge of ways to serve markets are each triggers for entrepreneurship in the individual-opportunity nexus framework of entrepreneurship (Shane, 2004). Broad questions about the process of new market creation examine: individuals' perception or non-perception of new market opportunities; other entrepreneurs' uncertainty that a new market will truly emerge, including the exact timing of the new market; and the process by which other entrepreneurs ultimately learn about and exploit the new market opportunity. Particularly during the growth stage of an industry, one expects to see the emergence of several new markets. Conversely, one expects to see a declining rate of new market creation as an industry enters maturity and decline.

Technological innovation can lower barriers to entry in an industry and stimulate new investments fostering the creation of new markets (Malerba et al., 1999). How entrepreneurs search for new markets is captured in March's (1991) exploration-versus-exploitation quandary. Namely, at any given time, entrepreneurs must balance their efforts to capitalize on existing capabilities that are valuable in known markets with other efforts to expose and identify new market opportunities. Generally, while new market creation is tightly linked to entrepreneurship, there is a relatively small literature on new market creation in entrepreneurship research and in creative industries research in particular.

Creative influences are the set of recognized social predecessors in a creative industry ('forefathers' or 'foremothers') who are credited for prior achievements in a creative industry. The creative influences of artists in a creative industry can and do vary widely, but they are particularly interesting because artists openly recognize and celebrate their influences – the raw material from which they attempt to fashion industry-changing innovations. We examine each artist's structural pattern of creative influences as idiosyncratic resources from which they may pioneer the creation of new markets.

Collectively, the exploration, perception and validation of new markets is a social process, by both individuals and organizations embedded in networks. This research, similarly, takes a decidedly social approach in considering the role of others, particularly creative influences, in the pioneering of new markets. John Lennon of The Beatles once commented: 'At least the first forty songs we wrote were Buddy Holly-influenced.' Buddy Holly, it follows, was a creative influence to The Beatles who, in turn, went on to influence thousands of other artists, and ultimately shape the market terrain of the popular music industry.

In this chapter, we consider how previously unidentified or unmet needs are identified and exploited by alert industry entrepreneurs (here examined as musical artists) who recognize an opportunity to create new value. We posit that certain patterns of creative influences – and particularly certain structural positions in the complete network of influences – should aid artists in pioneering new markets. Trying to understand new market pioneers, those who lead the creation of new markets, our dependent variable is first-movership or creating into a market in the first year of a market's existence. To predict first-movership, we analyse structural differences in each artist's creative influences networks, considering more than 14 000 influence ties among all major artists in the industry between 1950 and 2008. Our main predictor variables include: the centrality of the artist in the complete influences network (does the artist draw from centrally positioned or peripherally positioned artists?); each artist's out-degree (the total number of different influences an artist cites); and each artist's in-degree (how commonly the artist is cited as an influence to others).

We aim to contribute to the entrepreneurship literature while probing the evolution of a $4 billion popular music industry. Interestingly, we find that artists who draw from centrally positioned versus peripherally positioned artists and creative influences are more likely to pioneer new markets. Additionally, we find that artists with higher total numbers of creative influences are no more likely to be market pioneers. So, the centrality of an artist's influences, versus the abundance of their direct influences, is a better predictor of pioneering a new market. Quite opposite to the prevailing view that a tortured, socially isolated artist is most likely to generate industry-changing innovations, we find that highly socialized, and particularly centrally influenced artists, are most likely to pioneer new markets.

THE IMPORTANCE OF NETWORKS IN CREATIVE INDUSTRIES

Entrepreneurs and entrepreneurial firms in creative industries commonly develop innovations and generate new wealth by exploiting resources in their professional and personal networks. Looking at software – both in start-ups and at larger companies like Microsoft – 'flash teams' assemble and disband to exploit the potential of new technologies and business models by drawing on specialized expertise, depending on the unique demands of bringing a specific innovation to market. Considering the rapid-growth gaming industry, leading game developers such as Electronic Arts cultivate and exploit far-flung networks of game developers, interaction designers, programmers, licensing specialists and marketing partners to pioneer new markets in their industry. The Nintendo Wii is a particularly compelling example of how a gaming company disrupted existing dominance in the industry by Microsoft, by pioneering a new market (for example motion gaming) enabled by development of radical new user-interface technologies. Specifically, the breakthrough Wii system, with its novel controllers, enabled system owners to box, to bowl and to play tennis against each other through physically exerting gestures. Relatedly, the Nintendo Fit, an add-on controller, allows consumers to elevate their heart rate by practicing aerobics with a virtual trainer by standing on an interactive floor pad. Because leading in new markets is often a key to creating wealth – as well as to gaining access to emerging technologies and future networking capability – artists and companies in creative industries strive to build and exploit the most innovative networks with diverse expertise in different markets and varied technological platforms.

Supporting this overall process, researchers have demonstrated that worker free agency in Silicon Valley – and particularly lax non-competition arrangements, fluid organizational boundaries and strong informal networks of talent – are critical to the pursuit of fast-changing opportunities in dynamic industries such as the information technology (IT) and life sciences industries. Regional advantages, it follows, have been shown to emerge from heightened labour mobility and accepted norms of moving between and networking within organizations (Saxenian, 1996). Relatedly, if one looks to the popular music industry, artists responsible for major innovations have often combined new technologies, new group members and fused different musical styles to fashion new musical experiences (for example The Beatles, David Bowie, Pink Floyd, Stevie Wonder and Herbie Hancock). More broadly, considering the traditional creative industries of film, music and publishing, loose personal and professional affiliations are a treasure chest for locating critical talent, for sourcing funding for risky new ventures and for assembling teams to commercialize and industry-shaping innovation.

Although it can be difficult to document creative influences, software architects, game designers and film directors all operate in a social context where they are influenced by the creative products of their predecessors and peers. One's creative influences may shape what one believes is possible or desirable within a creative industry. As such, this research aims to disentangle the relative importance of one's individual talent versus the importance of one's creative influences in leading the creation of a new market.

To summarize, networks are instrumental to innovation in creative industries. Looking at the birth of 193 new markets in the popular music industry (1950–2008), we examine the ability of artists to pioneer new markets (that is, be first movers) based on their position in the complete network of creative influences. We posit that certain structural positions in a network of creative influences should be more fertile for spawning innovations which alter the industry's market structure. In the following short section, we explore resource dependency theory and, briefly, structural hole theory to motivate our main hypotheses further.

RESOURCE DEPENDENCY THEORY AND STRUCTURAL HOLE THEORY

Theory and research on networks provide insight into why networks – and particularly entrepreneur positions in networks – matter (Bavelas, 1951; Milgram, 1967; Granovetter, 1985; Burt, 1992; Krackhardt, 1995; Powell et al., 1996; Hills et al., 1997; Singh et al., 1999; Ahuja, 2000; Borgatti and Foster, 2003; Freeman, 2004; Smith-Doerr and Powell, 2005). For example, resource dependency theory, a foundational theory of networks research, predicts that one's adaptability and chances of survival in an industry depends on one's access to scarce resources in a business environment (Pfeffer and Salancik, 1978). Particularly, social contacts, or one's position in a social network, may enable or constrain access to critical resources needed for basic operation, growth and innovation. Critical resources obtained though social contacts may include financial resources, such as funds needed to develop a technical innovation, or social capital such as important social contacts needed to assemble or distribute an innovation. From this perspective, certain social ties – and particularly resources obtainable in the external environment – are what shape the survival and innovation capacity of certain industry players. A chief point in this theoretical perspective is that social ties can enable or constrain strategic actions by industry entrepreneurs.

In the context of software design, for instance, this may mean that a software company's ability to lead in a market is constrained by its ability to locate and attract top talent through its industry contacts, which may be facilitated by its centrality in industry networks. Relatedly, in the gaming industry, a game development team may be successful (or limited) based on its awareness of emerging technologies through formal and informal networks. One risk is to be peripheral (versus central) in key industry networks. Lastly, in music, we posit that an artist may face advantages or disadvantages in pioneering a new market based on the structural pattern of their creative influences, the raw material from which innovations may be fashioned. Our aim in this research is to isolate the importance of the network, and particularly certain structural positions in the network, in relation to one specific innovation outcome: being a first mover, or pioneer, in a new market.

A second theory, structural hole theory (Burt, 1992), which complements resource dependency theory, suggests that brokers in networks should have advantages in recognizing entrepreneurial opportunities and fashioning innovations because they sit at the nexus of unique information, also known as non-redundant information. Specifically, those artists who are connected to other network actors – where those network actors are otherwise unconnected – can exploit unique information flows and perceive entrepreneurial opportunities that only partially present themselves to others (who, by contrast, have inferior access to unique information by virtue of their network positions). Brokerage is a specific example of a network position that should be favourable for initiating innovations according to the network perspective.

To summarize, network theorizing and methods have found broad application in the study of business strategy, entrepreneurship and innovation processes, and earlier in epidemiology and politics (Wasserman and Faust, 1994; Smith-Doerr and Powell, 2005). Network analysis examines the architecture of direct and indirect social ties among network actors – such as people, teams, organizations and nations – and focuses on the relations among actors as opposed to the attributes of actors as is more common focus in the social sciences. Network research asks: does one's position in the network affect one's outcomes? Also, it asks: are there superior (or inferior) positions in the network from which certain actions initiate – here examined as pioneering a new market?

INDUSTRY MARKET STRUCTURE AND THE POPULAR MUSIC INDUSTRY (1950–2008)

Overview

The birth and evolution of the popular music industry (1950–2008) is a fascinating context to explore the importance of direct and indirect creative influences on innovation in an industry. Specifically, a culture of openness about creative influences – both near and distant – allows one to analyse artists' positions in the complete network of influences. By analyzing each artist's unique position in the complete network of musical influences, we can examine relationships between social structure and new market pioneering in this creative industry. Particularly, for each artist (or group), we determined: their exhaustive list of creative influences; the markets (that is, styles) the artist created into; and, most importantly, the timing of entry into each market. In our analysis, a first mover in a new market – our dependent variable and proxy for new market pioneering – is someone who created into a market the first year of a market's existence. For each market an artist created into, we measured their year of entry (year 0, 1, 5, 10, for example, or later) where zero means the artist created into the new market in the first year of the market's existence. Because we have year-of-entry data for all artists for all markets, we have continuous data showing first (early) and last (late) entry into each market for the industry.

Industry Market Structure

Since its inception, the $4 billion popular music industry has evolved into 13 broad market categories and 193 constituent markets (Recording Industry Association of America). The 13 broad market categories (that is, subgenres) include: folk/county rock, art-Rock/experimental, British invasion, and alternative/Indie rock as a sampling. The constituent 193 markets include specialized artists and target customers such as: Christian punk, post-Grunge, Scandinavian metal, Japanese pop, post-punk and Aboriginal rock, among others. In sum, we build out a continuous lineage of creative influences among all major artists cutting across all 193 new markets going back to the formation of the industry – a complete network. We located the birth, or pioneering, of individual new markets within this lineage. Considering theory and empirical findings presented above, we looked to test the following hypotheses:

Hypothesis 1: The structural pattern of creative influences for market pioneers will be different than for non-pioneers.

Hypothesis 2: Artists with a higher total number of direct influences will be more likely to pioneer new markets than artists with few direct influences.

Hypothesis 3: Artists who draw from centrally positioned versus peripherally positioned artists and influences will be more likely to pioneer new markets.

The three hypotheses above derive directly from our consideration of resource dependency. Namely, we expect that an artist's structural position vis-à-vis their creative influences should impact upon access to critical resources necessary to fashion an industry-changing innovation. Specifically, Hypothesis 2 predicts that artists with a higher total number of direct influences will be more likely to pioneer new markets. This prediction is based on the idea that several (versus few) influences should theoretically offer artists many influences to draw from, or recombine, in their efforts to pioneer the creation of a new market. While structural, this perspective only considers the number of direct influences immediately 'surrounding' the artist and is therefore a localized measure of direct resource availability. A step change, Hypothesis 3, predicts that artists who draw from centrally positioned versus peripherally positioned artists and influences will be more likely to pioneer new markets. Broadly, this hypothesis sets up two ideas: (1) that new market creation builds on core influences in the industry – and less so the exploitation of peripheral influences in the industry; and (2) that having centrally positioned creative influences is an especially efficient way to access the direct and indirect influences of others. An artist with centrally positioned influences, by definition, is more likely to be centrally positioned in the complete influences network, which is what we measure. Consistent with our prior discussion, the three hypotheses capture the broad idea that the pioneering of a new market is a decidedly social rather than isolated process.

METHOD

Data

The data come from allmusic.com, a top industry information provider whose database is the platform for both America Online's and Yahoo! Music's e-commerce websites. The archive provides data including each artist's name (individual or group), markets associated with the artist's music, discographies of albums and songs and, most importantly, lists of artists that have influenced each artist (1950s–2008). In total, there are more than 14 000 'influenced by' ties for nearly 1000 artists. These data allow for a seamless and complete network picture of all major artists in the industry and their creative influences over the past six decades (see www.allmusic.com for details). Relatedly, Figure 10.2 on page 214 provides a network visualization showing only the creative influences among the most influential artists in the industry (that is, those cited most as creative influences to all the other artists in the industry).

For this study, we used UCINET 6.0 (Borgatti et al., 2002) to build out the complete network and to measure the network positions associated with each artist. As mentioned, within the popular music industry there are 193 markets. For each artist, we created variables that measure their year of entry into new markets (that is, year 0, 1, 2 or 3, and so on) from when the market came into existence, our dependent variable. Entry in year zero (0) is considered being a first mover, or pioneer, in a market since entry occurred during the first year of the market's existence. We looked at the dependent variable in two ways. First, as a binary outcome variable where artists are either first movers or not (that is, either create into new markets in year zero, or at some later unspecified time). Second, we looked at first movership as a continuous dependent variable and considered each artist's year of entry into new markets (year 0, 1, 5, 10, for example, or later). With this second method, the requirement for first-movership was loosened to include the (several) first years of a market's existence. Here, entry into in a new market in year 2, for instance, represents first-movership when compared to other artists entering in year 15 of the market's existence.

For overall context concerning the creation of new markets, Figure 10.1 shows the percentage of 'Top Ten' Billboard albums in popular music coming from each of the 13 broad market categories in the period between 1950 and 2008.

As one can see, certain broad market categories – and therefore certain constituent markets – were not in existence for large periods of the industry's history. An artist's creation of music into several markets (that is, styles) is an indication of an artist's versatility. Figure 10.3 on page 215 shows creative influences among artists who created into 'eight or more markets, an elite group within the industry.

Analysis

First using the binary measure of first-movership (that is, where artists are either first movers or not), we analysed the characteristics of first movers in markets as well as comparisons between numbers of 'Top Ten' Billboard albums, an artist's number of record labels, and an artist's nationality (US or not). Motivated by our hypotheses we examined the centrality of the artist in the complete influences network (does the artist draw from centrally positioned or peripherally positioned artists?), each artist's out-degree (the number of different influences an artist cites), and each artist's in-degree (how commonly the artist is cited as an influence to others). More specifically, for centrality, we measured betweenness centrality, or the average number of times an artist was on the shortest network path lengths between all other artists. These variables were calculated for the

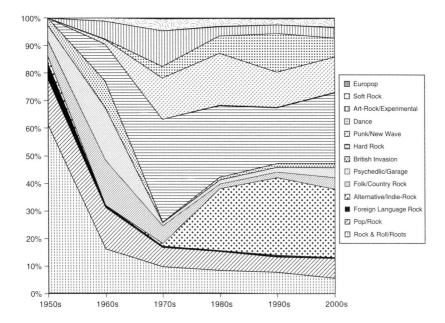

Legend:
- Europop
- Soft Rock
- Art-Rock/Experimental
- Dance
- Punk/New Wave
- Hard Rock
- British Invasion
- Psychedlic/Garage
- Folk/Country Rock
- Alternative/Indie-Rock
- Foreign Language Rock
- Pop/Rock
- Rock & Roll/Roots

Source: Data from allmusic.com.

Figure 10.1   Percentage of 'Top Ten' albums coming from 13 subgenres, 1951–2008

years 1950–2008. These bivariate and multivariate comparisons using ANOVA provided variables for use in our final continuous model of first movers. We fitted a logistic model to the dataset using a binary dependent variable (1 = first mover, 0 = non-first mover). The results of the logistic model in Table 10.1 show the strongest differentials between first movers and non-first movers, controlling for other variables.

Applying these stringent requirements, 5 per cent of the artists in the all-music.com database are first movers in a market and, of these, 0.9 per cent are first movers in two markets. Significant differences ($p < 0.05$) between means for first movers and non-first movers are seen in the number of 'Top Ten' Billboard albums (7.9 vs 1.6), in-degree (34.4 vs 3.0), and centrality (498.9 vs 37.8). The results of the logistic model predicting first mover vs non-first mover are given in Table 10.1.

The logistic model was highly significant ($p < 0.001$) with a pseudo-R-square of 0.461. The odds ratios indicate that first movers are: (1) twice as likely to have more 'Top Ten' Billboard albums; (2) almost twice as likely to have issued albums on more than one label; (3) four times more likely to

Table 10.1   Results of the logistic model of first movers in a market

	Sig.	Exp(B) = OddsRatio
Number_albums	0.382	0.959
Number_of_top10_bba	0.050**	2.100
Number_labels	0.035**	1.700
US or not	0.043**	4.110
Centrality/betweenness	0.026**	10.335
Out-degree/normalized	0.340	1.528
In-degree/normalized	0.007***	3.200

Table 10.2   Results of the regression model examining years to first album in a market

	Unstandardized coefficients		Sig.
	B	Std. error	
(Constant)	10.427	1.393	0.000
AlbumsperYear	−1.283	0.147	0.000
is_solo	11.378	1.043	0.000
Number_of_top10_bba	−0.646	0.154	0.000
Number_markets	1.262	0.281	0.000
First mover (Yes/No)	−4.817	1.225	0.004
Centrality/betweenness	−0.133	0.003	0.045

be from the US; (4) more than ten times more likely to be centrally located in the network and have centrally positioned creative influences; and (5) over three times more likely to have a high in-degree.

In addition to this logistic model, we also created a linear regression model using year of entry as our continuous dependent variable. This model examined whether an artist entering early into a market has similar characteristics to the (binary) first mover explored above in the logistic regression. The linear regression predicting the year of entry, our continuous variable for first-movership, was also highly significant ($p < 0.0001$) with an R-square of 0.540. Important parameters are albums per year, number of 'Top Ten' Billboard albums, whether or not the artist is a first mover (included as a dummy variable), and having centrally positioned creative influences. As shown in Table 10.2, all variables are significant and have a negative coefficient, indicating that the later an artist enters a market, the less likely an artist is to be a first mover. Interestingly, later movers in a market are much more likely to be solo artists.

Combined, the two models support Hypothesis 1, which predicts that the structural pattern of creative influences for market pioneers will be different than for non-pioneers. Neither model, however, supports Hypothesis 2, which predicts that artists with a higher total number of direct influences will be more likely to pioneer new markets than artists with few direct influences. Finally, both models support Hypothesis 3 which predicts that artists who draw from centrally positioned versus peripherally positioned artists and influences will be more likely to pioneer new markets. Broadly, the results suggest that first movers (that is, pioneers) build on core influences in the industry – and less so on the exploitation of peripheral influences in the industry.

IMPLICATIONS AND VALUE

This research draws attention to the unique social nature of new market creation in a creative industry. Specifically, despite the widespread stereotype of the socially isolated tortured artist, our findings suggest that pioneers of new markets likely fuse together several different creative influences versus fashioning innovations from an absence of influences. Particularly, our findings suggest that pioneers draw from centrally – versus peripherally – important artists in the industry. Put differently, this suggests that new market pioneering in the popular music industry – one particular type of industry innovation – results from recombining cultural touchstones more than from introducing and exploiting distant, unknown influences.

It is important to note, however, that these particular findings could be explained by what innovation an industry will bear and what is ripe, versus too far afield, for consolidation into a new market at a given point in time in the evolution of the industry's market structure. However, overall, the findings de-emphasize the importance of one's individual talent versus one's idiosyncratic pattern of creative influences in new market creation in a creative industry.

As discussed, Resource Dependency Theory strongly suggests that one's position in a network should impact upon one's ability to pioneer a new market, particularly if one has superior access to resources that others do not. Here, access is meant in a creative or inspirational sense, where all artists have creative influences but only some have certain structural patterns among their influences and occupy certain unique structural positions in the complete network of influences among all major music artists. Being influenced by centrally positioned artists, through one lens, is an especially efficient way to access the direct and indirect influences of other

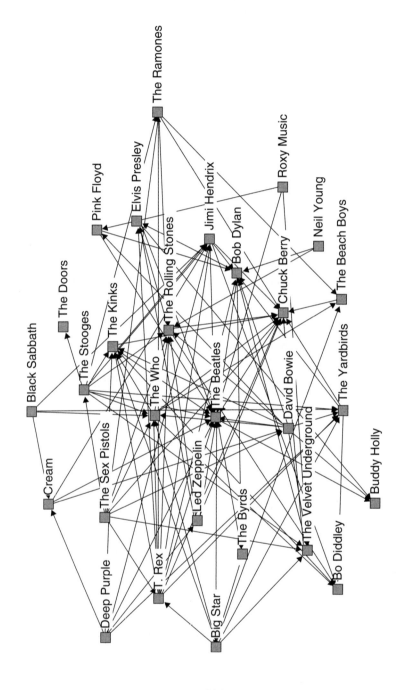

Figure 10.2 Network graphics of major creative influencers

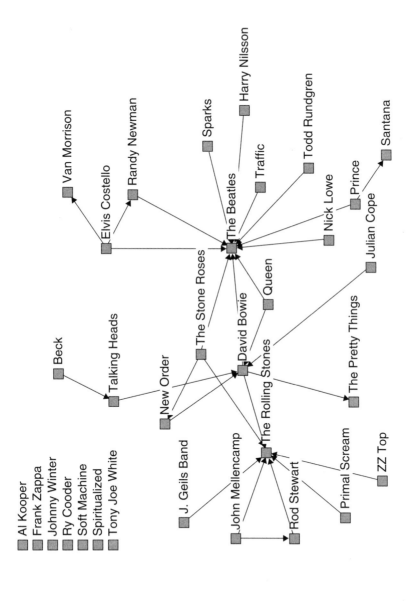

Figure 10.3   Artists who created into eight or more markets

artists (as opposed to having a comparable number of peripherally located influences).

By generalizing findings, this research may contribute to our understanding of the role of networks in new market creation in other creative industries. Specifically, the research has the potential to identify network positions among other artists (for example software architects or game designers) that may be fertile for initiating innovation, including but not limited to the pioneering of new markets. Moreover, taking a portfolio perspective, this research may suggest that music recording companies, such as BMG, Sony Music or Universal, might examine their aggregate artist portfolio positions in influence networks to maximize the probability of pioneering new markets in the future. Such an inquiry might suggest that music recording companies are strongly or weakly positioned for future industry evolution. Broadly, if extended, this research may inform artists and executives in other creative industries, such software, gaming, film and publishing, about strategies to generate and sustain innovation when established markets wane in an industry.

Future research examining networks in creative industries should examine how artist positions in networks impact upon commercial success, which often differs dramatically from what is regarded historically and contemporarily as innovation (for example pioneering a new market). While there are artists in creative industries that are widely regarded for creating commercially successful innovations, a common outcome is innovation without commercial success or commercial success without innovation. Clearly, research on creative industries needs to examine both market and financial outcomes in relation to these questions. More broadly, this research presents the opportunity to disentangle the importance of individual talent – which is so commonly viewed as a primary driver of innovation – and the importance of idiosyncratic social influences on innovation.

The network visualization in Figure 10.2 shows creative influences among artists who were most influential in the popular music industry (1950–2008). An arrow indicates the direction of influence; influence is most often unidirectional but can be bidirectional.

The network visualization in Figure 10.3 shows creative influences among artists who created into eight or more of the 193 studied markets. Creating into several markets indicates an artist's versatility and delineates where the artist does – and does not – have recognized contributions in the industry. Artists shown at the upper-left have created into eight or more markets, but are not influenced directly by other artists depicted in the visualization.

REFERENCES

Ahuja, G. (2000), 'Collaboration networks, structural holes, and innovation: a longitudinal study', *Administrative Science Quarterly*, **45**, 425–55.

Alvarez, S.A. and J.B. Barney (2007), 'Discovery and creation: alternative theories of entrepreneurial action', *Strategic Entrepreneurship Journal*, **1**, 11–26.

Bala, V. and S. Goyal (1994), 'Birth of a new market', *Economic Journal*, **104** (423), 289–90.

Bavelas A. (1951), 'Communication patterns in task-oriented groups', in D. Lerner and H.K. Lasswell (eds), *The Policy Sciences*, Stanford, CA: Stanford University Press, 193–202.

Borgatti, S.P., M.G. Everett and L.C. Freeman (2002), *UCINET for Windows: Software for Social Network Analysis*, Harvard, MA: Analytic Technologies.

Borgatti, S.P. and P.C. Foster (2003), 'The network paradigm in organizational research: a review and typology', *Journal of Management*, **29**, 991–1013.

Burt, R.S. (1992), *Structural Holes*, Cambridge, MA: Harvard University Press.

Burt, R.S. (2005), *Brokerage and Closure: An Introduction to Social Capital*, Oxford: Oxford University Press.

Freeman, L.C. (2004), *The Development of Social Network Analysis*, Vancouver, BC: Empirical Press.

Geroski, P.A. (2003), *The Evolution of New Markets*, Oxford: Oxford University Press.

Granovetter, M. (1985), 'Economic action, social structure, and embeddedness', *American Journal of Sociology*, **91**, 481–510.

Hayek, F. (1945), 'Use of knowledge in society', *American Economic Review*, **35**, 519–30.

Hills, G., G.T. Lumpkin and R.P. Singh (1997), 'Opportunity recognition: perceptions and behaviors of entrepreneurs', *Frontiers of Entrepreneurship Research*, Wellesley, MA: Babson College.

Kirzner, I. (1973), *Competition and Entrepreneurship*, Chicago, IL: University of Chicago Press.

Kirzner, I. (1997), 'Entrepreneurial discovery and the competitive market process: an Austrian approach', *Journal of Economic Literature*, **35**, 60–85.

Krackhardt, D. (1995), 'Entrepreneurial opportunities in an entrepreneurial firm: a structural approach', *Entrepreneurship Theory and Practice*, Spring, 53–69.

Malerba, F., R. Nelson, L. Orsenigo and S. Winter (1999), 'History friendly models of industry evolution: the computer industry', *Industrial and Corporate Change*, **1**, 3–41.

March, J.G. (1991), 'Exploration and exploitation in organizational learning', *Organization Science*, **2** (1), 71–87.

Milgram, S. (1967), 'The small world problem', *Psychology Today*, **2**, 60–67.

Pfeffer, J. and G. Salancik (1978), *The External Control of Organizations*, New York: Harper & Row.

Powell, W.W., K.W. Koput and L. Smith-Doerr (1996), 'Interorganizational collaboration and the locus of innovation: networks of learning in biotechnology', *Administrative Science Quarterly*, **41**, 116–45.

Rogers, E.M. (1995), *Diffusion of Innovations*, 4th edn, New York: Free Press.

Sarasvathy, Saras D. and N. Dew (2005), 'New market creation through transformation', *Journal of Evolutionary Economics*, **5**, 533–65.

Saxenian, A. (1996), *Regional Advantage: Culture and Competition in Silicon Valley and Route 128*, Boston, MA: Harvard University Press.

Schumpeter, J. (1934), *The Theory of Economic Development*, Cambridge, MA: Harvard University Press.

Shane, S. (2004), *A General Theory of Entrepreneurship: The Individual – Opportunity Nexus*, Cheltenham, UK and Northampton, MA, USA: Edward Elgar.

Shane, S. and S. Venkataraman (2000), 'The promise of entrepreneurship as a field of research', *Academy of Management Review*, **25**, 217–26.

Singh, R.P., G.E. Hills, R.C. Hybels and G.T. Lumpkin (1999), 'Opportunity recognition through social networks of entrepreneurs', in P.D. Reynolds, W.D. Bygrave, S. Manigart, C.M. Mason and G.D. Meyer (eds), *Frontiers of Entrepreneurship Research*, Wellesley, MA: Babson College, pp. 228–41.

Smith-Doerr, L. and W. Powell (2005), 'Networks and economic life', *Handbook of Economic Sociology*, Princeton, NJ: Russel Sage Foundation and Princeton University Press.

Wasserman, S. and K. Faust (1994), *Social Network Analysis: Methods and Applications*, Cambridge: Cambridge University Press.

White, H. (1981), 'Where do markets come from?', *American Journal of Sociology*, **87**, 517–26.

Index